Tibetan

Phrasebook & Dictionary

Acknowledgments
Product Editor Shona Gray
Book Designer Wibowo Rusli
Language Writer Sandup Tsering
Cover Image Researcher Naomi Parker

Thanks
James Hardy, Campbell McKenzie, Catherine Naghten, Rachel Rawling, Angela Tinson, Juan Winata

Published by Lonely Planet Global Limited
CRN 554153

6th Edition – Feb 2020
ISBN 978 1 78657 584 5
Text © Lonely Planet 2020
Cover Image Sunrise on Mt Everest, Ducoin-ana / 4Corners Images ©
Printed in Singapore   10 9 8 7 6 5 4 3 2 1

Contact lonelyplanet.com/contact

MIX
Paper from
responsible sources
FSC™ C021741
www.fsc.org

acknowledgments

about the author

Sandup Tsering is a Tibetan Buddhist Scholar, interpreter and language teacher, and was born in Purang in Western Tibet. In 1959 his parents fled to India, where they live in a refugee settlement. Sandup moved to Australia in 1984. He has a Bachelor of Arts and a Masters in Buddhism and was the President of the Tibetan Community of Victoria for five years from 1993 until 1998.

from the author

My special thanks goes to Ven Thupten Donyo and Kelsang Dhondup for their assistance with typing Tibetan script, and my wife and children for their support. I would also like to thank Alo Bhuti, Sonam Dolkar and Lobsang Dhargye for their help and input.

from the publisher

Scaling the heights of the Tibetan phrasebook was no small task. Sally Steward, Peter D'Onghia and Quentin Frayne arranged all necessary permits and Emma Koch helped with initial preparations. Editor Sophie Putman came on board to organise equipment and supplies, while proofer Adrienne Costanzo lent her keen eye to ensure all went as planned. Experienced trekkers Karina Coates, Karin Vidstrup Monk and Rachel Williams joined the party and offered support across the most challenging terrain. Jim Jenkin served as a guide along the entire trail, Ben Handicott proved a dependable porter and Annelies Mertens guaranteed no-one was lost for words. Hunor Csutoros provided the trusty map, while Meg Worby contributed to navigation plans with her clever contents. Fabrice Rocher coordinated the final ascent and designers Belinda Campbell, Patrick Marris, Yukiyoshi Kamimura and David Kemp ensured it went without a hitch. Yukiyoshi's talented illustrations of the Tibetan people, flora and fauna, inspired us all. The result: a euphoric summit celebration with châng all round.

acknowledgments

make the most of this phrasebook …

Anyone can speak another language! It's all about confidence. Don't worry if you can't remember your school language lessons or if you've never learnt a language before. Even if you learn the very basics (on the inside covers of this book), your travel experience will be the better for it. You have nothing to lose and everything to gain when the locals hear you making an effort.

finding things in this book

For easy navigation, this book is in sections. The Basics chapters are the ones you'll thumb through time and again. The Practical section covers basic travel situations like catching transport and finding a bed. The Social section gives you conversational phrases, pick-up lines, the ability to express opinions – so you can get to know people. Food has a section all of its own: gourmets and vegetarians are covered and local dishes feature. Safe Travel equips you with health and police phrases, just in case. Remember the colours of each section and you'll find everything easily; or use the comprehensive Index. Otherwise, check the two-way traveller's Dictionary for the word you need.

being understood

Throughout this book you'll see coloured phrases on each page. They're phonetic guides to help you pronounce the language. You don't even need to look at the language itself, but you'll get used to the way we've represented particular sounds. The pronunciation chapter in Basics will explain more, but you can feel confident that if you read the coloured phrase slowly, you'll be understood.

communication tips

Body language, ways of doing things, sense of humour – all have a role to play in every culture. 'Local talk' boxes show you common ways of saying things, or everyday language to drop into conversation. 'Listen for …' boxes supply the phrases you may hear. They start with the phonetic guide (because you'll hear it before you know what's being said) and then lead in to the language and the English translation.

CONTENTS

CONTENTS

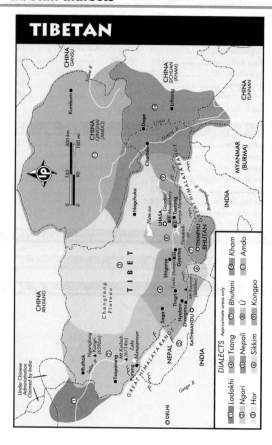

Tibetan belongs to the Tibeto-Burman linguistic group of the Sino-Tibetan language family, with Burmese its closest relative. It's spoken by around six million people, mainly in Tibet, but also in neighbouring Nepal, India and Bhutan, and used by Mongolians to study Buddhism.

There are many different Tibetan dialects and, due to differences in pronunciation and vocabulary, it can be difficult for people from different regions to understand one another. The main provinces, U-tsang, Amdo and Kham – all of which have been renamed by China – have their own dialects (and sub-dialects). Other Tibetan dialects can be found in bordering countries. However, greater social interaction among Tibetans from various regions in recent times has led to the development of a standard Tibetan language. In contrast to any of the traditional dialects, it's much closer to classical Tibetan and is also the focus of this book.

Written Tibetan was devised in the 7th century AD by Thumi Sambhota, the minister of the famous Tibetan ruler, King Songtsen Gampo. He was one of 15 scholars sent to India by the king to compile Tibetan scripts so that Buddhist literature could be translated into Tibetan. Under the guidance of his main Indian teachers, Brahmin Lipikara and Devavidyasinha, Sambhota learned a number of classical Indian languages. He developed the Tibetan language based on the Sanskrit characters of the Devanagari script (used for many Indian languages). He also compiled grammar texts which are still the primary source for studying Tibetan grammar today.

Since its introduction, the writing system has barely changed, although the spoken language has evolved considerably. As a result, written and spoken Tibetan are quite different.

Speaking Tibetan is the key to understanding the unique culture, lifestyle and history of the country. This phrasebook will help you communicate with Tibetans and enrich your experience in Tibet.

introduction

9

how to use this phrasebook

you can speak another language

Anyone can speak another language. Don't worry if you haven't studied languages before, or that you studied a language at school for years and can't remember any of it. You don't need to sit down and memorise endless grammatical details or long lists of vocabulary. You just need to start speaking. Once you start, you'll be amazed how many prompts will help you build on those first words. You'll hear people speaking, pick up sounds from TV, catch a word or two that you think you know from the local radio, see something on a billboard – all these things help to build your understanding.

plunge in

There's just one thing you need to start speaking another language – courage. Your biggest hurdle is overcoming the fear of saying aloud what may seem to you to be just a bunch of sounds.

The best way to start overcoming your fear is to memorise a few key words. These are the words you know you'll be saying again and again, for example, 'thank you' tu-jay-chay (ཐུགས་རྗེ་ཆེ།).

There's no exact equivalent for 'Hello' in Tibetan – sometimes the greeting ta-shi de-lek (བཀྲ་ཤིས་བདེ་ལེགས།), which literally means 'Good fortune' is used, or Tibetans may just ask a question such as kay-râng ka-bah pay-kay (ཁྱེད་རང་ག་བར་ཕེབས་གས།), 'Where are you going?'. If you're having trouble understanding someone, say ha ko ma-song (ཧ་གོ་མ་སོང་), 'I don't understand' or yâng-kya ka-lee ka-lee soong nâng da (ཡང་སྐྱར་ག་ལེར་ག་ལེར་གསུང་གནང་དང་) 'Could you speak more slowly please?'. Other phrases to help you with language difficulties are on page 52.

abbreviations used in this book

adj	adjective	n	noun
f	feminine	pl	plural
inf	informal	pol	polite
lit	literal translation	sg	singular
m	masculine	v	verb

ABOUT TIBETAN

legend

The following notation is used throughout this phrasebook:

( ) parentheses

- indicate words that can be replaced with words of your choice:

  I've been travelling for (two) months.

  nga dü-shü da-wa (nyi)　ང་བགྱལ་བཤུད་ཟླ་བ་（གཉིས）
  chay-pa yin　　　　　　བྱས་པ་ཡིན།

- indicate the words are optional:

  Can you show me (on the map)?

  (sâp-ta di-nâng)　　（ས་བཀྲ་འདི་ནང་）
  tön nâng-da　　　　སྟོན་གནང་དང་།

/ forward slash

- indicates when single words on either side of the slash are interchangeable:

  Turn left/right.

  yön-la/yeh-la　　　གཡོན་ལ་/གཡས་ལ་སྐྱོགས་གནང་།
  kyog-nâng

- indicates when single words are synonyms:

  necklace　　kay-gyen/gü-gyen　　སྐེ་རྒྱན་/མགུལ་རྒྱན།

; semicolon

- separates two (or more) alternatives where one (or more) consists of <u>more</u> than one word:

  earrings　　ahm-cho gyen;　　ཨམ་ཅོག་རྒྱན་/རྣ་རྒྱན།
  　　　　　　　na-gyen

[ ] square brackets

- contain two (or more) different constructions, separated by a semicolon, or a slash in script. One construction is compulsory in the phrase:

Please [slow down; go faster].

[ka-lee ka-lee; gyok-tsi]
do-nâng

[ག་ལེར་ག་ལེར/མགྱོགས་ཙི]
འགྲོ་གནང་།

The guide [has paid; will pay].

rin-ba nay-shay gya-khen-gi
tay-song/tay-gi-ray

རིན་པ་གནས་བ་གད་རྒྱག་མཁན་གྱིས
སྤྲད་སོང་/སྤྲད་ཀྱི་རེད།

- **bullet points**
- are used in the dictionary only to separate synonyms:

   often   yâng yang • yâng-se   ཡང་ཡང་ • ཡང་སེ

If it is necessary to clarify the difference between alternatives,
this is indicated in parentheses after each word.

pronunciation

Although there are a few sounds that are not common in English, pronunciation of Tibetan is generally not too difficult. The transliteraton system used in this book has been designed to help you pronounce Tibetan sounds correctly and with ease.

Remember that people will welcome your efforts and won't be concerned if you mispronounce the odd word.

transliteration

To assist with pronunciation, all syllables in the transliterations have been hyphenated. As long as you pronounce each of the syllables clearly, you should be understood.

vowels

Although there are only five vowels indicated in the writing system (see **The Tibetan Writing System**, page 15), their pronunciation can vary. The vowel ˆ, for example, can be pronounced as i or ee, depending on the sounds around it.

Transliteration	Pronunciation
a	as the 'u' in 'cup'
â	as the 'a' in 'alone'
aw	as the 'aw' in the British 'paw'
e	as the 'e' in 'bet'
i	as the 'i' in 'in'
ee	as the 'ee' in 'see'
o	as the 'o' in 'so'
ö	as the 'er' in 'her'
u	as the 'u' in 'glue'
oo	as the 'oo' in 'soon'
ü	similar to the 'u' in 'flute', but with a raised tongue
ay	as the 'ay' in 'say'

consonants

Most consonants are pronounced as in English; those that aren't are listed in the box below in Tibetan alphabetical order.

Some consonants in Tibetan can be aspirated or unaspirated. Aspirated consonants are pronounced with a puff of air. An h following the consonant is used to denote aspiration; for

Unaspirated	Aspirated	Pronunciation
k		as the 'k' in 'skill'
	kh	as the 'k' in 'kill'
g		always hard, as the 'g' in 'garden'
ng		as the 'ng' in 'sing'
c		as the 'ch' in 'charge'
	ch	as the 'ch' and the following 'h' in 'punch hard'
j		as the 'j' in 'jar'
ny		as the 'ny' in 'canyon'
t		as the 't' in 'stop'
	th	as the 't' in 'time'
p		as the 'p' in 'spot'
	ph	as the 'p' in 'pit'
ts		as the 'ts' in 'weights'
	tsh	as the 'ts' and the following 'h' in 'fights hard'
dz		as the 'd' in 'adds'
z		similar to the 'z' in 'zoo'
zh		similar to the 's' in 'pleasure'
r		pronounced deep in the throat, without rolling
s		as the 's' in 'suck'
sh		as the 'sh' in 'shut'

example, kh is the aspirated counterpart of k (see below). The difference in pronunciation is important, as it can change the meaning of a word – khãng-pa means 'house', whereas kãng-pa means 'leg'.

Be careful not to confuse th (aspirated t) with the English 'th' in 'thin' – or ph (aspirated p) with the English 'ph' in 'pharmacy'. In the case of zh and sh, however, the h does not indicate aspiration (see below).

nasalised sounds

An n, m or ng following a vowel indicates a nasalised sound. When pronouncing nasal vowels, the breath escapes partly through the nose and partly through the mouth. The last consonants aren't pronounced, but indicate the nasalisation of the preceding vowel. Imagining an 'ng' at the end of the syllable, as in the word 'sing' can help you make this nasal sound (as long as you remember that the 'g' isn't actually pronounced).

the tibetan writing system

Tibetan consists of 30 basic characters and four vowels, which can be added to these characters. You'll notice that each of the consonants in the writing system includes an a. This is because consonants in Tibetan are represented as syllabic units and all have an inherent a in their basic form. Symbols are added above or below the consonant to indicate different vowel sounds (see page 16).

ཀ	ཁ	ག	ང	ཅ	ཆ	ཇ	ཉ
ka	kha	ga	nga	ca	cha	ja	nya
ཏ	ཐ	ད	ན	པ	ཕ	བ	མ
ta	tha	da	na	pa	pha	ba	ma
ཙ	ཚ	ཛ	ཝ	ཞ	ཟ	འ	ཡ
tsa	tsha	dza	wa	zha	za	'a	ya
ར	ལ	ཤ	ས	ཧ	ཨ		
ra	la	sha	sa	ha	a		

The symbols added above or below the consonants to indicate different vowel sounds, other than a, are:

Vowel Sound	i	u	e	o
Symbol	ˆx	x̬	ˋx	˜x
Position	above	below	above	above

In the following box, we've taken the first consonant ka (ཀ) as an example:

Tibetan	Pronunciation
གི	ki
གུ	ku
གེ	ke
གོ	ko

The Tibetan for each vowel can be pronounced in different ways. Take for example choong, ཆུང ('small') and shu-mah, བཤུམར ('lamp'). Both contain the symbol ˬ but the pronunciation is affected by the letters around it. As a result, the symbol is pronounced as oo and u respectively (see Vowels, page 13, for pronunciation).

spelling

In Tibetan, certain words may be pronounced the same but have different meanings depending on spelling – just like 'through' and 'threw' in English.

སྔ	nga	before/early
ལྔ	nga	five
རྔ	nga	drum

consonant stacks

You'll often see characters on top or below other characters, so-called 'consonant stacks'. Some characters take a special form when being stacked; others remain the same. Consonant stacks are generally only formed with certain characters.

sanskrit characters

An additional set of 11 characters was created for the purpose of transcribing certain Sanskrit words which can't be represented by the Tibetan writing system, but appear frequently in Tibetan Buddhist literature and occasionally in other contexts. It's unlikely you'll come across any of them while visiting Tibet, but it's useful to know of their existence.

The additional characters are divided into two groups: reverse characters and thick characters. Reverse characters are literally characters of the Tibetan alphabet that have been reversed. Thick characters sound emphatic when pronounced. Again all have an inherent a sound.

Reverse Characters		Thick Characters	
ཊ	ta	གྷ	gha
ཋ	tra	དྷ	dha
ཌ	da	བྷ	bha
ཎ	na	ཛྷ	zha
ཥ	ka	ཌྷ	dhra
ཀྵ	kya		

tones

Tones (changes in pitch) do exist in Tibetan, but unlike in some Asian languages, they're not crucial to meaning. For this reason, tones haven't been indicated in this book.

stress

There's no strong word stress in Tibetan. Generally, if you give equal stress to each syllable, you'll be understood.

Tibetan grammar is quite straightforward, with just a few exceptions. This chapter will give you the basics and you'll soon be stringing your own sentences together.

Although the focus of this book is spoken Tibetan, we've included certain aspects of written Tibetan in this chapter, where relevant to the spoken language.

word order

Word order in Tibetan generally follows the pattern subject-object-verb, as opposed to the usual English word order subject-verb-object:

I like Lhasa.	nga lha-sa ga-po yö
	(lit: I Lhasa like)
I need a map.	ngah sâp-ta chig gö
	(lit: I map one need)

articles

definite article

Although the definite article 'the' exists in Tibetan (te), it's rarely used. Where 'the' is used in English, a demonstrative adjective is usually used in Tibetan:

this	di	**these**	din-tsö
that	pha-gi	**those**	phân-tsö
The car is white.		mo-ta pha-gi ka-po ray	
		(lit: car that white is)	
The rooms are dirty.		nye-khâng din-tsö	
		tsog-ba ray	
		(lit: room these dirty are)	

For further examples, see **Demonstratives**, page 21.

A number of basic grammatical terms are used in this chapter. Here's a general summary of them:

adjective	adds information about a noun *red* wine
adverb	adds information about a verb or adjective He runs *quickly*. *very* big
conjunction	joins together sentences or parts of a sentence Wash the car *and* walk the dog.
noun	a person (John), thing (book), place (beach) or concept (happiness)
object	refers to the noun or pronoun that is affected by the verb Paul washes the *dog*.
preposition	introduces information about time, place or direction *at* the market *towards* the city
pronoun	usually takes the place of a noun *he* sings instead of Paul sings
subject	refers to the noun or pronoun that is performing an action *The man* washes the dog.
verb	an action or doing word He *runs* fast.

indefinite article

The indefinite article 'a/an' is expressed in spoken Tibetan by chig, literally meaning 'one':

a yak	yâk chig
	(lit: yak one)
a book	teb chig
	(lit: book one)

nouns

plurals

Tibetan nouns have no plural form. Plurals may be indicated through context alone or through the absence of the indefinite article, chig:

There are mountains in Tibet.	bö-la ri yö-ray
	(lit: Tibet-in mountain are)

Plurals can also be expressed by adding a plural demonstrative adjective (din-tsö, 'these' or phân-tsö, 'those') after the noun:

The bicycles are here.	kâng-ga-ri din-tsö day du
	(lit: bicycle these here are)

Another alternative is to add a plural word (eg, mâng-po, 'many', nyoong-nyoong, 'a few', nyi, 'two' and ka-shay, 'some') or a numeral (see page 179) after the noun or pronoun:

There are many mountains in Tibet.	bö-la ri mâng-po yö-ray
	(lit: Tibet-in mountain many are)

demonstratives

Demonstratives are used far more in Tibetan than they are in English. Wherever possible, they're used instead of 'the' to be more specific. There are also more demonstratives in Tibetan than in English, for example, ya-gi, 'that up there' and mân-tsö, 'those down there'.

this	di	**these**	din-tsö
that	pha-gi	**those**	phân-tsö
that up there	ya-gi	**those up there**	yân-tso
that down there	ma-gi	**those down there**	mân-tsö

Demonstratives are placed after the nouns they refer to:

This country is very beautiful.   loong-pa-di nying-je-po
shay-ta du
**(lit: country-this
beautiful very is)**

That parcel is mine.   cha-lâg pha-gi ngay ray
(lit: parcel that mine is)

That bird up there.   chi-hu ya-gi
(lit: bird that-up-there)

adjectives

Generally, adjectives consist of two syllables in Tibetan. The first syllable is referred to as the root adjective stem and is important when forming comparatives (see opposite) and superlatives (see page 24). Adjectives follow the noun they describe:

red suitcase   tog-tay mah-po
(lit: suitcase red)

dirty room   nye-khâng tsog-ba
(lit: room dirty)

comparatives

Comparatives are formed differently in spoken and written Tibetan. In spoken language, comparatives are usually formed by replacing the second syllable of the adjective with the final consonant (along with its inherent a, see the Tibetan alphabet page 15) of the root adjective stem:

good	yâg-po
better	yâg-ga

Sometimes the written form is used in spoken language. The written form replaces the second syllable with pa or wa. There's no rule governing whether to add pa or wa, but even if you add the wrong one you'll still be understood:

good	yâg-po
better	yâg-pa

Here are a few of the more common adjectives with the appropriate endings added. The spoken form is listed first, followed in brackets by the written form. Where the written form is used in spoken language, only one form is given:

bad	dhuk-cha	**worse**	dhuk-ka (dhuk-pa)
cold	dâng-mo	**colder**	dâng-nga (dâng-wa)
good	yâg-po	**better**	yâg-ga (yag-pa)
hot	tsha-po	**hotter**	tsha-wa
high	tho-po	**higher**	tho-wa
many	mâng-po	**more**	mâng-nga (mâng-wa)
small	choong-choong	**smaller**	choong-nga (choong-wa)

Occasionally, the root adjective stem changes its form when pa or wa is added. Such exceptions are very rare, however:

big	chen-po	**bigger**	chay-wa

To compare two nouns in a sentence, attach -lay (roughly meaning 'than') to the noun that would follow 'than' in English. Note the order of the two nouns is reversed in Tibetan:

Mt Everest is higher than Mt Kailash.
gâng rim-po-che-lay jo-mo lâng-ri tho-wa yö-ray
(lit: Mt Kailash-than Mt Everest higher is)

superlatives

In both spoken and written language, superlatives are formed by replacing the second syllable of the adjective with -shö. Any root adjective stem changes are the same as for comparatives:

bad	dhuk-cha	**worst**	dhuk-shö
big	chen-po	**biggest**	chay-shö
cold	dâng-mo	**coldest**	dâng-shö
good	yâg-po	**best**	yâg-shö
high	tho-po	**highest**	tho-shö
hot	tsha-po	**hottest**	tsha-shö
many	mâng-po	**most**	mâng-shö
small	choong-choong	**smallest**	choong-shö

pronouns

personal pronouns

Whether it's acting as the subject (eg, 'I'), or the object (eg, 'me') of a sentence, the pronoun is the same in Tibetan, so nga, for example, means both 'I' and 'me'.

There are many forms of personal pronouns in honorific (for speaking to monks and nuns) and written Tibetan. Those listed below are the most commonly used in the spoken language. You'll notice that all plural pronouns end in -tso.

Singular		Plural	
I/me	nga	**we/us**	ngân-tso
you	kay-râng	**you**	kay-râng-tso
he/him (inf)	kho	**they/them (inf/pol)**	khong-tso
she/her (inf)	mo		
he/she/him/ her (pol)	khong		
it	te		

When used with intentional verbs (see page 26), the subject changes to mean 'by me', 'by you' etc:

Singular		Plural	
by me	ngay	**by us**	ngân-tsö
by you	kay-râng-gi	**by you**	kay-râng-tsö
by him (inf)	khö	**by them (m/f, inf)**	kho-tsö
by her (inf)	mö	**by them (m/f, pol)**	khong-tsö
by him/her (pol)	khong-gi		
by it	tay		

possessives

Possessive adjectives (eg, 'my') are the same as possessive pronouns (eg, 'mine'), so ngay is used to mean both 'my' and 'mine'. All plurals end in -tsö:

Singular		Plural	
my/mine	ngay	**ours**	ngân-tsö
your(s)	kay-râng-gi	**your(s)**	kay-râng-tsö
his (inf)	khö	**their(s) (m/f, inf)**	kho-tsö
her/hers (inf)	mö	**their(s) (m/f, pol)**	khong-tsö
his/her (pol)	khong-gi		
its	tay		

Possessive adjectives, unlike other adjectives, appear before the noun they possess, whereas possessive pronouns always follow the noun to which they refer:

This is my car.	di ngay mo-ta ray
	(lit: this my car is)
This car is mine.	mo-ta-di ngay-ray
	(lit: car-this mine-is)

verbs

Tibetan verbs fall into two classes. One class contains verbs that the subject controls, referred to here as 'intentional verbs'; the other class contains those that represent actions or feelings that the subject does not have direct control over, referred to here as 'unintentional verbs'. 'To eat' and 'to watch' would therefore be intentional verbs, while 'to feel sick' and 'to feel sad' would be unintentional verbs.

Some verbs can have both an intentional and an unintentional form. For example, the verb 'to sleep' has an intentional form, meaning the person went to sleep of their own volition, and an unintentional form, meaning the person fell asleep without wanting or trying to.

It's important to remember that each tense comprises three parts: a main verb, a tense particle and an auxiliary verb, 'to be' (see page 28). For example, 'I'm reading' is ngay log-gi-yö (lit: I read-present-am). In this sentence, the main verb is log 'to read', the tense particle is gi, and yö is the auxiliary verb.

The main verb usually takes the same form in the present, past and future tenses. (See page 30 for a list of Key Verbs.)

The auxiliary verbs and tense particles vary according to subject (me, you, he, she etc) and tense – it's good to try to learn these. The two classes of verbs take different auxiliary verbs and tense particles, so there are two sets to learn.

intentional verbs

	Present		Past		Future	
	Tense Particle	Auxiliary Verb	Tense Particle	Auxiliary Verb	Tense Particle	Auxiliary Verb
I/we		-yö	-pa	-yin		-yin
you/he/she/they	-gi	-du	-pa song	-ray	-gi	-ray

I listen to music.	ngay rö-ja nyen-gi-yö (lit: I music listen-present-am)
She listened to music.	mö rö-ja nyen-pâ-ray; mö rö-ja nyen song (lit: she music listen-past-was)
They will listen to music.	khong-tsö rö-ja nyen-gi-ray (lit: they music listen-future-will)

unintentional verbs

For unintentional verbs, the tense particle only changes according to person (I, we, he, she etc) in the past tense and the auxiliary verb doesn't change at all according to person. Note that in the past tense, no auxiliary verb is required at all:

	Present		Past	Future	
	Tense Particle	Auxiliary Verb	Tense Particle	Tense Particle	Auxiliary Verb
I/we			-choong		
you/he/she/they	-gi	-du	-song	-gi	-ray

I'm sick.	nga na-gi-du (lit: I sick-present-am)
She was sick.	mo na-song (lit: I sick-past)
They will be sick.	khong-tso na-gi-ray (lit: I sick-future-will)

to be

Whereas English uses one verb ('to be') to express both location ('the book is here') and equivalence ('the book is red'), Tibetan uses three different verbs:

1. The verb du is used to express location and also for information gained first-hand.

   The forest is here.   shing-nâg-te day du
                                (lit: forest-the here is)

   When used with 'I' or 'we', the verb du becomes yö:

   I'm here.   nga day yö
                         (lit: I here am)

2. To express equivalence the verb ray is used:

   He's Buddhist.   kho nâng-pa ray
                            (lit: he Buddhist is)
   The rooms are dirty.   nye-khâng din-tsö
                            tsog-ba ray
                            (lit: room these dirty are)

   The verb ray becomes yin when it's used with 'I' or 'we':

   I'm a teacher.   nga ge-gan yin
                            (lit: I teacher am)

3. The verb yö-ray is used to express facts that are general or common knowledge and can be used to express both location and equivalence.

   There are yaks in Tibet.   bö-la yâk yö-ray
                            (lit: Tibet-in yak are)
   He's a good person.   khong mi yag-po chig yö-ray **(pol)**
                            (lit: he person good one is)

All three verbs change when forming a negative sentence (see page 34).

to have

There's no equivalent for the verb 'to have' in Tibetan. The idea of possession is expressed by adding -la (usually indicating location, see Postpositions, page 35) to the end of the subject, as well as using the auxiliary verb du/yö at the end of the sentence. Again du is used in all cases except for I/we, when yö is used.

He has a map.   kho-la sâp-ta du
        (lit: he-la **map has**)

I have a car.   nga-la mo-ta chig yö
        (lit: I-la **car one have**)

modals

want, need, must

In Tibetan, the verb gö is used to mean 'want', 'need' and 'must':

I want tea.   nga cha gö
        (lit: **I tea want**)

I need two beds.   nga nye-ti nyi gö
        (lit: **I bed two need**)

When used in conjunction with another verb, gö takes an auxiliary verb at the end of the sentence:

I must see the   nga shing-nâg-te mig ta-gö-yö
forest.   (lit: **I forest-the see must**)

To form a question, gö becomes gö-bay, but the word order remains the same:

Do you want tea?   kay-râng cha gö-bay?
        (lit: **you tea want?**)

Alternatively, you can use a question word/phrase, such as 'how much', kâ-tsö: (See page 32 for more question words.)

How much money   kay-râng-la ngü kâ-tsö gö?
do you want?   (lit: **you-la money how-much want?**)

To make a negative sentence, add mö to the beginning of gö:

I don't want this.   nga-la di mö-gö
        (lit: **I-la this not-want**)

key verbs

Most verbs remain the same for all tenses, but some take a different form depending on the tense, as indicated below. Where present and future columns are blank, those tenses take the same form as the past tense.

Remember the forms listed can be used regardless of the subject (I, you, he, she etc) of the sentence – you just need to add the relevant endings (see page 27).

	Past	Present	Future
to agree	thün		
to arrive	jor		
to borrow/lend	yar		
to break	châg	chok	châg
to bring/take	kay		
to buy	nyö	nyo	nyo
to come	yong		
to cry	ngü	ngu	ngu
to dance	tâb		
to depart (leave)	thön		
to do	chay		
to drink	toong		
to eat	say	sa	sa
to give	tay	tö	tö
to go	chin	doh	doh
to hire	lay	la	la
to hit	doong		

	Past	Present	Future
to know (someone/something)	shay		
to like	gah		
to listen	nyen		
to make	sö	so	so
to meet	thoog		
to move	gü	nyo	nyo
to need	gö		
to prefer	dâm	dem	dem
to pull	ten		
to receive	jor		
to remember	den		
to say	lâb		
to see	tong		
to send	kur		
to sleep	nyey		
to stay	day	dö	day
to steal	kü	ku	ku
to stop	kâg	gok	gâk
to tell	lâb	so	so
to want	gö		
to wear	gyön		
to write	di		

questions

There are two main ways to form questions in Tibetan, depending on whether you want to form a question that requires a 'yes/no' response, or one that asks for more information.

information questions

To form information questions, you'll need to use a question word. Question words are generally placed before the verb:

What?	kâ-ray?	**What did you eat?** kay-râng kâ-ray say-bâ-yin? **(lit: you what ate?)**
Who?	su?	**Who's he?** khong su ray? **(pol)** **(lit: he who is?)**
Where?	ka-bah?	**Where's the post office?** da-khâng ka-bah yö-ray? **(lit: post-office where is?)**
When?	ka-dü?	**When did you leave?** kay-râng ka-dü thön-gay? **(lit: you when left?)**
Whose?	sü?	**Whose is this?** di sü ray? **(lit: this whose is?)**
How?	kân-te-si?	**How do I get to ...?** ...-la kân-te-si do-gö-ray? **(lit: to how go?)**
How much/ many?	kâ-tsay/ kât-sö?	**How much is the room?** khâng-mi te-la gong kâ-tsay ray? **(lit: room the cost how-much is?)**
Why?	kâ-ray chay-nay?	**Why did you go?** kay-râng kâ-ray chay-nay chin-bâ-yin? **(lit: you why went?)**

'yes/no' questions

To form a question from a sentence that uses one of the three equivalents of the verb 'to be', the endings are as follows:

	du/yö	ray/yin	yö-ray
I/he/she/it/we/they	du-gay	re-bay	yö re-bay
you	yö-bay	yin-bay	

Do you have a pen?   kay-râng-la nyu-gu-chig
yö-bay?
(lit: you pen-one have?)

For all other verbs, use the following endings:

intentional verbs

	Present	Past	Future
I/we	-gi du-gay	-pa re-bay	-gi re-bay
you	-gi yö-bay	**verb**-bay	-gi yin-bay
he/she/it/they	-gi du-gay	-pa re-bay	-gi re-bay

unintentional verbs

	Present	Past	Future
I/we/you/he/she/it/they	-gi du-gay	song-ngey	-gi re-bay

Are you watching the show?   kay-râng tay-mo ta-gi yö-bay?
(intentional)   **(lit: you show
watch-present-are?)**

Did you see the show?   kay-räng tay-mo tong song-ngey?
(unintentional)   **(lit: you show
see-past-were?)**

negatives

To make a 'to be' sentence negative, use the following forms:

	du/yö	ray/yin	yö-ray
I/we	may	min/ma-yin	yo-ma-ray
you/he/she/it/they	min-du	ma-ray	

This is not a restaurant. di sa-khâng ma-ray
(lit: this restaurant is-not)

There are no hotels here. day sa-khâng yö-ma-ray
(lit: here hotels are-not)

For all other verbs, add the following endings to the main verb:

intentional verbs

	Present	Past	Future
I/we	-gi-may	-pa-min	-gi-min
you/he/she/it/they	-gi-min-du	-pa-ma-ray	-gi-ma-ray

unintentional verbs

	Present	Past	Future
I/we	-gi-min-du	ma-choong	-gi-ma-ray
you/he/she/it/they		-ma-song	

I don't listen to music. ngay rö-ja nyen-gi-may
(intentional) (lit: I music listen-present-not)

I'm not sick. nga na-gi-min-du
(unintentional) (lit: I sick-am-present-not)

conveying 'yes' & 'no'

In Tibetan, the verb form used in the question determines how you say 'yes' and 'no'. Listen out for one of the following forms at the end of a question, and answer with the appropriate 'yes' or 'no':

Question Form	du-gay	yö-bay	re-bay	yin-bay	yö re-bay
Yes	du	yö	ray	yin	yö-ray
No	min-du	may	ma-ray	men	yö mâ-ray

Are yaks big?	yâk chen-po yö re-bay?	
	(lit: yaks big are?)	
Yes./No.	yö-ray/yö mâ-ray	
Do you live here?	kay-râng-day shu-gi yö-bay?	
	(lit: you-here live-present-are?)	
Yes./No.	yö/may	

There are some exceptions, for example, the past-tense question ending song-ngey (see page 33):

Did you see the show?	kay-râng tay-mo tong song-ngey?
	(lit: you show see-past-were?)
Yes./No.	song/ma-song

postpositions

Postpositions are equivalent to prepositions in English; where in English the preposition comes before the noun, in Tibetan it comes after the noun. 'To', 'at', 'for' and 'into' can all be expressed by -la.

I will go to India.	nga gya-ka-la do-gi yin
	(lit: I India-to go-future-am)

Below is a list of other common postpositions:

above	gâng-la
around	nye-ko-la
behind	gyâb-la/jay-la
beside	tih-la
from	nay
in	nâng-la
in front of	dün-la
of	ki/gi/yi
next to	tih-la
on	gâng-la
opposite	pha-chog-la/kha-trö-la/tog-chog-la
under	wog-la
with	nyâm-du

In front of the house.	khâng-bay dün-la
	(lit: house in-front-of)

conjunctions

Conjunctions are placed in the same position as in English.

and	dâng
because	gâng-yin say-na
but	yin-nay
or	yâng-na
since	tsâng/nay
so (therefore)	te-dah song-tsâng
so that (in order to)	ton-dâ-la/chay-du
then	te-nay/te-dü

I'd like to go to Tsetang, but I don't have time.	nga tse-tang-la don-dhö-yö, yin-nay nga-la dü-tsö may
	(lit: I Tsetang-to like but I time have-no)

cardinal numbers

གྱི་གྲངས

The Tibetan counting system is quite logical – as long as you follow the pattern below, you won't have a problem.

0	༠	lay-koh	ཀླད་ཀོར
1	༡	chig	གཅིག
2	༢	nyi	གཉིས
3	༣	soom	གསུམ
4	༤	shi	བཞི
5	༥	nga	ལྔ
6	༦	doog	དྲུག
7	༧	dün	བདུན
8	༨	gye	བརྒྱད
9	༩	gu	དགུ
10	༡༠	chu/chu-tâm-pa	བཅུ/བཅུ་ཐམ་པ
11	༡༡	chu-chig	བཅུ་གཅིག
12	༡༢	chu-nyi	བཅུ་གཉིས
13	༡༣	chu-soom	བཅུ་གསུམ
14	༡༤	chu-shi	བཅུ་བཞི
15	༡༥	chö-nga	བཅོ་ལྔ
16	༡༦	chu-doog	བཅུ་དྲུག
17	༡༧	chu-dün	བཅུ་བདུན
18	༡༨	chö-gye	བཅོ་བརྒྱད
19	༡༩	chu-gu	བཅུ་དགུ
20	༢༠	nyi-shu; nyi-shu tâm-pa	ཉི་ཤུ/ ཉི་ཤུ་ཐམ་པ
21	༢༡	nyi-shu tsa-chig	ཉི་ཤུ་རྩ་གཅིག
22	༢༢	nyi-shu tsa-nyi	ཉི་ཤུ་རྩ་གཉིས
30	༣༠	soom-chu; soom-chu tâm-pa	སུམ་ཅུ/ སུམ་ཅུ་ཐམ་པ
31	༣༡	soom-chu so-chig	སུམ་ཅུ་སོ་གཅིག

numbers & amounts

37

40	ৼO	shib-chu; shib-chu tâm-pa	བཞི་བཅུ/བཞི་བཅུ་ཐམ་པ
41	ৼኃ	shib-chu shay-chig	བཞི་བཅུ་ཞེ་གཅིག
50	५O	ngâb-chu; ngâb-chu tâm-pa	ལྔ་བཅུ/ལྔ་བཅུ་ཐམ་པ
51	५ኃ	ngâb-chu ngay-chig	ལྔ་བཅུ་ང་གཅིག
60	৬O	doog-chu; doog-chu tâm-pa	དྲུག་བཅུ/དྲུག་བཅུ་ཐམ་པ
61	৬ኃ	doog-chu re-chig	དྲུག་བཅུ་རེ་གཅིག
70	২/O	dün-chu; dün-chu tâm-pa	བདུན་བཅུ/བདུན་བཅུ་ཐམ་པ
71	২/ኃ	dün-chu dön-chig	བདུན་བཅུ་དོན་གཅིག
80	८O	gyay-chu; gyay-chu tâm-pa	བརྒྱད་བཅུ/བརྒྱད་བཅུ་ཐམ་པ
81	८ኃ	gyay-chu gya-chig	བརྒྱད་བཅུ་གྱ་གཅིག
90	९O	goob-chu; goob-chu tâm-pa	དགུ་བཅུ/དགུ་བཅུ་ཐམ་པ
91	९ኃ	goob-chu go-chig	དགུ་བཅུ་གོ་གཅིག
100	႟OO	gya; gya tâm-pa	བརྒྱ/བརྒྱ་ཐམ་པ
101	႟Oኃ	gya dâng chig	བརྒྱ་དང་གཅིག
155	႟५५	gya dâng ngâb-chu ngay-nga	བརྒྱ་དང་ལྔ་བཅུ་ང་ལྔ
1000	႟OOO	chig-tong; chig-tong tâm-pa	ཆིག་སྟོང/ཆིག་སྟོང་ཐམ་པ
10,000	႟OOOO	chig-ti/tong-tâg-chu	ཆིག་ཁྲི/སྟོང་ཕྲག་བཅུ
100,000	႟OOOOO	chig-boom/	ཆིག་འབུམ/
		boom-tâg-chig	འབུམ་ཕྲག་གཅིག

one million	႟OOOOOO	sa-ya-chig/boom-chu	ས་ཡ་གཅིག/འབུམ་བཅུ
ten million	႟OOOOOOO	chay-wa-chig	བྱེ་བ་གཅིག
one hundred million	႟OOOOOOOO	doong-chu-chig	དུང་ཕྱུར་གཅིག

ordinal numbers

རིམ་གྲངས

Ordinal numbers are easy to form in Tibetan – just add the suffix -pa (པ) to the relevant cardinal number. The only exception is with chig (གཅིག), 'one', which becomes dâng-po (དངརྤོ), 'first'.

1st	dâng-po	དང་པོ
2nd	nyi-pa	གཉིས་པ
3rd	soom-pa	གསུམ་པ
4th	shi-pa	བཞི་པ
5th	nga-pa	ལྔ་པ

fractions

ཆ་གྲངས།

a quarter	shi-cha-chig	བཞི་ཆ་གཅིག
a half	chay-ka	ཕྱེད་ཀ
a third	soom-cha-chig	གསུམ་ཆ་གཅིག
three-quarters	shi-cha-soom	བཞི་ཆ་གསུམ

digital counting

When using their fingers to count, Tibetans touch the tip of their thumb to each finger or the joint lines of each finger, so each can be used three times.

useful amounts

རྒྱུན་མཁོའི་གྲངས་འབོར།

How much?	gong kâ-tsay	གོང་ག་ཚོད།
How many?	kâ-tsö	ག་ཚོད
Could you please give me …?	ngah … nâng-da	ངར་ … གནང་དང་།
I need …	ngah … gö	ངར་ … དགོས།
all	tsâng-ma	ཚང་མ
a bottle	shay-tâm-chig	ཤེལ་དམ་གཅིག
a bottle of water	chu shay-tâm chig	ཆུ་ཤེལ་དམ་གཅིག
double	nyi-tsâg	ཉིས་ཚེག
a dozen	dha-tsen-chig	དར་ཚོན་གཅིག
half a dozen	dha-tsen chay-ka	དར་ཚོན་ཕྱེད་ཀ
half a dozen eggs	go-nga dha-tsen chay-ka	སྒོ་ང་དར་ཚོན་ཕྱེད་ཀ
enough	dâng-ngay/dâng-pa	འདང་ངེས/འདང་པ
a few	nyoong-nyoong	ཉུང་ཉུང
few	ka-shay/te-si	ཁ་ཤས/དེ་ཙམ
gram	ga-râm	གྲ་རམ
100 grams	ga-râm gya	གྲ་རམ་བརྒྱ

numbers & amounts

English	Transliteration	Tibetan
a kilogram	ki-lo chig	གི་ལོ་གཅིག
a kilogram of rice	day ki-lo chig	འབྲས་གི་ལོ་གཅིག
half a kilogram	ki-lo chay-ka	གི་ལོ་ཕྱེད་ཀ
less	nyoong-wa	ཉུང་བ
litre	li-tar	ལི་ཏར
two litres of oil	noom li-tar nyi	སྣུམ་ལི་ཏར་གཉིས
half a litre	li-tar chay-ka	ལི་ཏར་ཕྱེད་ཀ
a little	te-si	དོག་ཙམ
many; much; a lot	mâng-po	མང་པོ
more	mâng-wa	མང་བ
none	tsa-nay may-pa	རྩ་ནས་མེད་པ
once	teng-chig	ཐེངས་གཅིག
a packet	châg-pa chig;	ཁུག་པ་གཅིག/
	gâm-chig	སྒམ་གཅིག
a packet of cigarettes	tha-ma gâm-chig	ཐ་མག་སྒམ་གཅིག
a packet of green onions	tsong ngön-po châg-pa chig	ཙོང་སྔོན་པོ་ཁུག་པ་གཅིག
a pair	cha-chig	ཆ་གཅིག
a slice	lheb-chig	ལེབ་གཅིག
some	ka-shay	ཁ་ཤས
a tin	tin-chig	ཊིན་གཅིག
too many/much	mâng-dâg-pa	མང་དྲགས་པ
twice	teng-nyi	ཐེངས་གཉིས

telling the time

ཆུ་ཚོད་ག་ཚོད

Telling the time is very straightforward in Tibetan – just re-member to use ordinal numbers (see **Numbers & Amounts**, page 180) in your sentences.

What time is it?

    tân-da chu-tsö kâ-tsay-ray?   ད་ལྟ་ཆུ་ཚོད་ག་ཚོད་རེད།

It's two o'clock.

    chu-tsö nyi-pa ray   ཆུ་ཚོད་གཉིས་པ་རེད།
    (lit: hour second is)

It's five o'clock.

    chu-tsö nga-pa ray   ཆུ་ཚོད་ལྔ་པ་རེད།
    (lit: hour fifth is)

Quarter to three.

    soom-pa sin-ba ka-ma cho-nga   གསུམ་པ་སྲིན་པ་སྐར་མ་བཅོ་ལྔ
    (lit: third to minutes fifteen)

Twenty to six.

    doog-pa sin-ba ka-ma nyi-shu   ལྤ་པ་སྲིན་པ་སྐར་མ་ཉི་ཤུ
    (lit: sixth to minutes twenty)

There are some unusual expressions, however, which must be learnt separately:

It's midnight.

    gong-da chu-tsö chu-nyi ray   དགོང་དག་ཆུ་ཚོད་བཅུ་གཉིས་རེད།

It's noon.

    nyin-goong chu-tsö chu-nyi ray   ཉིན་གུང་ཆུ་ཚོད་བཅུ་གཉིས་རེད།

The term for 'half past' is chay-ka (ཕྱེད་ཀ), literally meaning 'half', and for 'quarter past' is ka-ma chö-nga (སྐར་མ་བཅོ་ལྔ), literally meaning 'minutes fifteen':

It's two thirty.

chu-tsö nyi-dâng chay-ka ray   ཆུ་ཚོད་གཉིས་དང་ཕྱེད་ཀ་རེད།
(lit: hour two-and half is)

It's quarter past six.

chu-tsö doog-dâng ka-ma   ཆུ་ཚོད་དྲུག་དང་སྐར་མ་བཅོ་ལྔ་རེད།
chö-nga ray
(lit: hour six-and minutes fifteen is)

days of the week

Monday	sa da-wa	གཟའ་ཟླ་བ
Tuesday	sa mig-ma	གཟའ་མིག་དམར
Wednesday	sa lhâg-bâ	གཟའ་ལྷག་པ
Thursday	sa phu-bu	གཟའ་ཕུར་བུ
Friday	sa pa-sâng	གཟའ་པ་སངས
Saturday	sa pem-pa	གཟའ་སྤེན་པ
Sunday	sa nyi-mâ	གཟའ་ཉི་མ

months

Tibet uses both the traditional lunar calendar, where each month has 30 days, and the Gregorian calendar, as used in the West. There are 12 months in each, which are simply referred to as the '1st month', the '2nd month' etc. However, the Lunar New Year is about six weeks after the Western New Year.

1st month	da-wa dâng-po	ཟླ་བ་དང་པོ
2nd month	da-wa nyi-pa	ཟླ་བ་གཉིས་པ
3rd month	da-wa soom-pa	ཟླ་བ་གསུམ་པ
4th month	da-wa shi-pa	ཟླ་བ་བཞི་པ

5th month	da-wa nga-pa	ཟླ་བ་ལྔ་པ
6th month	da-wa doog-pa	ཟླ་བ་དྲུག་པ
7th month	da-wa dün-pa	ཟླ་བ་བདུན་པ
8th month	da-wa gye-pa	ཟླ་བ་བརྒྱད་པ
9th month	da-wa gu-pa	ཟླ་བ་དགུ་པ
10th month	da-wa chu-pa	ཟླ་བ་བཅུ་པ
11th month	da-wa chu-chig-pa	ཟླ་བ་བཅུ་གཅིག་པ
12th month	da-wa chu-nyi-pa	ཟླ་བ་བཅུ་གཉིས་པ

To be more precise, you can substitute chin-da (ཕྱི་ཟླ), 'Western month', or bön-da (བོད་ཟླ), 'Tibetan month', for da-wa (ཟླ་བ) 'month'. February, for example, would be either chin-da nyi-pa (ཕྱི་ཟླ་གཉིས་པ) or bön-da nyi-pa (བོད་ཟླ་གཉིས་པ).

dates

ཚེས་པ

What date is it today? (Western calendar)

te-ring chi-tsay kâ-tsö ray?　　དེ་རིང་ཕྱི་ཚེས་ག་ཚོད་རེད།

It's 28 June.

te-ring chin-da doog-bay tsay　　དེ་རིང་ཕྱི་ཟླ་དྲུག་པའི་ཚེས་
nyi-shu tsâb-gye ray　　ཉི་ཤུ་རྩ་བརྒྱད་རེད།
(lit: today Western-month sixth
of-date twenty eight is)

It's 1 April.

te-ring chin-da shi-bay tsay　　དེ་རིང་ཕྱི་ཟླ་བཞི་པའི་ཚེས་གཅིག་རེད།
chig ray
(lit: today Western-month fourth
of-date one is)

present

ད་ལྟ

today	te-ring	དེ་རིང
this morning	te-ring shoh-gay	དེ་རིང་ཞོགས་ཀས
this afternoon	te-ring chi-toh	དེ་རིང་ཕྱི་དྲོ

this evening	dho-gong	དོ་གོང་
tonight	dho-gong-tshen	དོ་གོང་མཚན་
this week	dün-tâ di; sa-koh-di	བདུན་ཕྲག་འདི་/གཟའ་འཁོར་འདི་
this month	da-wa di	ཟླ་བ་འདི་
this year	tâ-lo/lo-di	ད་ལོ་/ལོ་འདི་

past

yesterday	kay-sa	ཁ་ས་
day before yesterday	kay nyin-mo	ཁ་ཉི་ཉིན་མོ་
yesterday morning	kay-sa shoh-gay	ཁ་ས་ཞོགས་གང་
yesterday afternoon	kay-sa chi-toh	ཁ་ས་ཕྱི་དྲོ་
yesterday evening	dâng-gong	མདང་དགོང་
last night	kay-sa gong-ta	ཁ་ས་དགོང་དག
last week	dün-ta ngön-ma; sa-koh ngön-ma	བདུན་ཕྲག་སྔོན་མ་/གཟའ་འཁོར་སྔོན་མ་
last month	da-wa ngön-ma	ཟླ་བ་སྔོན་མ་
last year	da-nyi/lo ngön-ma	ཟླ་ཉིང་/ལོ་སྔོན་མ་
(half an hour) ago	(chu-tsö chay-ka) ngön-la	(ཆུ་ཚོད་ཕྱེད་ཀ)སྔོན་ལ་
(three) days ago	nyin-(soom) ngön-la	ཉིན་(གསུམ)སྔོན་ལ་
(five) years ago	lo (nga) ngön-la	ལོ་(ལྔ)སྔོན་ལ་
since (May)	(chin-da nga-pa) nay soong	(ཕྱི་ཟླ་ལྔ་པ)ནས་བཟུང་

future

tomorrow	sa-nyin	སང་ཉིན་
day after tomorrow	nâng-nyin	གནངས་ཉིན་
tomorrow morning	sâng-shoh	སང་ཞོག
tomorrow afternoon	sâng chi-toh	སང་ཕྱི་དྲོ་
tomorrow evening	sâng-nyi gong-da; sâng-noob	སང་ཉིན་དགོང་དག/སང་ནུབ་

next week	dün-ta je-ma;	བདུན་ཕྲག་རྗེས་མ/
	sa-koh je-ma	གཟའ་འཁོར་རྗེས་མ
next month	da-wa je-ma	ཟླ་བ་རྗེས་མ
next year	lo je-ma/tü-sâng	ལོ་རྗེས་མ/སང་ལོ/དུས་སང་
in (five) minutes	ka-ma (ngay) nâng	སྐར་མ (ལྔ) ནང་
in (six) days	nyin-ma (doog) nâng	ཉིན་མ (དྲུག) ནང་
within an hour/	chu-tsö/da-wa	ཆུ་ཚོད/ཟླ་བ
month	chig nâng	གཅིག་ནང་
until (June)	(chin-da doog-pa)	(ཕྱི་ཟླ་དུག་པ)
	bah-tu	བར་དུ

during the day

ཉིན་གུང་ལ

It's early.	nga-po ray-sha	སྔ་པོ་རེད་ཤག
It's late.	chi-po ray	ཕྱི་པོ་རེད།
afternoon	chi-toh	ཕྱི་དྲོ
dawn	toh-reng/kya-reng	ཐོ་རེངས/སྐྱ་རེངས
day(time)	nyin-mo	ཉིན་མོ
early	nga-po	སྔ་པོ
evening	gong-da	དགོང་དག
late	chi-po	ཕྱི་པོ
lunchtime	nyin-goong kha-la dü-tsö	ཉིན་གུང་ཁ་ལག་དུས་ཚོད
midday	nyin-goong	ཉིན་གུང་
midnight	nâm-chay	ནམ་ཕྱེ
morning	shoh-gay	ཞོགས་སྐད
night	tsen-mo	མཚན་མོ
noon	nyin-goong	ཉིན་གུང་
sunset	nyin-ma noob-dü	ཉི་མ་ནུབ་དུས
sunrise	nyin-ma shar-dü	ཉི་མ་ཤར་དུས

useful words

ཀྱུན་སྤྱོད་ཀྱི་མིང་ཚིག

a while ago	dü-yün-kay ngön-la	དུས་ཡུན་ཁག་གཅིག་སྔོན་ལ་
after	jay-la	རྗེས་ལ་
always	tâg-pa/châr-chen	རྟག་པར་/འཆར་ཅན་
before	ngön-la	སྔོན་ལ་
every day	nyin-tar	ཉིན་ལྟར་
forever	tâg-tu	རྟག་ཏུ་
immediately	tân-ta-râng	དལྟ་རང་
long ago	nga-mo nga-mo	སྔ་མོ་སྔ་མོ་
never	nâm-yang	ནམ་ཡང་
not any more	yâng-kya-min/ chin-chay-min	ཡང་སྐྱར་མིན་/ ཕྱིན་ཆད་མིན་
not yet	tân-da-yâng may	དལྟ་ཡང་མེད་
now	tân-da	དལྟ་
recently	nye-char	ཉེ་ཆར་
sometimes	tshâm tshâm	མཚམས་མཚམས་
soon	gyok-po/lâm-sâng	མགྱོགས་པོ་/ལམ་སང་

festivals & holidays

དུས་ཆེན་དང་གུང་སེང་

If your trip coincides with a Tibetan festival, there's a good chance you'll see a châm performance. Châm is a ritual dance performed by monks and lamas and held over several days. The performers wear colourful masks and each movement has special significance.

All festivals are held according to the **Tibetan lunar calendar** (see page 170).

lo-sar ལོ་གསར་(བོད་ཟླ་ ༡ ཚེས་ ༡)
This is the New Year Festival, and so begins on the first day of the first lunar month.

mön-lâm chen-mo སྨོན་ལམ་ཆེན་མོ་(བོད་ཟླ་ ༡ ཚེས་ ༡༥)
The Great Prayer Festival runs from the 1st to 15th of the first lunar month and celebrates Buddha's miracles and victory over the six non-Buddhist masters at Sravasti in India.

sa-ga da-wa
ས་གཱ་ཟླ་བ (བོད་ཟླ་ ༤ ཚེས་ ༡༥)

The anniversary of Buddha's birth, death and enlightenment is celebrated on the 15th day of the fourth lunar month. Outdoor operas (see page 176) take place and throngs of pilgrims follow the Barkhor circuit.

zâm-ling chi-sâng
འཛམ་གླིང་སྤྱི་བསངས (བོད་ཟླ་ ༥ ཚེས་ ༡༥)

Occuring on the 15th day of the fifth lunar month, this festival marks the successful completion of the first Tibetan monastery – the Samye Monastery. Incense is burned and prayer flags are strung up for world peace.

lha-sa sho-ton
ལྷ་ས་ཞོ་སྟོན (བོད་ཟླ་ ༧ ཚེས་ ༢)

Held on the 2nd day of the seventh lunar month. Operas and masked dances take place and locals enjoy picnics.

lha-sa wong-koh
ལྷ་ས་འོང་བསྐོར (བོད་ཟླ་ ༧)

The Lhasa Farmer Festival generally occurs during the seventh lunar month. Farmers around Lhasa burn incense and string up prayer flags to honour the local deities who control the region's peace and stability, as well as the fertility of the soil.

toong-kah dü-chen བཙུངས་སྐར་དུས་ཆེན (ཕྱི་ཟླ་ ༧ ཚེས་ ༦)
His Holiness the Dalai Lama's birthday is celebrated on 6 July.
It commemorates the birth of the 14th Dalai Lama in Amdo,
Eastern Tibet, in 1935.

cho-kor dü-chen ཆོས་འཁོར་དུས་ཆེན (བོད་ཟླ་ ༦ ཚེས་ ༤)
The remembrance of Buddha's first discourse, when he taught
the Four Holy Truths to his five disciples, takes place on the 4th
day of the sixth lunar month.

lha-bâb dü-chen ལྷ་བབས་དུས་ཆེན (བོད་ཟླ་ ༩ ཚེས་ ༢༢)
Held on the 22nd day of the ninth lunar month, this celebration
commemorates Buddha's descent from heaven. You'll find
many pilgrims in Lhasa on this day.

legendary lhamo!

Lha-mo (ལྷ་མོ) is Tibetan opera and is very popular at festival
times. It recounts historical events and ancient legends and
tells of heroes and villains.

gân-den ngâm-chö དགའ་ལྡན་ལྔ་མཆོད (བོད་ཟླ་ ༡༠ ཚེས་ ༢༥)
Sometimes referred to as the Tsong Khapa anniversary, this
event is held on the 25th day of the tenth lunar month. Tsong
Khapa (1357-1419) was a renowned Tibetan lama, scholar and
meditator who founded the Gelugpa School of Tibetan Buddhism.

ngan-pa gu-zom ངན་པ་དགུ་འཛོམས (བོད་ཟླ་ ༡༡ ཚེས་ ༦)
The 6th day of the eleventh lunar month is considered a day
of nine inauspicious signs – a very bad day to start a trip or
any projects.

sang-po chu-zom བཟང་པོ་བཅུ་འཛོམས (བོད་ཟླ་ ༡༡ཚེས་ ༧)
The 7th day of the eleventh lunar month is a day of 10 auspicious signs – a good day for picnicking and generally having fun.

tse gu-tor ཚེ་དགུ་གཏོར (བོད་ཟླ་ ༡༢ ཚེས་ ༢༩)
This is a festival to banish evil spirits and takes place on the
29th day of the twelfth lunar month.

new year

The Year End Festival, nyi-shu-gu (ཉི་ཤུ་དགུ), is held on the 29th day of the twelfth lunar month. People go to watch the spiritual dance associated with a ritual to banish the evil forces.

In the evening, families make a special porridge soup, gu-thuk (དགུ་ཐུག), into which they put balls of dough, each containing a roll of paper with a message. The messages are supposed to be humourous, as well as revealing of the individual personalities.

On New Year's Day, everyone gets up as early as possible to try to get the first of the water for good luck. For the rest of the day, however, people stay home as it's believed that too much socialising and spending money on the first day will decrease good fortune. From the second day onwards, people attend public celebrations, socialise and party!

Day before New Year's Eve	nyi-shu-gu	ཉི་ཤུ་དགུ
(29th of the twelfth Tibetan month)		
Tibetan New Year's Eve	nâm-gâng	གནམ་གང་
New Year's Day	lo-sar	ལོ་གསར་
New Year 1st Day	lo-sar tse-chig	ལོ་གསར་ཚེས་གཅིག
New Year 2nd Day	lo-sar tse-nyi	ལོ་གསར་ཚེས་གཉིས་
New Year 3rd Day	lo-sar tse-soom	ལོ་གསར་ཚེས་གསུམ་
Happy New Year!	lo-sar ta-shi de-lek	ལོ་གསར་བཀྲ་ཤིས་བདེ་ལེགས།

---

seven weeks in tibet

When people are cremated in Tibet, the day of the cremation is organised in accordance with astrological charts. In order to rest the spirit and help it find a better rebirth, people make offerings to the temple and give charity to the needy. Once a week for seven weeks following the death, a special religious service is held. Seven weeks is believed to be the maximum amount of time needed for the spirit to find its rebirth.

birthdays

When's your birthday?

kay-râng-gi kye-tsay   ཁྱེད་རང་གི་སྐྱེས་ཚེས་ག་དུས་རེད།
ka-dü ray?

My birthday is on (25 January).

ngay kye-tsay (chin-da tâng-pö   ངའི་སྐྱེས་ཚེས་(ཕྱི་ཟླ་དང་པོའི་ཚེས་ཉེར་ལྔ་)
tse nye-nga) la ray   ལ་རེད།

Happy birthday!

kye-kah-nyin ta-shi de-lek   སྐྱེས་སྐར་ཉིན་བཀྲ་ཤིས་བདེ་ལེགས།

birthday cake	kye-kah kek	སྐྱེས་སྐར་ཀོག
candles	yân-lah	ཡང་ལྭ

weddings

Traditional Tibetan weddings begin with a one-day celebration at the bride's home, with her family and friends. The actual wedding then takes place at the groom's home, with lots of singing and all the guests offering ka-ta (see page 42). The partying and celebrating may continue for three or more days!

Congratulations!

ta-shi de-lek   བཀྲ་ཤིས་བདེ་ལེགས།

To the bride and groom!

bâg-ma dâng mâg-ba nyi-la   བག་མ་དང་མག་པ་གཉིས་ལ།

engagement	long-châng tong-wa	སྟོང་ཆང་གཏོང་བ
honeymoon	châng-sa gyâb-jay-ki toh-seng	ཆང་ས་བརྒྱབ་རྗེས་ཀྱི་སྟོ་གསེང
wedding	châng-sa	ཆང་ས

འགྲིམ་འགྲུལ་བྱེད་པ

finding your way

འགྲོ་ལམ་འཚོལ་བ

Where's the ...?	... ka-bah yö-ray	... ག་བར་ཡོད་རེད།
road to ...	...-la doh-say lâm-ga	...ལ་འགྲོ་སའི་ལམ་ཁག
What time does	... chu-tsö kâ-tsay-la	... ཆུ་ཚོད་ག་ཚོད་ལ་
the ... leave/arrive?	doh-ki-ray/leb-ki-ray	འགྲོ་གི་རེད། ས�্লེབས་ཀྱི་རེད།
aeroplane	nâm-du	གནམ་གྲུ
boat	dru-zing	གྲུ་གཟིངས།
What ... is this?	... di-ming-la ka-ray-sa	... འདི་མིང་ལ་ག་རེ་ཟ།
street	lâm-ga	ལམ་ཁག
village	loong-pa/dong-seb	ལུང་པ/གྲོང་གསེབ།

How do I get to ...?

...-la kân-teh-si doh-gö ray ...ལ་གང་འདྲས་འགྲོ་དགོས་རེད།

Is it far/near?

[ta ring-po; ta nye-po] re-bay [ཐག་རིང་པོ/ཐག་ཉེ་པོ]རེད་པས།

Can I &walk there?

gom-pa gyâb-nay leb thoob-ki གོམ་པ་བརྒྱབ་ནས་སྟེབས་ཐུབ་ཀྱི
re-bay རེད་པས།

Can you show me (on the map)?

(sâp-ta di-nâng) tön nâng-da (ས་བཀྲ་འདི་ནང་)སྟོན་གནང་དང་།

Are there other means of getting there?

pha-kay do-ya tâb-lâm ཕ་གིར་འགྲོ་ཡག་ཐབས་ལམ་གཞན་དག
shen-da yö re-bay ཡོད་རེད་པས།

directions

Turn (left/right)	...-la (yön/yeh)	...ལ་(གཡོན་/གཡས་)
at the ...	kyog-nâng	སྐྱོགས་གནང༌།
next corner	su-dong jay-ma	ཟུར་གདོང་རྗེས་མ།
traffic lights	lâm-gay log-da	ལམ་གའི་ལྒོག་འད།
Go straight ahead.	ka-toog-do	ཁ་ཐུག་འགྲོ།
Turn left/right.	yön-la/yeh-la	གཡོན་ལ་/གཡས་ལ།
	kyog-nâng	སྐྱོགས་གནང༌།
Thank you for	lâm-ga tön-nâng-wa	ལམ་ག་སྟོན་གནང་བར་
showing us the way.	tu-jay-chay	ཐུགས་རྗེ་ཆེ།

north	châng	བྱང༌།
south	lho	ལྷོ།
east	shâr	ཤར།
west	noob	ནུབ།
inside	nâng-lâ	ནང་ལ།
outside	chi-lo-lâ	ཕྱི་ལོག་ལ།
behind	gyâb-lâ	རྒྱབ་ལ།
in front of	dün-lâ	མདུན་ལ།
opposite	dog-cho/	ལྒོག་ཕྱོགས་/
	pha-chog/ka-trö	ཕར་ཕྱོགས་/ཀ་སྟྲོད
far	ta ring-po	ཐག་རིང་པོ།
near	tee-lâ/ta nye-po	འཐིབས་ལ་/ཐག་ཉེ་པོ
here	day	འདིར།
there	pha-kay	ཕ་གིར།

---

distance learning

Along the roads in Tibet, distance is typically cited in do-ban (དོ་བ�ན༌), the road repair stations which can be seen every 10 km.

How many doban is it to the Saga district?

sa-ga zong bâ-tu do-ban	ས་སྒ་རྫོང་བར་དུ་དོའི་སྤྲང༌
kâ-tsay yö-ray	གཅོད་ཚོད་ཡོད་རེད།

52

taxi

ཏེག་སི

Where can I find a taxi?
tek-si la-sa ka-bah yö-ray
ཏེག་སི་ག་ལ་ས་ག་པར་ཡོད་རེད།

Please hire us a taxi.
tek-si-chig dâ-la tong nâng-dâng
ཏེག་སི་གཅིག་ང་ཚོ་ལ་གླ་གཏོང་གནང་དང་།

Is this taxi free?
tek-si-di tong-pa re-bay
ཏེག་སི་འདི་སྟོང་པ་རེད་པས།

Can you take me to ...?
...-la kye-rog nâng
...ལ་སྐྱེལ་རོགས་གནང་།

I want a taxi to the airport.
nâm-tâng-ba tek-si-chig gö-ki-du
གནམ་ཐང་བར་ཏེག་སི་གཅིག་དགོས་ཀྱི་འདུག

How much is it to go to ...?
...-la doh-wa-la la-ja kâ-tsay yin
...ལ་འགྲོ་བ་ལ་གླ་ཆ་ག་ཚོད་ཡིན།

How much is the fare?
khor-la-la kâ-tsay yin
འཁོར་གླ་ལ་ག་ཚོད་ཡིན།

Do we pay extra for luggage?
cha-lâg-la la-ja tö-ba tay-gö re-bay
ཅ་ལག་ལ་གླ་ཆ་འཕར་ལ་གླ་སྤྲོད་དགོས་རེད་པས།

instructions

ལམ་སྟོན་བྱེད་པ

Continue!	mu thü-nâng	མུ་མཐུད་གནང་།
Please wait here.	day gu-rog nâng	འདིར་བསྒུག་རོགས་གནང་།
Stop here!	day kâg-rog nâng	འདིར་བཀག་རོགས་གནང་།

Stop at the corner.
su-dong-tay kâg-rog nâng
གསུར་གདོང་དེར་བཀག་རོགས་གནང་།

It's the next street to the left/right.
lâm-ga jay-ma-tay yön-la/
ལམ་ག་རྗེས་མ་དེར་གཡོན་ལ་/
yeh-la kyog-nâng
གཡས་ལ་སྐྱོགས་གནང་།

Please [slow down; go faster].
[ka-lee ka-lee; gyok-tsi]
[ག་ལེར་ག་ལེར་/མགྱོགས་ཙི]
doh-nâng
འགྲོ་གནང་།

getting around

buying tickets

འཕྲ་སརྗེ་གགས་ཉི་ཚོང

Where can I buy a ticket?

   ti-ka-si nyo-sa ka-bah yö-ray   ཏེ་གགས་ཉི་ས་ག་བར་ཡོད་རེད།

I want to buy a ticket to ...

   nga ...-la doh-ya-gi ti-ka-si   ང་ ...ལ་འགྲོ་ཡག་གི་ཏེ་གགས་
   nyo-gö-yö   ཉི་དགོས་ཡོད།

How much is a ticket to ...?	...-la doh-ya ti-ka-si gong kâ-tsay ray	...ལ་འགྲོ་ཡག་ གི་ཏེ་གགས་གོང་ག་ཚོད་རེད།
Ganden	gân-den	དགའ་ལྡན
Gyantse	gyân-tse	རྒྱལ་རྩེ
Shigatse	shi-gâ-tse	གཞིས་ག་རྩེ

Do I need to book?

   (ti-ka-si) ngön-la nyo-gö re-bay   (ཏེ་གགས་)སྔོན་ལ་ཉི་དགོས་རེད་པས།

Can I reserve a place?

   dö-sa ngön-nay ngâg thoob-ki   སྡོད་ས་སྔོན་ནས་མངགས་ཐུབ་ཀྱི་རེད་པས།
   re-bay

It's full.

   kâng tsa-sha   གང་ཚར་ཤག

Please refund my ticket.

   ti-ka-si ngü tsoo lo-rog nâng   ཏེ་གགས་དངུལ་ཚུར་སྒྱུག་རོགས་གནང་།

Can I get a stand-by ticket?

   dö-sa tan ma-kay-way ti-ka-si   སྡོད་ས་གཏན་མ་ཁེལ་བའི་ཏེ་གགས་
   thob-ki re-bay   འཐོབ་ཀྱི་རེད་པས།

I'd like (a) ...	ngah ... gö	ངར་ ... དགོས།
one-way ticket	ya-lâm chig-pö ti-ka-si	ཡར་ལམ་གཅིག་པོའི་ ཏེ་གགས་
return ticket	ya-lâm ma-lâm nyi-kay ti-ka-si	ཡར་ལམ་མར་ལམ་ གཉིས་ཀའི་ཏེ་གགས་
two tickets	ti-ka-si nyi	ཏེ་གགས་གཉིས་

air

When's the next flight to ...?

...-la doh ya-gi nâm-du
jay-ma-de kâ-dü ray

...ལ་འགྲོ་ཡས་གནམ་གྲུ་རྗེས་མ་དེ་ག་དུས་རེད།

How long does the flight take?

nâm-dru-nâng yün ring-lö
doh-gö ray

གནམ་གྲུ་ནང་ཡུན་རིང་ལོས་འགྲོ་དགོས་རེད།

Is it a direct route?

sha-kyâg doh-ya re-bay

ཤ་རྐྱག་འགྲོ་ཡས་རེད་པས།

What time do I have to check in at the airport?

ti-ka-si to-dâm-che nâm-tâng-la
chu-tsö ka-tsay jor-gö-ray

ཏི་ཀ་སེ་དོ་དམ་ཆེད་གནམ་ཐང་ལ་ཆུ་ཚོད་
ག་ཚོད་འབྱོར་དགོས་རེད།

Where's the baggage claim?

tog-tay tsi-len chay-sa ka-bah
yö-ray

རྟོག་ཐིས་རྩི་ལེན་བྱེད་ས་ག་བར་
ཡོད་རེད།

My luggage hasn't arrived.

ngay tog-tay jor min-du

ངའི་རྟོག་ཐིས་འབྱོར་མིན་འདུག

at customs

I have nothing to declare.

nyen-seng shu gö-yeh
cha-lâg kay may

སྙན་སེང་ཞུ་དགོས་ཡས་ཅ་ལག་གང་ཡི་མེད།

I have something to declare.

ngah nyen-seng shu gö-yeh
cha-lâg-chig yö

ངར་སྙན་སེང་ཞུ་དགོས་ཡས་ཅ་ལག་ཅིག་ཡོད།

Do I have to declare this?

di nyen-seng shu gö re-bay

འདི་སྙན་སེང་ཞུ་དགོས་རེད་པས།

This is all my luggage.

ngay cha-lâg di-ga-râng yin

ངའི་ཅ་ལག་འདི་དགའ་རང་ཡིན།

That's not mine.

pa-gi ngay ma-ray

ཕ་གི་ངའི་མ་རེད།

I didn't know I had to declare it.

te nyen-seng shu-gö-pa ngay
ha-go-ma-song དེ་སྐྱེན་སེང་ཤུ་དགོལ་པར་དངས་ཏ་གོ་མ་སོང་།

car

Where can I hire a car (and driver)?

mo-ta (dâng mo-ta tong-khen)
la-sa ka-bah yö-ray མོ་ཊ་(དང་མོ་ཊ་གཏོང་མཁན)
གླ་སགགབར་ཡོད་རེད།

I'd like to hire a ...	nga ...-chig yar dhö-yö	ང་...གཡར་འདོད་ཡོད།
jeep	jip	ཇིབ
landcruiser	len cu-ru-sa	ལེནཀུ་རུ་ས
minibus	chi-chö lâng-kho choong-choong	སྤྱི་སྤྱོད་རྡང་འཁོར་ ཆུང་ཆུང་

For ... day(s). nyin-ma ... ཉིནམ ...

How much does it cost per kilometre?

ki-lo-mi-tar re-ray-la gong
kâ-tsay nay-ki ray ཀི་ལོ་མི་ཊར་རེ་རེ་ལགོང་ཚོན་ཆ་གནད་ཀྱི་རེད།

Does that include insurance?

tay khong-su in-shu-ren
thob-tâng tsi yö re-bay དེའི་ཁོངས་སུ་ཨིན་ཤུ་རེན་འཐོབ་ཐང་
རྩི་ཡོད་རེད་པས།

I'll pay half now, and half at the end of the trip.

khor-la che-kâ dân-ta tay-ki
yin, che-kâ jay-ma doh-tsa-nay
tay-ki yin འཁོར་ལ་ཕྱེད་ཀ་ད་ལྟ་སྤྲོད་ཀྱི་ཡིན། ཕྱེད་ཀ་རྗེས་
མ་འགྲོ་ཚར་ནས་སྤྲོད་ཀྱི་ཡིན།

I'd like to see the car.

nga mo-ta mig tân-dhö yö ང་མོ་ཊ་མིག་བལྟ་འདོད་ཡོད།

I'd like to meet the driver.

nga mo-ta tong-khen
thoog-dhö yö ང་མོ་ཊ་གཏོང་མཁན་ཐུག་འདོད་ཡོད།

How many people does the vehicle take?

mo-tay-nâng mi kâ-tsay
shong-gi ray

མོ་ཏའི་ནང་མི་ཚོ་ག་ཚོད་ཤོང་གི་རེད།

How much is it daily/weekly?

[nyin ray-ray; dun-tâg ray-ray]
gong kâ-tsay ray

[ཉིན་རེ་རེར་/བདུན་ཕྲག་རེ་རེར་]
གོང་ག་ཚོད་རེད།

Does that include mileage?

may-le kâ-tsay doh-men-gi
gong-tsay nyâm-tu tsi yö
re-bay

མེ་ལེ་ག་ཚོད་འགྲོ་མན་གྱི་གོང་ཚོད་མཉམ་དུ་
བརྩིས་ཡོད་རེད་པས།

How long can we park here?

day mo-ta yun ring-lö shah
cho-gi ray

འདིར་མོ་ཊ་ཡུན་རིང་ལོས་བཞག་ཆོག་གི་རེད།

Does this road lead to ...?

lâm-ga-di ... doh-ya re-bay

ལམ་ཀ་འདི་ ... འགྲོ་ཡག་རེད་པས།

Please stop (the car).

(mo-ta) kâ-rog nâng

(མོ་ཊ་)བཀག་རོགས་གནང་།

fastest route	lâm-chog gyog-shö	ལམ་ཕྱོགས་མགྱོགས་ཤོས།
short route	lâm-chog tâg nye-wa	ལམ་ཕྱོགས་ཐག་ཉེ་བ།

bicycle

�སྐང་ག་རི་ལ།

Is it within cycling distance?

kâng-ga-ri-tog leb thoob-ya-ki
sa-tâg re-bay

ཀང་ག་རི་ལ་ཕྱོག་སླེབས་ཐུབ་ཡག་གི་ས
ཐག་རེད་པས།

Is there a bike path?

kâng-ga-ri tong-yeh lâm-ga
du-kay

ཀང་ག་རི་ལ་གཏོང་ཡས་ལམ་ཀ་འདུག་གས།

Where can I hire a bicycle?

kâng-ga-ri la-sa ka-bah yö-ray

ཀང་ག་རི་ལ་གླས་ས་ག་བར་ཡོད་རེད།

Do you hire bicycles?

    kâng-ga-ri la-ya yö-bay   ཀང་སྐྲ་རི་ལ་གཡག་ལག་ཡོད་པས།

You have to leave your passport here (as security).

    kay-râng-gi pa-se-pot   ཁྱེད་རང་གི་སྦུ་སེ་པོ་
    (ta-ma-chay) day shâ-go-ray   (གཏའ་མ་ཆེད་)འདིར་བཞག་དགོས་རེད།

Where can I find (second-hand) bikes for sale?

    kâng-ga-ri (nying-pa) nyo-sa   ཀང་སྒ་རི་(རྙིང་པ་)ཉོ་ས་
    ka-bah yö-ray   ག་བར་ཡོད་རེད།

How much is it ... la-ja kâ-tsay ray   ... ལ་ཚ་ག་ཚོད་རེད།
for a/an ...?

hour	chu-tsö-chig	ཆུ་ཚོད་གཅིག
morning	sho-kay-chig	ཞོགས་ཀར་གཅིག
afternoon	chi-toh-chig	ཕྱི་དྲོ་གཅིག
day	nyin-ma-chig	ཉིན་མ་གཅིག
week	dün-tâ-chig	བདུན་ཕྲག་གཅིག
month	da-wa-chig	ཟླ་བ་གཅིག

Can you fix this bicycle?

    kâng-ga-ri-di sob-chö gya   ཀང་སྒ་རི་འདི་བཟོ་བཅོས་རྒྱག་ཐུབ་ཀྱི་རེད་པས།
    thoob-ki re-bay

It has a puncture.

    khor-lo dhö sha   འཁོར་ལོ་འདོ་ཤ་ལ།

bicycle path	kâng-ga-ri lâm-ga	ཀང་སྒ་རི་ལམ་ག
brakes	kha kâ-ya bay-rek	ཁ་བཀག་ལ་ལ་ས་རེག
chain	khor-lö châg-tâg	འཁོར་ལོ་ལྕགས་ཐག
gears	so-khor gi-yar	སོ་འཁོར་གི་ཡར
handlebars	lâg-ju yook-ba	ལག་འཇུ་དཀྱུལ་པ
helmet	châg-sha	ལྕགས་ཤ
inner tube	khor-lo nâng-gi-shoob	འཁོར་ལོ་ནང་གི་ཤུབ
lights	log	གློག
mountain bike	ri-zek kâng-ga-ri	རི་འཛེག་ཀང་སྒ་རི
padlock	go-châg	སྒོ་ལྕགས
pump	poom-da/pom	ཕུ་མ་དར་/ཕོམ
saddle	(kâng-gâ-ri) koob-kyâg	(ཀང་སྒ་རི)སྐུབ་ཀྱག
tools	lâg-cha	ལག་ཆ

accommodation

 སྡོད་གནས།

There's a variety of accommodation in Lhasa, Shigatse and Tse-tang, ranging from small inns to luxury hotels. In more remote areas, your options will be limited – you'll either have to take a tent or try a local family- or monestery-run guesthouse. Alternatively, you could try a truck stop. Truck stops offer basic, often dorm-style, rooms and can be found in all districts (zong, རྫོང་, or shen, ཤན་) in Tibet.

finding accommodation

སྡོད་གནས་འཚོལ་བ

See **Trekking**, page 139 for words and phrases on camping.

I'm looking for a ...	...-chig mig ta-gi-yö	...གཅིག་མིག་བལྟ་གི་ཡོད།
campsite	gur gyâb-nay	གུར་བརྒྱབ་ནས་སྡོད་
	dö-say sa-cha	སའི་ས་ཆ
guesthouse	drön-khâng	མགྲོན་ཁང་
hotel	drü-khâng/fan-dian	འགྲུལ་ཁང་/ཕན་ཏི་ཡན་

Where can I	drü-khâng ...-chig	འགྲུལ་ཁང་ ...གཅིག་
find a ... hotel?	ka-bah ra-gi ray	རག་གི་རེད།
clean	tsâng-ma	གཙང་མ
good	yâg-po	ཡག་པོ་
nearby	tâg nye-po	ཐག་ཉེ་པོ་

Where's the	drü-khâng ... ka-bah	འགྲུལ་ཁང་ ...
... hotel?	yö-ray	ག་བར་ཡོད་རེད།
best	yâg-shö	ཡག་ཤོས
cheapest	ke-shö	ཁེ་ཤོས

What's the address?

ka-châng kâ-ray ray   ཁ་བྱང་ག་རེ་རེད།

Could you write down the address?

ka-châng day ti-rog nâng   ཁ་བྱང་འདིར་འབྲི་རོགས་གནང་།

booking ahead

 སྔོན་ནས་བླ་འབྲི་གནས་པ།

I'd like to book a (single/double) room, please.

khâng-mi [mi-chig kay-kyâng dö-sa; mi-nyi dö-sa]-chig la gö-yö

ཁང་མིག[མི་གཅིག་ཨེར་རྐྱང་སྡོད་ས། མི་གཉིས་སྡོད་ས]ཅིག་ལ་དགོས་ཡོད།

For (three) nights.

tsen (soom) ring

མཚན་(གསུམ)རིང་

How much for ...? ...-la gong kâ-tsay ray
...ལ་གོང་གཚོད་རེད།

one night	tsen chig	མཚན་གཅིག
a week	dun-tâ chig	བདུན་ཕྲག་གཅིག
two people	mi-nyi	མི་གཉིས

I'll/We'll be arriving at ...

nga/ngân-tso ...-la yong-gi-yin

ང་/ངན་ཚོ ...ལ་ཡོང་གི་ཡིན།

My name's ...

ngay ming ... yin

ངའི་མིང ... ཡིན།

checking in

འབྱོར་བརྡ་གཏོང་བ།

Do you have any rooms/beds available?

khâng-mi/nye-ti tong-pa yö-bay

ཁང་མིག/ཉལ་ཁྲི་སྟོང་པ་ཡོད་པས།

Do you have a room with two beds?

nye-ti-nyi chay-pay khâng-mi yö-bay

ཉལ་ཁྲི་གཉིས་བྱེད་པའི་ཁང་མིག་ཡོད་པས།

---

they may say ...

gong-da, khâng-mi tong-pa min-du
Sorry, we're full.

PRACTICAL

60

Do you have a room with a double bed?

mi-nyi shong-say nye-ti   མི་གཉིས་ཤོང་སའི་ཉལ་ཁྲི་
chay-pay khâng-mi yö-bay   བྱེད་པའི་ཁང་མི་ཡོད་པས།

I'm not sure how long I'm staying.

nga yün-ring-lö day-gö   ང་ཡུན་རིང་ལོས་བསྡད་དགོས་
ten-ten may   གཏན་གཏན་མེད།

Are there any private rooms here?

day nye-khâng kâb-tsâng yö   འདིར་ཉལ་ཁང་ཁབ་གཙང་ཡོད་
re-bay   རེད་པས།

I'd like ...	ngah ...-chig gö	ང་ ...ཅིག་དགོས།
to share a dorm	chi-khâng-nâng dö-sa	སྤྱི་ཁང་ནང་སྡོད་ས
a single room	mi chig-kay-kyâng dö-say khâng-mi	མི་གཅིག་ཁེར་རྐྱང་སྡོད་ སའི་ཁང་མི།

I need ... bed(s).	nga-la nye-ti ... gö	ང་ལ་ཉལ་ཁྲི་ ... དགོས།
one	chig	གཅིག
two	nyi	གཉིས
three	soom	གསུམ

I/We want a room with (a) ...	nga/ngân-tso ... yö-pay khâng-mi-chig gö	ང་/ངན་ཚོ་ ... ཡོད་པའི་ཁང་མི་ ཅིག་དགོས།
air-conditioning	dâng-log	གྲང་ལྒོག
bathroom	trü-khâng	ཁྲུས་ཁང་
hot water	chu tsa-po	ཆུ་ཚ་པོ་
private toilet	sâng-chö râng-da	གསང་སྤྱོད་རང་བདག
shower	soog-po tru-ya	གཟུགས་པོ་ཁྲུ་ཡ
	tor-chu	འཐོར་ཆུ་
telephone	kha-pah	ཁ་པར་
TV	dian-shi;	དེན་ཞི;
	soog-tong nyen-tin	གཟུགས་མཐོང་ཉན་འཛིན
window	gay-koong	སྒེ་ཁུང་

Can I see the room?

nye-khâng mig ta-na di-gi re-bay   ཉལ་ཁང་མིག་བལྟ་ན་འགྲིག་གི་རེད་པས།

I don't like this room.

khâng-mi-di lo-la bah ma-song ཁང་མི་འདི་བློར་འབབ་ཀྱི་མིན་འདུག

Do you have another (room)?

(nye-khâng) shen-da yö-bay (ཉལ་ཁང་)གཞན་དག་ཡོད་པས།

It's fine. I'll take it.

yâg-po du. khâng-pa-di
la-gi yin

ཡགཔོ་འདུག ཁང་པ་འདི་
ལ་གི་ཡིན།

requests & queries

འབོད་སྐུལ་དང་འདི་རྩད་བྱེད་པ

Can I get ... here?	day ... râ-gee re-bay	འདིར་ ... རག་གི་རེད་པས།
food/meals	kha-la	ཁ་ལག
boiled water	chu khö-ma	ཆུ་འཁོལ་མ

Where's the bathroom?

trü-khâng ka-bah ཁྲུས་ཁང་ག་བར།

Where's the toilet?

sâng-chö ka-bah yö-ray གསང་སྤྱོད་ག་བར་ཡོད་རེད།

Is there hot water (all day)?

chu tsa-po (nyin-gâng) yö re-bay ཆུ་ཚ་པོ་ (ཉིན་གང་)ཡོད་རེད་པས།

Is there electricity (all day)?

(nyin-gâng) log yö re-bay (ཉིན་གང་)གློག་ཡོད་རེད་པས།

Where's breakfast served?

shog-cha ka-bah tâng-gi-ray ཞོགས་ཇ་ག་བར་གཏང་གི་རེད།

Is there somewhere to wash clothes?

du-log trü-sa yö-bay དུག་ལོག་འཁྲུས་ས་ཡོད་རེད་པས།

Can we use the kitchen?

tâb-tsâng bay-chö chay-na
di-gi re-bay

ཐབ་ཚང་བེད་སྤྱོད་བྱེད་ན་འགྲིག་གི་རེད་པས།

Can we use the telephone?

kha-pah bay-chö chay-na
di-gi re-bay

ཁ་པར་བེད་སྤྱོད་བྱེད་ན་འགྲིག་གི་རེད་པས།

I need a/another ...

ngah ...-chi/-shen-da-chi gö

ངར་ ...ཅིག/གཞན་དག་ཅིག་དགོས།

**Do you have a safe where I
can leave my valuables?**

rin-tâng-chen cha-lâg
chö-sa yö-bay

རིན་པར་ཅན་ཅ་ལག་འཇོག་ས་ཡོད་པས།

Could you store this/these for me?

di/din-tsö nyâh nâng-gay

འདི/འདི་ཚོ་ཉར་གནང་གས།

Could I have a receipt for them?

choong-zin-chig nâng-dâ

བྱུང་འཛིན་ཅིག་གནང་དང་།

Do you change money here?

day chi-gye-ngü jay-gee yö-bay

འདིར་ཕྱི་རྒྱལ་དངུལ་བརྗེ་གྱི་ཡོད་པས།

Do you arrange tours?

yu-kor tow-châm doh-ya ko-dik
shu-gi yö-bay

ཡུལ་སྐོར་སྤྲོ་འཆམ་འགྲོ་ཡལ་གོ་སྒྲིག་ཞུ་གྱི་ཡོད་པས།

Can I leave a message?

len-chi shâg-na di-gi re-bay

ལན་གཅིག་བཞག་ན་འགྲིག་གི་རེད་པས།

Is there a message for me?

ngah len du-gay

ངར་ལན་འདུག་གས།

Please wake me up sa-nyin ... nyi
at ... tomorrow. say-rog nâng
   five o'clock chu-tsö nga-pah
   six o'clock chu-tsö doog-pah

སང་ཉིན་ ... གཉིད་
སད་རོགས་གནང་།
ཆུ་ཚོད་ལྔ་པར་
ཆུ་ཚོད་དྲུག་པར་

Please change the sheets.

cha-tah-di je-rog-nâng

ཚག་དར་འདི་བརྗེ་རོགས་གནང་།

The room needs to be cleaned.

khâng-mi-di tsâng-ma so-gö-du

ཁང་མིག་འདི་གཙང་མ་བཟོ་དགོས་འདུག

Can you wash this?

di trü thoob-gi re-bay

འདི་བཀྲུ་ཐུབ་ཀྱི་རེད་པས།

Please iron these.

din-tso u-ti kyön nâng-dâ

འདི་ཚོ་ཡུ་ཏི་བཀྱོན་གནང་དང་།

Could we have (a/an) …?

ngân-tsoh … gö

ང་ཚོ་ … དགོས།

(extra) blanket	nye-chay (tö-bâ)	ཉལ་ཆས་(ལྷག་པ།)
(extra) quilt	pho-gay (tö-bâ)	ཕོ་ཁེབས་(ལྷག་པ།)
mosquito net	nye-gur	ཉལ་གུར་
pillow	nyen-go	སྔས་མགོ།
pillowcase	nyen-shoob	སྔས་ཤུབ།
our key	ngân-tsö di-mig	ང་ཚོའི་ལྡེའི་མིག
sheet	cha-tah/nye-keb	ཅ་འདག་/ཉལ་ཁེབས།

I've locked myself out of my room.

ngay go-châg gyâb-nay di-mig
nâng-la lâg-sha

ངས་སྒོ་ལྕགས་བརྒྱབ་ནས་ལྡེའི་མིག་ནང་ལ་
ལུག་ཤག

We left the key at reception.

di-mig ngân-tsö nay-len-sah
shâg yö

ལྡེའི་མིག་ང་ཚོས་སྣེ་ལེན་སར་བཞག་ཡོད།

complaints

སྐྱོན་བརྗོད།

I can't open/close the window.

gay-koong chay/gyâb thoob-ki
min-du

སྐེ་ཁུང་ཕྱེ་/བརྒྱབ་ཐུབ་ཀྱི་མིན་འདུག

The toilet won't flush.

sâng-chö-di kâg sha

གསང་སྤྱོད་འདི་འགགས་ཤག

Can I change to another (room)?

(khâng-mi) shen-ta chig-la
po-na di-gi re-bay

(ཁང་མིག་)གཞན་དག་གཅིག་ལ་
སྤོ་ན་འགྲིག་གི་རེད་པས།

The … doesn't work.

… di kyön shor-sha

… འདི་སྐྱོན་ཤོར་ཤག

heater — tsa-log

ཚ་ལོག

lamp	shu-mah	གཞུ་མར་
light bulb	log shay-do	གློག་ཤེལ་རྡོག
telephone	kha-pah	ཁ་པར་
TV	dian-shi;	དེན་ཤི/
	soog-tong nyen-tin	གཟུགས་མཐོང་ཉན་འཕྲིན

This room is dirty.

nye-khâng-di tsog-pa ray-sha ཁང་མིག་འདི་བཙོག་པ་རེད་ཤག

This room is	khâng-mi-di ...	ཁང་མིག་འདི་ ... དྲག་ཤག
too ...	ta-shâg	
big	chay	ཆེ་
cold	dâng	གྲང་
dark	nâg	ནག
light/bright	öh chay	འོད་ཆེ་
noisy	kay-jö tsa	སྐད་ཅོར་ཚ་
small	choong	ཆུང་

This ... is not clean.	... di tsâng-ma min-du	... འདི་གཙང་མ་མིན་འདུག
blanket	nye-chay	ཉལ་ཆས་
pillow	nyen-go	སྔས་མགོ
pillowcase	nyen-shoob	སྔས་ཤུབ་
sheet	cha-tah/nye-keb	ཅ་དར/ཉལ་ཁེབས

Please fix ...	... so-ro nâng	... བཟོ་རོགས་གནང་
this	di	འདི་
the bed	nye-ti-di	ཉལ་ཁྲི་འདི་

accommodation

checking out

འབྱོན་བརྡ་གཏོང་ང་

What time do we have to check out?

ngân-tso chu-tsö ka-tsay
tön-gö-ray

ང་ཚོ་ཆུ་ཚོད་ག་ཚོད་
འབྱོན་དགོས་རེད།

I'd like to check out ...

nga ... tön-gi yin

ང་ ... འབྱོན་གྱི་ཡིན།

now	tân-da	ད་ལྟ་
at noon	nyin-goong	ཉིན་གུང་
tomorrow	sa-nyin	སང་ཉིན་

We had a great stay, thank you.

ngân-tso kyi-po shay-ta choong,
tu-jay-chay nâng

ང་ཚོ་སྐྱིད་པོ་ཞེ་དྲག་བྱུང་།
ཐུགས་རྗེ་ཆེ་གནང་།

You've been wonderful.

kay-râng-nay pay-mi-si yâk-po
nâng-choong

ཁྱེད་རང་ནས་དཔེ་མི་སྲིད་ཡག་པོ་
གནང་བྱུང་།

Thank you for all your help.

kay-râng-nay rog nâng-wa
tsâng-mah tu-jay-chay

ཁྱེད་རང་ནས་རོགས་གནང་བར་
ཚང་མར་ཐུགས་རྗེ་ཆེ།

The room was perfect.

nye-khâng pay-mi-si yâg-po du

ཉལ་ཁང་དཔེ་མི་སྲིད་ཡག་པོ་འདུག

We hope we can return some day.

ngân-tso jay-ma yâng-kya yong
thoob-pay re-wa-yö

ང་ཚོ་རྗེས་མ་ཡང་བསྐྱར་
ཡོང་ཐུབ་པའི་རེ་བ་ཡོད།

I'd like to pay the bill.

ngü-tsi gya-gi yin

དངུལ་རྩིས་རྒྱག་གི་ཡིན།

Can I pay with a travellers cheque?

drü-shü ngü-zin-tog ngü pü-na
di-gi re-bay

འགྲུལ་བཞུད་དངུལ་འཛིན་ཐོག་དངུལ་སྤྲོད་ན
འདི་གི་རེད་པས།

Can I pay by credit card?

ngü bu-lön shog-jâng-tog
tay-na di-gi re-bay

དངུལ་བུ་ལོན་ཤོག་བྱང་ཐོག
སྟེར་ན་འདི་གི་རེད་པས།

There's a mistake in the bill.

ngü-tsi-nâng non-tü shor-sha དངུལ་ཚིས་ནང་ནོར་འཁྲུལ་ཤོར་ཤག

Can I leave my luggage here?

ngay cha-lâg day shâg-na di-gi
re-bay རེད་པས། ངའི་ཅ་ལག་འདིར་བཞག་ན་འགྲིག་གི་

We'll be back in (three) days.

ngân-tso nyin-ma-(soom)
je-la yong-gi-yin ང་ཚོ་ཉིན་མ་(གསུམ)
རྗེས་ལ་ཡོང་གི་ཡིན།

Can you call a taxi for me?

ngah tek-si-chig kay tong-da ངར་ཊེག་སི་ཤིག་ཨཱ་ཅོ་སྐད་གཏོང་དང་།

renting

I'm here about your ad for a room to rent.

khâng-la tong-ya kyâb-da nâng-du,
chay-tsâng nga day yong-wa-yin ཁང་ལ་གཏོང་ཡ་ཁྱབ་བསྒྲགས
གནང་དུས་གཟིགས་ཚང་ང་འདིར་ཡོང་བ་ཡིན།

Do you have any flats to rent?

khâng-la tong-ya khâng-pa
yö-bay ཁང་ལ་གཏོང་ཡ་ཁང་པ་ཡོད་པས།

**I'm looking for a flat to rent for
(two) months.**

ngah da-wa (nyi)-ring khâng-pa-chig
la-ya tâb-shay chay-ki yö ངར་ཟླ་བ་(གཉིས)་རིང་ཁང་པ་གཅིག
གླ་ཡག་ཐབས་ཤེས་བྱེད་ཀྱི་ཡོད།

I'm looking for something close to the ...	... tee-la khâng-pa-chig râg-gi yö-may ta-gi-yö	... འཛིན་ལ་ཁང་པ་གཅིག རག་གི་ཡོད་མེད་བལྟ་གི་ཡོད།
city centre	dong-kay-kyil	གྲོང་འཁྱེར་དཀྱིལ
market	trom	ཁྲོམ
monastery	gom-pa	དགོན་པ

How much is it per ...?	... ray-ray-la gong kâ-tsay ray	... རེ་རེ་ལ་གོང་ ག་ཚོད་རེད།
week	dün-tâ	བདུན་ཕྲག
month	da-wa	ཟླ་བ་

Is there anything cheaper?

gong ke-wa yö-bay

གོང་ཁེ་བ་ཡོད་པས།

Could I see it?

nga mig ta-na di-gi re-bay

ང་མིག་བལྟ་ན་འགྲིག་གི་རེད་པས།

Do you need a deposit?

ngü nga-dön tay gö-ki re-bay

དངུལ་སྔ་འདོན་སྤྲད་དགོས་ཀྱི་རེད་པས།

I'd like to rent it for (one) month.

da-wa (chig)-ring la-gi yin

ཟླ་བ་(གཅིག)་རིང་གླ་གྲུ་གྱི་ཡིན།

Lhasa is not only the capital, but the heart and soul of Tibet. The vast white and ochre Potala Palace dominates the city and is considered one of the wonders of Eastern architecture. The Jokhang, the most sacred and active of Lhasa's temples, is another key sight. Surrounding the Jokhang is the Barkhor circuit, the most famous of Lhasa's pilgrimage circuits and also a popular spot for souvenir shopping.

Modern Lhasa is divided into two sections: a western Chinese section and an eastern Tibetan section.

looking for ...

འཚོལ་བ། ...

I'm looking for a/the ...	... ka-bah yö-may ta-gi yö	... ག་བར་ཡོད་མེད་བལྟ་གི་ཡོད།
art gallery	lâg-tse dem-tön-khâng	ལག་རྩལ་འགྲེམས་སྟོན་ཁང་
bank	ngü-khâng	དངུལ་ཁང་
church/temple	lha-khâng	ལྷ་ཁང་
cinema	log-nyen ta-sa	གློག་བརྙན་བལྟ་ས།
city centre	drong-kay-kyil	གྲོང་ཁྱེར་དཀྱིལ།
... consulate	... dön-chö lay-khoong	... དོན་གཅོད་ལས་ཁུངས་
... embassy	... shung-tsâb lay-khoong	... གཞུང་ཚབ་ལས་ཁུངས་
... hotel	... drü-khâng	... འགྲུལ་ཁང་
market	trom	ཁྲོམ།
museum	dem-tön-khâng	འགྲེམས་སྟོན་ཁང་
police station	kor-soong lay-koong	སྐོར་སྲུང་ལས་ཁུངས་
post office	da-khâng	སྦྲག་ཁང་
public telephone	mi-mâng kha-pah	མི་དམངས་ཁ་པར།
public toilet	mi-mâng sâng-chö	མི་དམངས་གསང་སྤྱོད།
restaurant	sa-khâng	ཟ་ཁང་
telephone centre	kha-pah lay-khoong	ཁ་པར་ལས་ཁུངས་
tourist information	yu-kor to-châm	ཡུལ་སྐོར་སྤྲོ་འཆམ་གྱི

office	lay-khoong	ལས་ཁུངས་
town square	dong-kay mi-mâng	གྲོང་ཁྱེར་མི་དམངས་
	zom-sa te-wa	འཛོམས་ས་སྟེ་བ་

(See **Getting Around**, page 52, for directions.)

at the bank

དངུལ་ཁང་ནང་།

In rural areas it can be difficult to change large notes, so try to carry cash in small denominations.

What time does the bank open?
ngü-khâng chu-tsö kâ-tsay go chay-gi ray

དངུལ་ཁང་ཆུ་ཚོད་ག་ཚོད་ལ་སྒོ་ཕྱེ་གི་རེད།

I want to exchange some money.
nga chi-gay ngü jay-gö-yö

ང་ཕྱི་རྒྱལ་དངུལ་བརྗེ་དགོས་ཡོད།

Where can I cash a travellers cheque?
drü-shü ngü-zin jay-sa ka-bah yö-ray

འགྲུལ་བཞུད་དངུལ་འཛིན་བརྗེ་ས་ག་བར་ ཡོད་རེད།

Please change this travellers cheque.
drü-shü ngü-zin-dee jay nâng-da

འགྲུལ་བཞུད་དངུལ་འཛིན་འདི་བརྗེ་གནང་དང་།

Can I use my credit card to withdraw money?
bu-lön shog-châng-tog ngü tön cho-gee re-bay

བུ་ལོན་ཤོག་བྱང་ཐོག་དངུལ་ བཏོན་ཆོག་གི་རེད་པས།

Can I exchange money here?
day chi-gye-ngü jay-gi re-bay

འདིར་ཕྱི་རྒྱལ་དངུལ་འབརྗེ་གྱི་རེད་པས།

What's the exchange rate?
ngü-je-gong-tsay kâ-ray ray

དངུལ་བརྗེའི་གོང་ཚད་ག་རེ་རེད།

What's your commission?
kay-râng-gi keb-sâng ten-cha kâ-tsay ray

ཁྱེད་རང་གི་ཁེ་གསང་འཛིན་ཆ་ག་ཚོད་རེད།

Please write it down.

day di-rog nâng འདིར་འབྲི་རོགས་གནང་།

Where do I sign?

sa-yig ka-bah gya-go ray ས་ཨིག་ག་བར་རྒྱག་དགོས་རེད།

Can I have smaller notes?

ngü-shog rin-tâng choong-wa དངུལ་ཤོག་རིན་ཐང་ཆུང་བ་གནང་ཐུབ་ཀྱི་
nâng thoob-ki re-bay རེད་པས།

Can I have money transferred here from my bank?

ngay-ngü chö-say ngü-khâng-nay ངའི་དངུལ་བཙོལ་སར་དངུལ་ཁང་ནས་དངུལ་
ngü-day tâng thoob-ki re-bay འདི་རུ་གཏང་ཐུབ་ཀྱི་རེད་པས།

Can I transfer money overseas?

chi-gay-la ngü tâng thoob-ki ཕྱི་རྒྱལ་ལ་དངུལ་གཏང་ཐུབ་ཀྱི་རེད་པས།
re-bay

black market	nâg-tsong	ནག་ཚོང་
cashier	ngü-nye	དངུལ་གཉེར་
counterfeit	zü-ma	རྫུས་མ་
signature	sa-yig	ས་ཨིག་

at the post office སྦྲག་ཁང་ཉིན་ལ

The international postal service offered in Tibet is generally re-
liable and efficient. However, if you have mail to send, it's best
to do so in Lhasa, Shigatse or Tsetang.

I want to buy ...	nga ...-chig gö-yö	ང་ ...ཅིག་ཏུ་དགོས་ཡོད།
postcards	dâg-shog	སྦྲག་ཤོག་
stamps	ti-ka-si/dâg-tag	ཊི་ཀ་སི/སྦྲག་ཐགས་

| **I would like to send a ...** | nga ...-chig tâng-go yö | ང་ ...ཅིག་གཏང་དགོས་ཡོད། |

71

letter	yi-ge	ཡི་གེ།
parcel	cha-lâg	ཅ་ལག།
postcard	dâg-shog	སྐྱག་ཤོག

Please send it by air/surface mail.

nâm-tog/sa-tog tâng nâng-ro གནམ་ཐོག/ས་ཐོག་གཏང་གནང་རོགས།

How much does it cost to send this to ...?

di ... tâng-na gong kâ-tsay
nay-ki-ray

འདི ... གཏང་ན་གོང་ག་ཚད་གནས་ཀྱི་རེད།

Where's the poste restante section?

da-trö may-pay dâg-yi jo-khâng
ka-bah yö-ray

བདག་སྤྲོད་མེད་པའི་སྐྱག་ཡིག་འཇོག་ཁང་
ཀ་བར་ཡོད་རེད།

Is there any mail for me?

nga-la dâg du-gay ང་ལ་སྐྱག་འདུག་གས།

air mail	nâm-tog dâg-kay	གནམ་ཐོག་སྐྱག་སྐྱེལ།
envelope	yi-gok	ཡི་སྐོགས།
express mail	nyur-kyeA-dâg	མྱུར་སྐྱེལ་སྐྱག
mailbox	dâg-gâm	སྐྱག་སྒམ།
registered mail	teb-kay dâg	དེབ་སྐྱེལ་སྐྱག
surface mail	sa-tog dâg-kay	ས་ཐོག་སྐྱག་སྐྱེལ།

communications

ཁ་པར་བོག་འབྲེལ་སྒྲུག

Mobile-phone coverage is generally good. Most hotels in Lhasa have International Direct Dial telephones but levy a hefty surcharge on calls.

---

giving lip!

Don't be alarmed if someone pouts at you – they're probably just showing you which way to go. Tibetans often use their lips to indicate direction.

PRACTICAL

Where's the nearest public phone?

mi-mâng kha-pah tong-sa ཨི་དམངས་ཁབར་གཏོང་ས་ཐག་
tah nye-shö ka-bah yö-ray ཉེ་ཤོས་ཀ་བར་ཡོད་རེད།

Could I use the telephone?

kha-pah bay-chö chay-na ཁབར་བེད་སྤྱོད་བྱེད་ན་འགྲིག་གི་རེད་པས།
di-gi re-bay

I want to call ...

nga ...-la kha-pah tâng-go yö ང་ ...ལ་ཁབར་གཏང་དགོས་ཡོད།

How much does a (one)-minute call cost?

ka-ma-(chig) kay-cha shay-na སྐར་མ་(གཅིག)སྐད་ཆ་བཤད་ན་གོང་ག་
gong kâ-tsay ray ཚོད་རེད།

How much does each extra minute cost?

ka-ma tö-pa ray-ray-la སྐར་མ་མཆོད་པ་རེ་རེ་ལ་གོང་ག་ཚོད་གནད་ཀྱི་
gong kâ-tsay ray རེད།

The number is ...

kha-pah ahng-dâng ... ray ཁབར་ཨང་གྲངས་ ... རེད།

What's the area code for ...?

... sa-nay-ki kha-pah ahng-ta ... ས་གནས་ཀྱི་ཁབར་ཨང་རྟགས་ག་རེ་རེད།
kâ-ray ray

I want to make a long-distance call to (Australia).

nga (o-ta-li-ya)-la kha-pah ང་(ཨོ་ཏ་ལིཡ)ལ་ཁབར་གཏང་དགོས་ཡོད།
tâng-go yö

I want to make a reverse-charges/ collect call.

kha-pah tong-la phâ-chog-nay ཁབར་གཏོང་ལ་ཕ་ཕྱོགས་ནས་ཚིས་རྒྱལ་ཆོག་
tsi-gya chog-pay kha-pah-chi པའི་ཁབར་གཅིག་གཏང་དགོས་ཡོད།
tâng go-yö

It's engaged.

kha-pah de-wa ray-sha ཁབར་བྲེལ་བ་རེད་ཤག

I've been cut off.

nga kay-cha shay-ki shay-ki
kha-pah tsâm chay-song

ངས་སྐད་ཆ་བཤད་ཀྱི་བཤད་ཀྱི་ཁ་པར་མཚམས་ཆད་
སོང་།

engaged	de-wa	བྲེལ་བ་
modem	mo-dem	མོ་ཌེམ་
mobile/cell	mo-ba-yel/po-kay	མོ་སྦྱེལ་ཁ་པར་/
phone	kha-pah	སྤོ་འཕྲིན་ཁ་པར་
operator	kha-pah lay-chay-pa	ཁ་པར་ལས་བྱེད་པ་
phone book	kha-pah ahng-dâng-teb	ཁ་པར་ཨང་གྲངས་དེབ་
phone box	kha-pah tong-say khâng-choong	ཁ་པར་གཏོང་ས་འི་ཁང་ཆུང་
phone card	kha-pah tong-ya la-kay	ཁ་པར་གཏོང་ཡ་ལག་ལག་འབྱོར་
public telephone	mi-mâng kha-pah	མི་དམངས་ཁ་པར་
reverse charges	la pha-chog nay tsi gyâ-chog-pa	གླ་ཕ་ཕྱོགས་ནས་རྩིས་རྒྱ་ ཕྱོགས་པ་

making a call

ཁ་པར་གཏོང་བ་

Hello, do you speak English?

ta-shi de-lek, kay-râng in-ji-kay
shin-gi yö-bay

བཀྲ་ཤིས་བདེ་ལེགས།
ཁྱེད་རང་དབྱིན་ཇི་སྐད་ཤེས་ཀྱི་ཡོད་པས།

Hello, is ... there?

ha-lo, ...-la shoog du-gay

ཧ་ལོ། ...ལགས་བཞུགས་འདུག་གས།

Hello. (answering a call)

ha-lo

ཧ་ལོ།

Can I speak to ...?

nga ...-la kah-mö shu-gö yö

ང་ ...ལགས་གདང་མོ་ཞུ་དགོས་ཡོད།

Who's calling?

su yin-bâh

སུ་ཡིན་པ།

It's ...

nga ... yin

ང་ ... ཡིན།

Yes, he's/she's here.

la-wong, khong day shoog-du

ལགས་འོང་། ཁོང་འདིར་བཞུགས་འདུག

One moment, please.

teh-si gu-nâng

དོག་ཙམ་བསྒུག་གནང་།

I'm sorry, he's/she's not here.

khong day shoog min-du

ཁོང་འདིར་བཞུགས་མིན་འདུག

What time will he/she be back?

kho/mo chu-tsö kâ-tsay-la
yong-gi ray

ཁོ་/མོ་ཆུ་ཚོད་ག་ཚོད་ལ་ཡོང་གི་རེད།

Can I leave a message?

kha-len-chi shâ-na di-gi re-bay

ཁ་ལེན་གཅིག་བཞག་ན་འགྲིག་གི་རེད་པས།

Please tell ... I called.

...-la ngay kha-pah tâng-so
shu-rog

...ལ་ངས་ཁ་པར་བཏང་སོང་ཞུ་རོགས།

My number is ...

ngay kha-pah ahng-dâng ... ray

ངའི་ཁ་པར་ཨང་གྲངས ... རེད།

I don't have a contact number.

ngah kha-pah ahng-dâng may

ངར་ཁ་པར་ཨང་གྲངས་མེད།

I'll call back later.

ngay jay-la kha-pah tâng-go

ངས་རྗེས་ལ་ཁ་པར་གཏང་ངོ་

the internet

ཨིན་ཊ་ནེཊ་

Is there a local Internet cafe?

sa-nay-day in-ta-net bay-chö
tong-sa yö-pay cha-khâng
yö re-bay

ས་གནས་དེར་ཨིན་ཊ་ནེཊ་བེད་སྤྱོད་གཏོང་ས་ཡོད་པའི་ཇ་ཁང་ཡོད་རེད་པས།

I'd like to get Internet access.

nga in-ta-net bay-chö chay-go yö

ང་ཨིན་ཊ་ནེཊ་བེད་སྤྱོད་བྱེད་དགོས་ཡོད།

I'd like to check my email.

ngah ee-mel yö-may ta-go yö

ངར་ཨི་མེལ་ཡོད་མེད་བལྟ་དགོས་ཡོད།

I'd like to send an email.

nga ee-mel-chig tâng-go yö

ང་ཨི་མེལ་ཞིག་གཏང་དགོས་ཡོད།

sightseeing

Where can I get a local map?

sa-nay-ki sâp-ta kâ-nay ra-gi-ray · ས་གནས་ཀྱི་ས་བཀྲ་ག་ནས་རག་གི་རེད།

Do you have a guidebook in English?

in-ji kay-tog drü-shü
nay-yig yö-bay · དབྱིན་ཇི་སྐད་ཐོག་འགྲུལ་བཞུད་གནས་ཡིག་ ཡོད་པས།

What are the main attractions?

ta-kor dro-sa tso-wo
kâ-ray yö-ray · བལྟ་སྐོར་འགྲོ་ས་གཙོ་བོ་ག་རེ་ཡོད་རེད།

We only have [one day; two days].

ngân-tso nyin-ma
chig-lay/nyi-lay de-ya may · ང་ཚོ་ཉིན་མ་གཅིག་ལས་/གཉིས་ ལས་བསྡད་ཡག་མེད།

I'd like to see ...

... mig ta-dö yö · ... མིག་བལྟ་འདོད་ཡོད།

Is it OK if I take a photo?

par gyâb-na di-gi re-bay · པར་རྒྱབ་ན་འགྲིག་གི་རེད་པས།

Can I take your photograph?

kay-râng par gyâ-na di-gi re-bay · ཁྱེད་རང་པར་རྒྱག་ན་འགྲིག་གི་རེད་པས།

Could you take a photograph of me?

nga-la par-chig gyâ nâng-da · ང་ལ་པར་ཅིག་རྒྱག་གནང་དང་།

Would you like a copy?

kay-râng par gö-bay · ཁྱེད་རང་པར་དགོས་པས།

I'll send you one.

ngay-chig tâng yong-gö · ངས་གཅིག་གཏང་ཡོང་དགོས།

What's your address?

kay-râng-gi ka-châng kâ-ray ray · ཁྱེད་རང་གི་ཁ་བྱང་ག་རེ་རེད།

getting in

ནང་དུ་འཛུལ་བ།

What time does it open/close?

chu-tsö kâ-tsay-la go
chay-gi/gyâb-gi ray

ཆུ་ཚོད་ཀ་ཚད་ལ་སྒོ་ཕྱེ་/སྒོ་བརྒྱབ་གི་རེད།

Is there an admission charge?

zü-la tay-go re-bay

འཛུལ་གླ་སྤྲད་དགོས་རེད་པས།

You don't have to pay.

la tay-go ma-ray

གླ་སྤྲད་དགོས་མ་རེད།

Can I make a donation?

shen-deb bü-na di-gi re-bay

ཞལ་འདེབས་ཕུལ་ན་འགྲིག་གི་རེད་པས།

the sights

བལྟ་སྐོར།

What's that ...?	... pha-gi kâ-ray ray	... ཕ་གི་ག་རེ་རེད།
building	khâng-pa	ཁང་པ།
monument	den-ten	རྟེན་རྟེན།
place	sa-cha	ས་ཆ།

How old is it?	nying-lö ray	རེ་སྙིང་ལོས་རེད།

ancient	na ngâ-mo	གནའ་སྔ་མོ།
archaeological	na-ngö chay-pay	གནའ་རྫས་དཔྱད་པའི་
	rig-nay	རིག་གནས།
cinema	log-nyen ta-sa	གློག་བརྙན་བལྟ་ས།
concert	ro-yâng tro-tön	རོལ་དབྱངས་སྟོན་སྟོན།
crowded	tsâng-ga shi-shi	འཚང་ག་ཤིག་ཤིག
flag	dar-cho	དར་ཆོ།
gardens	may-tog doom-ra	མེ་ཏོག་ལྡུམ་ར།
market	trom	ཁྲོམ།
monastery	gom-pa	དགོན་པ།
mosque	ka-chay lha-khâng	ཁ་ཆེའི་ལྷ་ཁང་།
museum	dem-tön khâng	འགྲེམས་སྟོན་ཁང་།
old city	dron-kay nying-ba	གྲོང་ཁྱེར་རྙིང་པ།
palace	pho-dâng	ཕོ་བྲང་།
park	ling-ga	གླིང་ག
statues	dâ-ku	འདྲ་སྐུ།

around town

| temple | lha-khâng | ལྷ་ཁང་ |
| university | tsoog-la lob-ta chen-mo | གཙུག་ལག་སློབ་གྲྭ་ཆེན་མོ |

tours

བསྐོར་

Are there regular tours we can join?

cha-chen drü-pa ta-kor ti-gi
yö-na teh nyâm-tu ngân-tso
yong-na di-gi re-bay

ཆར་ཆེན་འགྲུལ་པ་ལ་བསྐོར་འབྱིད་ཀྱི་ཡོད་ན
དེའི་མཉམ་དུ་ང་ཚོ་ཡོ ན་འབྱོ ག་གི་རེད་པས།

How much is [the tour; a guide]?

[ta-kor do-ya; nay-shay
gya-khen] la-cha kâ-tsay ray

[བསྐོར་འགྲོ ཡག/གནས་བཤད་
རྒྱག་མཁན་]གླ་ཆ་ཚོ རེད།

How long is the tour?

ta-kor gyün ring-lö do-ya
yö-ray

བསྐོར་རྒྱུན་རིང་ལོ ས་འགྲོ་ཡག་ཡོ རེད།

Will we have free time?

ngân-tsoh dü-tsö tong-ba
yö re-bay

ང་ཚོ དུས་ཚོ སྟོ པ་ཡོ རེད་པས།

What time should we be back?

ngân-tso chu-tsö kâ-tsay
chi-log teb-ki ray

ང་ཚོ ཆུ་ཚོ ག་ཚོ ལ་ཕྱིར་ལོ ཐེབས་ཀྱི་རེད།

The guide [has paid; will pay].

rin-ba nay-shay gya-khen-gi
tay-song/tay-gi-ray

རིན་པ་གནས་བཤད་རྒྱག་མཁན་གྱིས་
སྤྲད་སོ /སྤྲད་ཀྱི་རེད།

I'm with them.

nga khong-tsö nyâm-du yö

ང་ཁོང་ཚོ མཉམ་དུ་ཡོ །

I've lost my group.

nga rog-pa tsâng-ma lâg-sha

ང་རོགས་པ་ཚང་མ་བརྫངས་ཤག

Have you seen a group of (Australians)?

kay-râng-nay (o-ta-li-ya) drü-ba
kyu-chig tong song-ngay

ཁྱེད་རང་ནས་(ཨོ་སི་ཊ་ལི་ཡ)
འགྲུལ་པ་རྒྱུ གཅིག་མཐོང་སོ ་ངས།

visiting temples

Tibetans are deeply religious and you'll see monks, nuns and other local people walking around temples, saying prayers, lighting butter lamps and incense, and turning prayer wheels to show their spiritual devotion. Throughout the year, there are many religious festivals (see **Festivals & Holidays**, page 46).

If you want to address a monk or a nun and you don't know their name, you can use the honorific titles ku-sho-la (ཨེ་ལགས་) for monks and ani-la (ཨ་ནི་ལགས་) for nuns. Other titles for people associated with Buddhism are:

abbot	khen-po	མཁན་པོ་
lama (teacher)	la-ma	བླ་མ་
layperson	kyâ-wo	སྐྱ་བོ་
monastic disciplinarian	gay-kö	དགེ་སྐོས་
shrine keeper	kö-nyey	བསྐོ་གཉེར་
student	gay-toog/lob-toog	དགེ་ཕྲུག་/སློབ་ཕྲུག་
What is that ... called?	... pha-gi ming-la kâ-ray ray	... ཕ་གིའི་མིང་ལ་ག་རེ་རེད།
monastery	gom-pa	དགོན་པ་
nunnery	ah-ni gom-pa	ཨ་ནི་དགོན་པ་
shrine/temple	lha-khâng	ལྷ་ཁང་

---

monumentally sacred

Chö-ten (མཆོད་རྟེན་) are religious monuments that can be found throughout Tibet. When Buddhism was first introduced, there were no images of Buddha and chö-ten became symbolic of Buddhism. Often you'll see piles of stones around the base of the chö-ten inscribed with the sacred words 'Om Mani Padme Hum' the mantra of Avalokiteshvara, the Bodhisattva of Compassion.

80

Am I allowed to go inside (the temple)?

(gom-bay)-nâng doh cho-ki re-bay

(དགོན་པའི་)ནང་འགྲོ་ཆོག་གི་རེད་པས།

Am I allowed to go upstairs?

toh-ga doh cho-ki re-bay

ཐོག་ཁར་འགྲོ་ཆོག་གི་རེད་པས།

How many monks/nuns are there?

tâ-pa/ah-ni kâ-tsay yö-ray

གྲྭ་པ/ཨ་ནེ་ག་ཚོད་ཡོད་རེད།

I'd like to meet the abbot.

nga khen-po-dâng jen-dö yö

ང་མཁན་པོ་དང་མཇལ་འདོད་ཡོད།

May I offer ...?   ...-chi bü-na di-gi re-bay

...ཕུལ་ན་འགྲིག་གི་རེད་པས།

  a butter lamp   chö-may   མཆོད་མེ

  incense   pö   སྤོས

Can I sit here for a while?

day te-tsi day-na di-gi re-bay

འདིར་རེ་ཙིག་ཚམ་བསྡད་ན་འགྲིག་གི་རེད་པས།

Please say a prayer for me.

ngah mön-lâm kyön nâng-ro

ང་ར་སྨོན་ལམ་བརྒྱབ་གནང་རོགས།

around town

81

I'd like to learn about meditation.

nga gom châng-dö yö གང་སྒོམ་སྦྱང་འདོད་ཡོད།

altar	chö-shom	མཆོད་བཤམས།
assembly hall	tsog-khâng	ཚོགས་ཁང་།
bell	tih-bu	དྲིལ་བུ།
Buddha	sâng-gye	སངས་རྒྱས།
circumambulation	ko-ra	སྐོར་ར།
cymbal	boog-chel	སྦུག་ཆལ།
drum	nga	རྔ།
gods/goddesses	lhâ/lhâ-mo	ལྷ་/ལྷ་མོ།
karma	lay	ལས།
meditate	gom	སྒོམ།
non-virtue	mi-ge-wa	མི་དགེ་བ།
offering	chö-pa	མཆོད་པ།
prayer wheel	mâ-ni kho-lo	མ་ཎི་འཁོར་ལོ།
prostrate	châg-tsay	ཕྱག་འཚལ།
reliquary	chor-ten	མཆོད་རྟེན།
rosary	tren-ngâ	ཕྲེང་བ།
spiritual dance	châm	འཆམ།
trumpet (small)	gyâ-ling	རྒྱ་གླིང་།
trumpet (big)	doong-chen	དུང་ཆེན།
vajra (a tantric ritual sceptre)	dor-je	རྡོ་རྗེ།
vase	boom-pa	བུམ་པ།
virtue	gay-wa	དགེ་བ།

For phrases on Pilgrimage & Religion, see **Specific Needs**, page 102.

paperwork

ཡིག་ཆ་ལས་ཀ

name	ming	མིང་།
address	ka-châng	ཁ་བྱང་།
date of birth	kye-tse	སྐྱེས་ཚེས།
place of birth	kye-yül	སྐྱེས་ཡུལ།

Buddhism first appeared in Tibet in the 7th century AD. It gained popularity during the reign of King Trisong Detsen (755-97) and King Tritsug Detsen Ralpachen (817-36). However, following the reign of the next king, Langdharma, the Tibetan state collapsed and Buddhism was attacked. The faith didn't revive until the 11th century, when Tibetans began travelling to India to study. New ideas were brought back and eventually three further schools of Buddhism developed: Kagyupa, Sakyapa and Gelugpa. The Nyingmapa order, referred to as the 'Old School' already existed.

birth certificate	kye-tse lâg-kay	སྐྱེས་ཚེས་ལག་ཁྱེར་
age	lo	ལོ་
sex	pho-mo tâg	ཕོ་མོ་རྟགས་
female	mo	མོ་
male	pho	ཕོ་
nationality	loong-ba	ལུང་པ་
profession/work	tso-tâb châng-sha	འཚོ་ཐབས་བྱུངས་ཤ་གཏོགས་པའི་
	tön-pay lay-rig/lay-ka	ལས་རིགས/ལས་ཀ
marital status	châng-sa gyâb yö-may nay-bâb	ཆང་ས་བརྒྱབ་ཡོད་མེད་གནས་བབ་
single	mi-hreng	མི་ཧྲེང་
married	châng-sa gyâb yö-ba	ཆང་ས་བརྒྱབ་ཡོད་པ་
divorced	sa-tsâng ka day-wa	བཟའ་ཚང་ཁ་བྲལ་བ་
widow	kyo-da de-pö mo-hreng	ཁྱོ་ག་འདས་པའི་མོ་ཧྲེང་
widower	kye-man de-pö pho-hreng	སྐྱེ་དམན་འདས་པའི་ཕོ་ཧྲེང་
religion	chö-loog	ཆོས་ལུགས་
identification	ngo-trö lâg-kay	ངོ་སྤྲོད་ལག་ཁྱེར་
passport	pa-se-pot/chi-kyö lâg-teb	པ་སེ་པོར་/ཕྱི་སྐྱོད་ལག་དེབ་
passport number	pa-se-pot âhng-dâng	པ་སེ་པོར་ཨང་གྲངས་
visa	vi-za/tong-chen	ཝི་ཟ/མཐོང་མཆན་
car owners title	mo-ta dâg-pö ming	མོ་ཊ་བདག་པོའི་མིང་
car registration	mo-tay teb-kye	མོ་ཊའི་དེབ་སྐྱེལ་
drivers licence	mo-ta tong-ya lâg-kay	མོ་ཊ་གཏོང་ཡག་ལག་ཁྱེར་
tourist card	yu-kor tro-châm lâg-kay	ཡུལ་སྐོར་སྤྲོ་མཆམས་ལག་ཁྱེར་

reason for travel	drü-kyö chay-ya gyu-tsen	འགྲུལ་སྐྱོད་བྱེད་ཡག་རྒྱུ་མཚན་
purpose of visit	drü-shü chay-ya gyu-tsen	འགྲུལ་གནང་བྱེད་ཡག་རྒྱུ་མཚན་
business	tsong-lay	ཚོང་ལས་
holiday	goong-seng	གུང་གསེང་
visiting relatives	nyen-tay	གཉེན་འཕྲད་
visiting the homeland	râng-gi pha-yu ta-ga	རང་གི་ཕ་ཡུལ་བལྟ་ག
border	sa-tsâm	ས་མཚམས་
customs	gâ-go	བགག་སྒོ་
immigration	gyâ-khâb shen-du	རྒྱལ་ཁབ་གཞན་དུ་
	shi châg-pa	གནས་ཆགས་པ་

The Barkhor circuit in Lhasa offers the best souvenir shopping. Lined with stalls, you'll find everything from jewellery and handicrafts to prayer shawls and prayer wheels.

looking for ...

... འཚོལ་བ

How far is the ... from here?	di-nay ... ta ring-lö kâ-tsay yö-ray	འདི་ནས ... ཐག རིང་ལོས་ག་ཚོད་ཡོད་རེད།
Where's the nearest ...?	... nyay-shö ka-bah yö-ray	... ཉེ་ཤོས་ག་བར་ཡོད་རེད།
bank	ngü-khâng	དངུལ་ཁང་
barber	ta sha-khâng	སྐྲ་བཞར་ཁང་
bookshop	teb tsong-khâng	དེབ་ཚོང་ཁང་
camera shop	par tsong-khâng	པར་ཚོང་ཁང་
clothing store	du-log tsong-khâng	དུག་ལོག་ཚོང་ཁང་
craft shop	lâg-sö cha-lâg tsong-khâng	ལག་བཟོས་ཅ་ལག་ཚོང་ཁང་
department store	de-tsen tsong-khâng	སྡེ་ཚན་ཚོང་ཁང་
general store	nay-zom tsong-khâng	སྣ་འཛོམས་ཚོང་ཁང་
laundry	du-log trü-khâng	དུག་ལོག་འཁྲུད་ཁང་
market	trom	ཁྲོམ
newsagency	tsâg-sho tsong-khâng	ཚགས་ཤོག་ཚོང་ཁང་
optician	mik-shay so-khen	མིག་ཤེལ་བཟོ་མཁན
pharmacy	men tsong-khâng	སྨན་ཚོང་ཁང་
music shop	rö-ja tsong-khâng	རོལ་ཆ་ཚོང་ཁང་
shoe shop	lhâm-ko tsong-khâng	ལྷམ་ཀོ་ཚོང་ཁང་
souvenir shop	dren-ten cha-lâg tsong-khâng	དྲན་རྟེན་ཅ་ལག་ཚོང་ཁང་
stationery shop	yig-chay tsong-khâng	ཡིག་ཆས་ཚོང་ཁང་
supermarket	râng-kho râng-dem tsong-khâng	རང་མགོ་རང་འདེམས་ཚོང་ཁང་

Tibetan rug store	bö-ki room-den tsong-khâng	བོད་ཀྱི་རུམ་གདན་ཚོང་ཁང་
travel agency	dim-drü-khâng	འགྲིམ་འགྲུལ་ཁང་

making a purchase

ཉོ་སྒྲུབ་བྱེད་པ

I'm just looking.

nga ta-gâ-si mig-tâ-gi-yö
ང་དགའ་སེ་མིག་བལྟ་གི་ཡོད།

Excuse me Mr/Ms, please come here.

cho-la/ah-cha-la, day-chi peb-dâng
ཇོ་ལགས། ཨ་ཅག་ལགས། འདིར་ཅིག་ཕེབས་དང་།

How much is this?

di gong kâ-tsay ray
འདི་གོང་ག་ཚོད་རེད།

Can you write down the price?

gong shu-gu-tog dih nâng-da
གོང་ཤོག་བུ་ཐོག་དིས་གནང་དང་།

I'd like to buy ...

nga ... chig nyo-dö yö
ང་ ... གཅིག་ཉོ་འདོད་ཡོད།

Do you have any ...?

kay-râng-la ... tsong-ya yö-bay
ཁྱེད་རང་ལ ... འཚོང་ཡག་ཡོད་པས།

We don't have any.

ngân-tsoh kyö-nay may
ང་ཚོ་ཁྱོན་ནས་མེད།

Which one? This one?

ka-gi gö. di gö-bay
ག་གི་དགོས། འདི་དགོས་པས།

Not that one. This one.

pha-gi man. di gö
ཕ་གི་མན། འདི་དགོས།

Do you have any others?

shen-ta yö-bay
གཞན་ད་ཡོད་པས།

Can you show me that?

pha-gi ngah mik tön-dâ
ཕ་གི་ངར་མིག་སྟོན་དང་།

I don't like it.

te lo-la doh-ma-song
དེ་བློར་འབབ་མ་སོང་།

Is this for sale?

di tsong-ya re-bay འདི་བཙོང་ཡ་རེད་པས།

How much is it?

gong kâ-tsay ray གོང་ག་ཚད་རེད།

I'll buy this one.

nga di nyo-gi yin ང་འདི་ཉོ་གི་ཡིན།

Do you accept credit cards?

bu-lön shog-jâng-tog བུ་ལོན་ཤོག་བྱང་ཐོག
rim-pa tay-na di-gi re-bay རིམ་པ་སྤྲད་ན་འགྲིག་གི་རེད་པས།

Could I have a receipt please?

choong-zin nâng thoob-ki re-bay བྱུང་འཛིན་གནང་ཐུབ་ཀྱི་རེད་པས།

Does it have a guarantee?

te-la gan-len gan-gya དེ་ལ་འགན་ལེན་འགན་རྒྱ་
tay-ki re-bay སྤྲད་ཀྱི་རེད་པས།

Can I have it sent overseas/abroad?

te chi-gye-la tâng-nâng དེ་ཕྱི་རྒྱལ་ལ་གཏང་གནང་
thoob-ki re-bay ཐུབ་ཀྱི་རེད་པས།

Please wrap it.

toom-sho gya-ro nâng ཐུམ་ཤོག་རྒྱག་རོགས་གནང་།

I'd like to return this please.

ku-chi, di chi-log chay སྐུ་མཁྱེན། འདི་ཕྱིར་ལོག་བྱེད་
chu-rog-nâng བཅུག་རོགས་གནང་།

It's faulty.

te kyön sho-sha དེ་སྐྱོན་ཤོར་ཤག

It's broken.

te châg-sha དེ་ཆག་ཤག

I'd like my money back.

ngay-ng tsuh lo-ro-nâng ངའི་དངུལ་ཚུར་སློག་རོགས་གནང་།

What is this made of?

dee gyoob-jâ kâ-ray ray འདིའི་རྒྱུ་ཆ་ག་རེ་རེད།

Where does this come from?

di loong-ba kâ-nay thön-ba ray འདི་ལུང་པ་ག་ནས་ཐོན་པ་རེད།

bargaining

Bargaining at market stalls is the norm in Lhasa – you may initially be quoted a price up to 10 times the real value.

It's too expensive.

gong chay-ta-sha གོང་ཆེ་དྲགས་འདག

What's your real price?

gong ngön-nay soong-dâ གོང་དངོས་གནས་གསུང་དང

Really?

ngön-nay དངོས་གནས

It's too much.

gong chay-tah-sha གོང་ཆེ་དྲགས་འདག

I don't have much money.

nga-la ngü shay-ta may ང་ར་དངུལ་ཞེ་དྲགས་མེད

Could you give me a discount?

gong châg thoob-ki re-bay གོང་བཅག་ཐུབ་ཀྱི་རེད་པས

Do you have something cheaper?

gong kay-pa yö-bay གོང་ཁེ་བ་ཡོད་པས

I'll give you ...

ngay ... tay go ངས་ ... སྤྲད་དགོས

No more than ...

...-lay mâng-wa tay-ki-man ...ལས་མང་བ་སྤྲད་ཀྱི་མིན

souvenirs

amber	pö-shay	སྤོས་ཤེལ
carpets	room-den	རུམ་གདན
earrings	ahm-cho gyen; na-gyen	ཨམ་ཅོག་རྒྱན/རྣ་རྒྱན
gold	say	གསེར
handicraft	lag-sö	ལག་བཟོ

necklace	ke-gyen/gü-gyen	སྐེ་རྒྱན།/མགུལ་རྒྱན།
pottery	za-chay	རྫ་ཆས།
ring	tsi-kok	མཚོན་ཞིབས།
rug	khâ-den	ཁ་གདན།
silver	ngü	དངུལ།
turquoise	yu	གཡུ།

essential groceries

དགོས་མཁོའི་ཚོང་ཆ།

| Where can I find (a) ...? | ... ka-bah ra-gi ray | ... ག་བར་རག་གི་རེད། |
| I'd like (a) ... | ngah ... gö | ངར་ ... དགོས། |

batteries	log-shu-men	གློག་བཞུ་སྨན།
bread	bâk-lay	བག་ལེབ།
butter	mâh	མར།
candles	yâng-la	ཡང་ལ།
cheese	chu-ra	ཆུ་ར།
chocolate	chok-let	ཅོག་ལེཊ།
eggs	go-nga	སྒོ་ང་།
flour (wholemeal)	dro-shib	གྲོ་ཞིབ།
gas cylinder	gas gâm	གྱས་སྒམ།
ham	phâg-sha dü-ma	ཕག་ཤ་དུས་མ།
honey	dâng-tsi	སྦྲང་རྩི།
margarine	mâh zü-ma	མར་བཟུས་མ།
matches	tsâg-ta/mu-si	ཚག་སྟ།/སྨུ་སེ།
milk	oh-ma	འོ་མ།
mosquito coil	du-dâng gog-ya-men	དུག་སྦྲང་འགོག་ཡག་སྨན།
pepper	ey-ma	ཨེ་མ།
salt	tsha	ཚ།
sugar	chay-ma-ka-ra/chi-ni	བྱེ་མ་ཀ་ར།/ཅི་ནི།
water purification tablets	chu tsâng-ma sö-ya men	ཆུ་གཙང་མ་བཟོ་ཡག་སྨན།
washing powder	du-log trü-ya po-ta	དུ་ལོག་འཁྲུ་ཡག་པོ་ཏར།
yogurt	sho	ཞོ།

clothing

 དུག་ལོག

belt	kay-râ	སྐེད་རགས
blouse	wâng-ju	འོན་འཇུག
boots	ju-ta yu-ring	འཇུ་ཏ་ཡུ་རིང
coat	ko-ti	ཀོ་ཏི
dress	mo-chay	མོ་ཆས
gloves	lâg-shoob	ལག་ཤུབས
hat	shah-mo	ཞྭ་མོ
jacket	ja-ke-ti	ཇ་ཀེ་ཏི
jeans	jeen	འཇིན
jumper	ba-len; o-mo-sü	སྤུ་ལེན/ཨུ་མོ་སུའི་སྟོད་ཐུང
(sweater)	tö-toong	
pants (trousers)	gö-toong/dho-ma	གོས་ཐུང/དོར་མ
raincoat	cha-keb	ཆར་ཁེབས
sandals	cha-pa-li	ཅ་པ་ལི
shirt	tö-toong/wâng-ju	སྟོད་ཐུང/འོན་འཇུག
shoes	lhâm-kok/ju-ta	ལྷམ་ཀོག/འཇུ་ཏ
shorts	ha-pan; gö-toong wog-dho	ཧ་པན/གོས་ཐུང་འོག་དོ
skirt	may-yog	སྨད་གཡོག
socks	u-su/o-mo-su	ཨུ་སུ/ཨུ་མོ་སུ
swimsuit	chu-kay gyön-chay	ཆུ་རྐྱལ་གྱོན་ཆས
T-shirt	gong-may tö-toong	གོང་མེད་སྟོད་ཐུང
	phu-che	ཕུ་ཐེད
underwear	nâng-gyön ha-pan	ནང་གོན་ཧ་པན

Can I try it on?

tsö-ta-che gyön-na
di-gi re-bay

ཚོད་བལྟ་ཆེད་གྱོན་ན་འགྲིག་གི་རེད་པས

My size is ...

ngay-tsay ... ray

ངའི་ཚད ... རེད

It doesn't fit.

tâg-tâg ray min-du

ཏག་ཏག་རེད་མིན་འདུག

Can it be altered?

so-chö gya thoob-ki re-bay

བཟོ་བཅོས་རྒྱབ་ཐུབ་ཀྱི་རེད་པས

It's too ...	te ... tâg-sha	དེ་ ... དྲགས་ཤག
big	chay	ཆེ་
small	choong	ཆུང་
short	toong	ཐུང་
long	ring	རིང་
tight	dâm	དམ་
loose	lhö	ལྷོད་

colours

ཚོས་གཞི།

black	nâg-po	ནག་པོ་
blue	ngön-po	སྔོན་པོ་
brown	gya-moog/mah-moog	རྒྱ་སྨུག/དམར་སྨུག
green	jâng-gu	ལྗང་གུ་
grey	kya-wo/ngön-kya	སྐྱ་པོ་/སྔོན་སྐྱ་
orange	mâ-say/li-wâng	དམར་སེར་/ལི་ཝང་
pink	sing-kya	ཟིང་སྐྱ་
purple	ngön-mah/mu-man	སྔོན་དམར་/སྨུག་མན་
red	mah-po	དམར་པོ་
white	ka-po	དཀར་པོ་
yellow	say-po	སེར་པོ་

I don't like this colour.

nga tsü-shi di-la gâ-bo min-du ང་ཚོས་གཞི་འདི་ལ་དགའ་པོ་མིན་འདུག

Do you have another (colour)?

(tsü-shi) shen-da yö-bay (ཚོས་གཞི་)གཞན་དག་ཡོད་པས།

---

true colours

To be more specific about colour, replace the second syllable of the relevant colour with nâg (ནག), 'dark', or kya (སྐྱ), 'light'. For example, 'blue' is ngön-bo (སྔོན་པོ) but 'dark blue' is ngön-nag (སྔོན་ནག) and 'light blue' ngön-kya (སྔོན་སྐྱ).

materials

brass	râg	རག
ceramic	za-sö	ཟ་བཟོའི
corduroy	shur-mâ	ཤུར་མ
cotton	tin-bay	སྲིན་བལ
felt	ching-pâ	ཕྱིང་པ
glass	shay	ཤེལ
gold	say	གསེར
leather	ko-wa	ཀོ་བ
metal	châg	ལྕགས
nylon	ni-len	ནེ་ལེན
plastic	pö-ka	སོལ་ག
silk	dru-zi	གྲུ་ཟི
silver	ngü	དངུལ
stainless steel	tsa mi-gya-pay si-tee	བཙའ་མི་རྒྱག་པའི་སི་ཌིལ
velvet	pu-mâ	སྤུ་མ
wood	shing	ཤིང
wool	bay	བལ
handmade	lâg-sö	ལག་བཟོས
synthetic	zay-jo sö-pay	རྫས་སྦྱོར་བཟོས་པའི

Is this ...?	di ... re-bay	འདི་ ... རེད་པས
amber	pö-shay	སྤོས་ཤེལ
gold	say	གསེར
jade	zü/yâng-ti	ཧྲུག/གཡང་ཏི
silver	ngü	དངུལ
turquoise	yu	གཡུ

toiletries

Some toiletries are hard to find even in Lhasa, including shaving cream, decent razor blades, insect repellent and tampons.

aftershave	ka-bu sha-je ju-ya di-sâng	ཁ་སྤུ་གཤགས་རྗེས་བྱུག་ཡ་སྲི་བསྲང
bath/shower gel	soog-po tru-dü ju-ya phik-phik-chi	གཟུགས་པོ་འཁྲུ་དུས་བྱུག་ཡ་ཕིག་ཕིག་ཅིག
comb	gyook-shay	ཀྲུག་ཤས
condoms	lig-shoob	ལིག་ཤུབས
dental floss	so tsâng-ma so-ya dar-kü	སོ་གཙང་མ་བཟོ་ཡ་དར་སྐུད
deodorant	lü-di gok-men di-yo do-ren	ལུས་དྲི་འགོག་སྨན་དྲི་ཡོ་དོ་རེན
face cream	shâb-sö	ཞབས་བསོས
hairbrush	gyook-shay/pân-do	ཀྲུག་ཤས/ཕྱག་མཛོ
hair dye	ta-tsö	སྐྲ་ཚོས
insect repellent	bu-dâng gok-men	འབུ་སྦྲང་འགོག་སྨན
moisturiser	shâb-sö	ཞབས་བསོས
razor (blades)	ta-di(-ka)	སྐྲ་དྲི(་ཁ)
sanitary napkins	tsâng-day shu-gu	གཙང་སྦྲའི་ཤོག་གུ
shampoo	ta trü-ya shâm-bu	སྐྲ་འཁྲུ་ཡ་ཤམ་བུ
shaving cream	ah-ra shar-dü ju-ya bhu-wa	ཨ་ར་བཞར་དུས་བྱུག་ཡ་ལྦུ་བ
soap	yi-tsi	ཡི་ཙི
sunblock	nyib-tâg gok-chay ju-ya men	ཉི་བཏགས་འགོག་བྱེད་བྱུག་ཡ་སྨན
talcum powder	soog-por ju-ya tel-kâm po-tah	གཟུགས་པོར་བྱུག་ཡ་ཏལ་ཀམ་པོ་ཏཱ
tampons	ma-kha gok-chay sin-bay	སྨ་ཁ་འགོག་བྱེད་སྲིན་བལ
tissues	lâg-chi shu-gu	ལག་ཕྱིས་ཤོག་གུ
toilet paper	sâng-chö shu-gu	གསང་སྤྱོད་ཤོག་གུ
toothbrush	so-trü	སོ་འཁྲུ
toothpaste	so-men	སོ་སྨན

for the baby

ཕྲུ་གུ་ལ་དགོས་ཡས།

baby powder	pu-gü soog-po	ཕྲུག་གུའི་གཙགགས་པོ
	ju-ya po-tah	བྱུག་ཡས་པོ་ཏར
bib	ka-lâg tay-dü pu-gü	ཁ་ལག་སྟེར་དུས་ཕྲུག
	kay gyön-chay	གུའི་སྐྱེར་གྱོན་ཆས
disposable	bay-chö sin-jay	བེད་སྤྱོད་ཟིན་ཇས་གཏགས
nappies	yu-roong pu-gü chu-den	རུ་ཕྲུག་གུའི་ཆུ་གདན
dummy/pacifier	jib-ru	འཇིབ་རུ
feeding bottle	pu-gu o-ma tay-ya	ཕྲུ་གུའི་འོ་སྟེར་ཡས་ཤེལ་དམ
	shay-tâm	
nappies	pu-gü chu-den	ཕྲུག་གུ་ཆུ་གདན
nappy rash cream	chu-den tor-sib	ཆུ་གདན་ཐོར་ སིབ་སེལ་འགོག་ བྱེད
	gok-chay ju-ya-men	བྱུག་ཡས་སྨན
powdered milk	o-tsâm	འོ་ཚམ
teat	jib-rü nu-ma	འཇིབ་རུའི་ནུ་མ
tinned baby food	pu-gu tay-ya	ཕྲུ་གུར་སྟེར་ཡས
	châg-tin say	ལྕགས་ཏིན་ཟས

stationery & publications

ཡིག་ཆས་དང་པར་སྐྲུན་དེབ།

**Is there an English-language
bookshop nearby?**

nye-dâm-la in-ji teb
tsong-khâng yö re-bay

ཉེ་འཁྲིས་ལ་དབྱིན་ཇི་དེབ་
ཚོང་ཁང་ཡོད་རེད་པས།

**Is there a local entertainment
guide in English?**

sa-nay-la tay-mo gâng ta-gyu
yö-may kyâb-ta-teb in-ji-tog
yö re-bay

ས་གནས་ལ་ལྟད་མོ་གང་ལྟ་རྒྱུ་
ཡོད་མེད་སྐྱབ་ལྟ་དེབ་དབྱིན་ཇི་ཐོག་
ཡོད་རེད་པས།

**Do you have any books in
English by …?**

kay-râng-la …-nay
tsâm-pay-teb in-ji-tog yö-bay

ཁྱེད་རང་ལ་…ནས་བརྩམས་པའི་དེབ་
དབྱིན་ཇི་ཐོག་ཡོད་པས།

PRACTICAL

Is there an English-language section?

in-ji teb-ki de-tsen yö re-bay ﾠ དབྱིན་ཇི་དེབ་ཀྱི་སྡེ་ཚན་ཡོད་རེད་པས།

Do you sell ...?	... tsong-ya yö-bay	... བཙོང་ཡག་ཡོད་པས།
books	(in-ji)-teb	(དབྱིན་ཇི་)དེབ
(in English)		
magazines	dü-teb	དུས་དེབ
newspapers	(in-ji) tsâg-ba	(དབྱིན་ཇི་)ཚགས་པར་
(in English)		
postcards	dâg-sho	སྒྲག་ཤོག

(Tibetan-English)	(bö-in) tshing-dzö	(བོད་དབྱིན་)ཚིག་མཛོད་
dictionary		
exercise book	jong-dah ti-teb	སྦྱོང་བརྡར་འབྲི་དེབ
envelope	yi-gok	ཡིག་སྒྲོགས
glue	jâr-tsi	སྦྱར་རྩི
... map	... sâp-ta	... ས་བཀྲ
city	dong-kye	གྲོང་ཁྱེར་
regional	sa-nay-ki	ས་གནས་ཀྱི་
road	lâm-kay	ལམ་ཁག
trekking	ri-loong do-ya	རི་ལུང་འགྲོ་ཡག
notebook	di-teb	འབྲི་དེབ
novel	doong-teb/nâm-thar	སྒྲུང་དེབ/རྣམ་ཐར་
pad (letter	(tân-yig) ti-say-teb	(ཤོག་དྲིལ་ཡིག་)འབྲི་དེབ
writing)		
paper	shu-gu	ཤོག་གུ
pen	nyu-gu	སྙུག་གུ
pencil	sha-nyoog/pen-see	ཞ་སྙུག/པན་སིལ་
scissors	jâm-tse	ཇེམ་ཙེ
writing paper	ti-shog	འབྲི་ཤོག

music

རོལ་ཆ

I'm looking for a ... CD.

nga ... si-di ra-gi yö-may ﾠﾠ ང་ ... སི་ཌི་རག་གི་ཡོད་མེད་
ta-ki-yö ﾠﾠﾠﾠﾠﾠﾠﾠﾠﾠﾠﾠ བལྟ་གྱི་ཡོད།

Do you have any ...?

kay-râng-la ... yö-bay

ཁྱེད་རང་ལ་ ... ཡོད་པས།

What's his/her best recording?

kö/mö shay yâg-shö ka-re ray

ཁོའི/མོའི་གཞས་ཡག་ཤོས་ག་རེ་རེད།

I heard a band/singer called ...

ngay [rö-ja tsog-pa; shay tong-khen] ... say-wa go nyong-sha

ངས་[རོལ་ཆ་ཚོགས་པ/གཞས་ གཏོང་མཁན] ... ཟེར་བ་གོ་མྱོང་ཤག

Can I listen to this CD here?

si-di-di day nyen-na di-gi re-bay

སི་ཌི་ཌི་འདིར་ཉན་ན་འགྲིག་གི་རེད་པས།

photography

How much is it for developing?

phing-sho trü-la kâ-tsay ray

ཕིང་ཤོག་བཏུ་ལ་ག་ཚད་རེད།

When will it be ready?

kâ-dü tsha-gi ray

ག་དུས་ཚར་གྱི་རེད།

I'd like a film for this camera.

par-chay di-la phing-sho chig gö

པར་ཆས་འདི་ལ་ཕིང་ཤོག་གཅིག་དགོས།

Do you fix cameras?

par-chay so-chö gya-ki yö-bay

པར་ཆས་བཟོ་བཅོས་རྒྱག་གི་ཡོད་པས།

battery	log-shu-men/bay-ti-ri	གློག་བཟུང་སྨན/སྦེ་ཊི་རི་
B&W film	phing-sho tshön-ta may-pa	ཕིང་ཤོག་ཚོན་ཁ་མེད་པ
camera	par-chay	པར་ཆས
film	phing-sho	ཕིང་ཤོག
flash	par-chay-ki log	པར་ཆས་ཀྱི་གློག
flash bulb	par-chay-ki log shay-dok	པར་ཆས་ཀྱི་གློག་ཤེལ་དོག
lens	par-shay	པར་ཤེལ
light meter	wö-tshay gyab-ya	འོད་ཚད་བརྒྱབ་ཡག

smoking

A packet of ... cigarettes, please.

... tha-ma gâm-chig nâng-da ... ཐ་མག་སྒམ་གཅིག་གནང་དང་།

Are these cigarettes strong or mild?

tha-ma din-tso gar-bo shay-ta ཐ་མག་འདི་ཚོ་གར་པོ་ཤེན་དྲག
yö-na, gar-la tsâm-bo yö-na ཡོད་ན། གར་ལ་འཚམས་པོ་ཡོད་ན།

Do you have a light?

kay-râng-la may par-ya yö-bay ཁྱེད་རང་ལ་མེ་སྤར་ཡག་ཡོད་པས།

Please don't smoke.

tha-ma ma-ten-rog nâng ཐ་མག་མ་འཐེན་རོགས་གནང་།

Do you mind if I smoke?

tha-ma ten-na dig-gi re-bay ཐ་མག་འཐེན་ན་འགྲིག་གི་རེད་པས།

I'm trying to give up.

nga tha-ma chö-yak tâb-shay ང་ཐ་མག་གཏོང་ཡག་ཐབས་ཤེས་བྱེད
chay-ki yö ཀྱི་ཡོད།

cigarettes	tha-ma	ཐ་མག
cigarette papers	tha-ma shu-gu	ཐ་མག་ཤོག་གུ
cigars	tha-ma si-gah	ཐ་མག་སི་གར
filtered	tsâg-gyâb-pa	འཚག་བརྒྱབ་པ
lighter	may par-ya	མེ་སྤར་ཡག
matches	tsâg-ta/mu-si	ཚག་ཏ/སུ་སི
pipe	tu-ten-dong	དུ་འཐེན་མོང
tobacco	doh-tâg shib-shib	མོད་མག་ཞིབ་ཞིབ

weights & measures

centimetre	sin-ti-mi-tar	སེན་ཏི་མི་ཏར
gram	ga-râm	སྐ་རམ
kilogram	ki-lo-ga-râm/chi-gya	ཀི་ལོ་སྐ་རམས/ཕྱི་རྒྱ
kilometre	ki-lo-mi-tar/	ཀི་ལོ་མི་ཏར/

	chi-lee/goong-li	ཆི་ལི།/གུང་ལི།
litre	li-tar	ལི་ཏར།
metre	mi-tar/chi-ti	མི་ཏར།/ཆི་ཏི།
millimetre	mi-li-mi-tar	མི་ལི་མི་ཏར།
pound	pön	པོནད།

sizes & comparisons

ཆེ་ཆུང་དང་མཚུངས་སྡུར།

big	chen-po	ཆེན་པོ།
few	ka-shay	ཁ་ཤས།
heavy	ji-bo	ལྗིད་པོ།
less	nyoong-nga	ཉུང་ང་།
light	yâng-po	ཡང་པོ།
long	ring-po	རིང་པོ།
many	mâng-po	མང་པོ།
more	mâng-wa	མང་བ།
much	shay-tah	ཞེ་དྲགས།
little (amount)	nyoong-nyoong	ཉུང་ཉུང་།
a little bit	tög-tsâm	ཏོག་ཙམ།
short	toong-toong	ཐུང་ཐུང་།
small	choong-choong	ཆུང་ཆུང་།
some	ka-shay	ཁ་ཤས།
tall	ring-bo/tho-po	རིང་པོ།/མཐོ་པོ།
too much/many	mâng tah-pa	མང་དྲགས་པ།

(See page 39 for Useful Amounts.)

PRACTICAL

98

accessible travel

དགུལ་པ་དབང་པོ་སྐྱོན་ཅན

I'm ...	nga ... yin	ང་ ... ཡིན།
blind	long-wa	ལོང་བ
deaf	wön-ba	འོན་པ
disabled	wâng-po kyön-chen	དབང་པོ་སྐྱོན་ཅན

I need assistance.

nga ... rog gö-ki-du   ང་ ... རོགས་དགོས་ཀྱི་འདུག

What services do you have for disabled people?

mi wâng-po kyön-chen-la
cha-kyen kâ-ray kâ-ray yö   མི་དབང་པོ་སྐྱོན་ཅན་ལ་ཆ
སྐྱེན་ག་རེ་ག་རེ་ཡོད།

Is there wheelchair access?

kho-lö koob-gya do-sa yö re-bay   འཁོར་ལོའི་སྐུབ་རྒྱ་འགྲོ་ས་ཡོད་རེད་པས།

I have a hearing aid.

nga ahm-cho go-ya-gi
trü-ja gyön-yö   ང་ཨམ་ཆོག་གོ་ཡག་གི
འཕྲུལ་ཆ་གྱོན་ཡོད།

Speak more loudly, please.

soong-kay chay-tsâm
kyön nâng-da   གསུང་སྐད་ཆེ་ཙམ་བསྐྱོན
གནང་དང་།

Are guide dogs permitted?

long-wa ti-khen-gi kyi tih
cho-gi re-bay   ལོང་བ་འཁྲིད་མཁན་གྱི་ཁྱི་འཁྲིས
ཆོག་གི་རེད་པས།

braille library	long-yi pen-zö-khâng	ལོང་ཨིག་དཔེ་མཛོད་ཁང་
disabled person	mi wâng-po kyön-chen	མི་དབང་པོ་སྐྱོན་ཅན
guide dog	long-wa ti-khen-kyi	ལོང་བ་འཁྲིད་མཁན་ཁྱི
wheelchair	kho-lö koob-gya	འཁོར་ལོ་སྐུབ་རྒྱ

travelling with children

ཉ+་མི་མཉམ་ཡུལ་སྐོར་སྐྱོད་འཆམ་འགྲོ་བ

Children are welcome visitors in Tibet, generally receiving a lot of attention, and travelling with children poses no more of a challenge than it would elsewhere.

Are there facilities for babies?

pu-gu mah-ja-la gö-ya
kho-chay du-gay

ཕུ་གུ་མར་འབྱར་ལ་དགོས་ཡའལག
མཁོ་ཆས་འདུག་གམ

Do you have a child-minding service?

pu-gu ta-khen yö re-bay

ཕུ་གུ་བལྟ་མཁན་ཡོད་རེད་པས

Where can I find a/an
(English-speaking) babysitter?

(in-ji-kay shin-khen) bu-zi-chi
ka-bah ra-gi-ray

(དབྱིན་ཇི་སྐད་ཤེས་མཁན)བུ་རྫི
གཅིག་གཱ་བར་རག་གི་རེད

Can you put a/an (extra)
bed in the room?

khâng-pay-nâng nye-ti
(tö-pa)-chig shâg nâng-da

ཁང་པའི་ནང་ཉལ་ཁྲི
(ཐོལ་པ)ཅིག་བཞག་གནང་དང

I need a car with a child seat.

ngah pu-gu dö-say koob-gya
yö-pay mo-ta-chi gö

ངར་ཕུ་གུ་སྡོད་སའི་ཀྲུབ་རྒྱ་ཡོད་པའི་མོ
ཊ་གཅིག་དགོས

Is it suitable for children?

te pu-gu-la ren-gi re-bay

དེ་ཕུ་གུ་ལ་རན་གྱི་རེད་པས

Is there a family discount?

kyim-tsâng-la chay-cha
yö re-bay

ཁྱིམ་ཚང་ལ་ཕྱེད་ཆ
ཡོད་རེད་པས

Are children allowed?

pu-gu ti-na di-gi re-bay

ཕུ་གུ་འཐི་ན་འགྲིག་གི་རེད་པས

Do you have a children's menu?

pu-gu-la ka-la ming-to yö-bay

ཕུ་གུ་ལ་ཁ་ལག་མིང་བྱོ་ཡོད་པས

Is there a playground nearby?

tih-la pu-gü tse-tâng yö re-bay

འཐིས་ལ་ཕུ་གུའི་རྩེད་ཐང་ཡོད་རེད་པས

on business

We're attending a ... n: ngân-tso ... tsog-gi yö   ངན་ཚོ ... འཛོགས་གི་ཡོད།
- **conference** dö-leng tsong-du   གྲོས་གླེང་ཚོགས་འདུ
- **meeting** tsong-du   ཚོགས་འདུ
- **trade fair** tsong-sog dem-tön   ཚོང་ཚོགས་འགྲེམས་སྟོན

I'm on a course.

nga lob-jong chay-ki yö   ང་སློབ་སྦྱོང་བྱེད་ཀྱི་ཡོད།

I have an appointment with ...

nga ... thoog-gyü dü-kâg gyâb-yö   ང ... ཐུག་རྒྱུའི་དུས་བཀག་བརྒྱབ་ཡོད།

Here's my business card.

di ngay tsong-gi ka-châng ray   འདི་ངའི་ཚོང་གི་ཁ་བྱང་རེད།

I need an interpreter.

ngah kay-gyu gö-ki-du   ངར་སྐད་སྒྱུར་དགོས་ཀྱི་འདུག

I'd like to use a computer.

nga câm-pu-tah bay-chö chay-gö yö   ང་ཀམ་པུ་ཏར་བེད་སྤྱོད་བྱེད་དགོས་ཡོད།

I'd like to send a/an fax/email.

nga faks/ee-mel tâng-gö yö   ང་ཕེགས/ཨི་མེལ་གཏང་དགོས་ཡོད།

mobile/cell	mo-ba-yel/po-kay	མོ་བྱེལ/སྤོ་འབྲེར
phone	kha-pah	ཁ་པར
client	tsong-sha	ཚོང་ཤག
colleague	lay-rog	ལས་རོགས
distributor	tsong-so dem-pay chay-ken	ཚོང་ཚོ་འགྲེམས་སྤེལ་བྱེད་མཁན
email	ee-mel	ཨི་མེལ
exhibition	dem-tön	འགྲེམས་སྟོན
manager	oo-zin	དབུ་འཛིན
profit	keb-sâng	ཁེ་བཟང
proposal	sâm-chah/dö-shi	བསམ་འཆར/གྲོས་གཞི

specific needs

101

pilgrimage & religion

གནས་མཇལ་དང་ཆོས་ལུགས་སྐོར

In Tibet, it's considered very important to undertake a pilgrimage at least once to each of the major Buddhist sites in the country, as well as those in India and Nepal. Tibetans believe that the sacred sites are blessed with positive energy and that simply being there brings hope, vision and clarity to their lives.

What's your religion?

kay-râng-gi chö-loog kâ-ray yin   ཁྱེད་རང་གི་ཆོས་ལུགས་ག་རེ་ཡིན།

I'm ...	nga ... yin	ང་ ... ཡིན།
Buddhist	nâng-pa	ནང་པ
Catholic	yig-su cay-tho-li	ཨེ་ཤུ་ཀོ་ཐོ་ལི
Christian	yig-shu	ཨེ་ཤུ
Hindu	hin-du	ཧིན་དུ
Jewish	ji-u	ཇི་ཡུ
Muslim	kha-che	ཁ་ཆེ

I'm not religious.

nga chö-la yi-chay may   ང་ཆོས་ལ་ཡིད་ཆེས་མེད།

I'm (Catholic), but not practising.

nga (yig-su cay-tho-li) yin-yâng   ང་(ཨེ་ཤུ་ཀོ་ཐོ་ལི)ཡིན་ཡང་ངས
nyâm-len chay-khen men   ཉམས་ལེན་བྱེད་མཁན་མིན།

I think I believe in God.

nga kön-chog-la yi-chay yö   ང་དཀོན་མཆོག་ལ་ཡིད་ཆེས་ཡོད་
sâm-gi-du   བསམ་གྱི་འདུག

---

divine intervention

The practice of divination (mo, མོ) is very common in Tibet and is relied on when making decisions about marriage, farming, travelling, health etc. People who practise divination generally consult a specific deity with whom they have formed a bond through meditation. Popular methods of divination involve rosaries, mirrors, dice or dough balls.

I believe in destiny/fate.

    nga len-day-la yi-chay-yö   ང་ལས་འབྲས་ལ་ཡིད་ཆེས་ཡོད།

I'm interested in astrology/philosophy.

    nga ka-tsi/doob-ta-la ying yö   ང་སྐར་ཅིས་/གྲུབ་མཐའ་ལ་དབྱིངས་ཡོད།

I'm agnostic.

    nga kön-chog sog yö-may   ང་དཀོན་མཆོག་སོགས་ཡོད་མེད་སྐྱ་
    sü-kyâng tog mi-nü shay   གུང་རྟོགས་མི་ནུས་ཞེས་སྨྲ་མཁན་ཡིན།
    ma-ken yin

Can I attend this service?

    tsog-la yong-na di-gi re-bay   ཚོགས་ལ་ཡོང་ན་འགྲིག་གི་རེད་པས།

Can I pray here?

    day ka-dön chay-na di-gi re-bay   འདིར་ཁ་འདོན་བྱེད་ན་འགྲིག་གི་རེད་པས།

Where can I pray/worship?

    ka-dön/cha-chö nyâm-len   ཁ་འདོན་/ཕྱག་མཆོད་ཉམས་ལེན་
    ka-bah chay-gö-ray   ག་བར་བྱེད་དགོས་རེད།

dalai lama

The Dalai Lama is considered to be a reincarnation of Avalokiteshvara, the patron saint of Tibet. The honorific title means 'Ocean of Wisdom'.

Tibetans use three additional titles for his Holiness the Dalai Lama – The Presence, The Wish-fulfilling Jewel and The Precious Refuge Protector.

Much as Tibetans enjoy talking about His Holiness the Dalai Lama, remember religion and politics are sensitive and risky issues in Tibet.

His Holiness the Dalai Lama	kün-dün/ye-shin nor-bu/kyâb-gön rin-po-che	སྐུ་མདུན/ཡིད་བཞིན་ནོར་བུ/ སྐྱབས་མགོན་རིན་པོ་ཆེ
funeral	ro-phoong kye-way cho-ga	རོ་སྤུང/སྐྱེ་བའི་ཆོ་ག
god	kön-chog	དཀོན་མཆོག
monastery	gom-pa	དགོན་པ
monk	ta-pa	གྲྭ་པ
nun	ah-ni	ཨ་ནི
prayer	shay-dön/mön-lâm	ཞལ་འདོན/སྨོན་ལམ
priest	la-ma	བླ་མ
reincarnation	kye-wa nga-chi	སྐྱེ་བ་སྔ་ཕྱི
relic	ring-say	རིང་བསྲེལ
saint	kye-bu dâm-pa	སྐྱེས་བུ་དམ་པ
shrine	chö-khâng/chö-ten	མཆོད་ཁང/མཆོད་རྟེན
temple	lha-khâng	ལྷ་ཁང

SOCIAL > meeting people

མཇལ་འཕྲད།

You'll find that most Tibetans enjoy having visitors to their country and are keen to talk to you. A good conversation starter is ta-shi de-lek (བཀྲ་ཤིས་བདེ་ལེགས།). Literally meaning 'good fortune', it's often used as an equivalent to 'hello'.

basics

ཞེས་དངོས་པ

Hello.	ta-shi de-lek	བཀྲ་ཤིས་བདེ་ལེགས།
Good morning.	nga-to de-lek	སྔ་དྲོ་བདེ་ལེགས།
Goodbye. (staying)	ka-lee pay	ག་ལེར་ཕེབས།
Goodbye. (leaving)	ka-lee shu	ག་ལེར་བཞུགས།
Excuse me;	tu-jay-sig	ཐུགས་རྗེ་གཟིགས།
Please. (pol)		
Thank you.	tu-jay-chay	ཐུགས་རྗེ་ཆེ།
Many thanks.	tu-jay shay-ta-chay	ཐུགས་རྗེ་ཞེ་དྲགས་ཆེ།

There's no single word for 'yes' and 'no' – it depends on the verb in the question. Either way, you'll notice that la (ལགས།) is used initially – this is a general marker that politely acknowledges the question. Often the verb that follows will be one of the 'to be' verbs (see Grammar, page 28):

Yes		No	
la, yin	ལགས། ཡིན།	la, men	ལགས། མིན།
la, ray	ལགས། རེད།	la, ma-ray	ལགས། མ་རེད།
la, yö	ལགས། ཡོད།	la, may	ལགས། མེད།
la, du	ལགས། འདུག	la, min-du	ལགས། མིན་འདུག

For instance, if asked kay-râng lob-toog yin-bay (ཁྱེད་རང་སློབ་ཕྲུག་ཡིན་པས།), 'Are you a student?', you would reply either la, yin (ལགས། ཡིན།), 'yes' or la, men (ལགས། མིན།), 'no'.

meeting people

greetings & goodbyes

Although ta-shi de-lek (བཀྲ་ཤིས་བདེ་ལེགས།) has become popular as a greeting in Lhasa, it may not always be understood as an equivalent to 'hello' elsewhere. Traditionally, Tibetans would ask each other where they were going by way of a greeting; nowadays, people often just start talking without any greeting at all.

Good morning.	nga-to de-lek	སྔ་དྲོ་བདེ་ལེགས།
Good day. (noon)	nyin-mo de-lek	ཉིན་མོ་བདེ་ལེགས།
Good afternoon.	chi-to de-lek	ཕྱི་དྲོ་བདེ་ལེགས།
Good evening.	gong-to de-lek	དགོང་དྲོ་བདེ་ལེགས།

thumbs up!

Giving a thumbs up with both hands means 'sorry' in Tibet.

There are two phrases for 'goodbye' in Tibetan: ka-lee shu (ག་ལེར་བཞུགས།) and ka-lee pay (ག་ལེར་ཕེབས།). The first is said by the person leaving and literally means 'Stay slowly'; the second is said to the person leaving and literally means 'Go slowly'. Other useful phrases include:

It's time to go.
ta doh-ran-sha   ད་འགྲོ་རན་ཤག

See you tomorrow.
sa-nyin jay-yong   སང་ཉིན་མཇལ་ཡོང་།

See you later.
je-ma jay-yong   རྗེས་མ་མཇལ་ཡོང་།

Come again soon.
yâng-kya pheb-ro-ah   ཡང་སྐྱར་ཕེབས་རོགས་ཨ།

We had a good time.
ngân-tso kyi-po choong   ངེད་ཚོ་སྐྱིད་པོ་བྱུང་།

Good night.
sim-ja nâng-go   གཟིམ་འཇགས་གནང་དགོས།

civilities

There are two words meaning 'please' in Tibetan: ku-chi (སྐུ་སྐྱིད) and tu-jay-sig (ཐུགས་རྗེ་གཟིགས). The former is the colloquial and the latter the polite version. However, neither is used as readily as 'please' in English. Generally, they're reserved for quite desperate or urgent requests, such as 'Please help me', ku-chi, nga-la rog nâng-dâ (སྐུ་སྐྱིད། ང་ལ་རོགས་གནང་དང་།). For day-to-day use, there's a number of polite expressions for situations where English speakers would use 'please' or 'thank you'.

(Please) Come in.
yah pay-nâng
ཡར་ཕེབས་གནང་།

(Please) Sit down.
shu-den ja
བཞུགས་གདན་འཇགས།

Excuse me; Sorry.
gong-da
དགོངས་དག

May I?; Do you mind?
di-gi re-bay
འགྲིག་གི་རེད་པས།

Thank you (very much).
tu-jay (shay-ta)-chay
ཐུགས་རྗེ་(ཞེ་དྲག)་ཆེ།

Thank you for your hospitality.
nay-len yak-po nâng-wa
tu-jay-chay
སྣེ་ལེན་ཡག་པོ་གནང་དབར་ཐུགས་རྗེ་ཆེ།

Thank you for your help.
nga rog nâng-wa tu-jay-chay
ང་ར་རོགས་གནང་བ་ཐུགས་རྗེ་ཆེ།

You're welcome.
la yin-dâng-yin
ལགས། ཡིན་དང་ཡིན།

Not at all; Don't mention it.
shu gö-ya yö-ma-ray
ཞུ་དགོས་ཡ་ལ་ཡོད་མ་རེད།

---

no offence!

Don't be offended if people don't say 'please' or 'thank you' to you – these phrases aren't very common in Tibetan.

requests

འདོད་སྐོར།

I'd like to ask you a favour.

ngay kay-râng-la ray-kü-chig
shu-ya yö

ངས་ཁྱེད་རང་ལ་རེ་སྐུལ་གཅིག་
ཞུ་ཡ་ཡོད།

May I ask you a question?

ngay kay-râng-la kân-ti-chig
shu-na di-gi re-bay

ངས་ཁྱེད་རང་ལ་བཀའ་འདྲི་གཅིག་
ཞུ་ན་འགྲིག་གི་རེད་པས།

Please can you help me?

ku-chi, nga-la rog nâng-da

སྐུ་མཁྱེན། ང་ལ་རོགས་གནང་དང་།

(Please) Could you repeat that?

(ku-chi) yâng-kya soong
nâng-da

(སྐུ་མཁྱེན།) ཡང་སྐྱར་གསུང་གནང་དང་།

(Please) Show me that.

pa-gi nga-la tön nâng da

ཕ་གི་ང་ལ་སྟོན་གནང་དང་།

Will you pass it to me please?

nga-la shu-ro nâng

ང་ལ་བཞུས་རོགས་གནང་།

Can I take ... now?

ta ... kye-na di-gi re-bay

ད་ ... འཁྱེར་ན་འགྲིག་གི་རེད་པས།

May I go now?

ta do-na di-gi re-bay

ད་འགྲོ་ན་འགྲིག་གི་རེད་པས།

Please don't forget!

ku-chi, ma-je-ro nâng

སྐུ་མཁྱེན། མ་བརྗེད་རོགས་གནང་།

What's the name of this?

dee ming-lâ kâ-ray ray

འདིའི་མིང་ལ་ག་རེ་རེད།

---

oh la la!

If someone calls you or tries to get your attention, a polite response to show you've heard is la (ལགས།). It can also be attached to the end of someone's name to be more polite when calling them. For example, if the person's name is Tashi, you would call out Tashi-la.

forms of address

བཏུད་ཆོག

To attract someone's attention, Tibetans use kinship terms, rather than say 'Excuse me'. Kinship terms vary according to the age and sex of the person you're speaking to. The standard term for someone of about your own age is cho-la (ཇོ་ལགས), literally 'elder brother', for a man, and ah-cha-la (ཨ་ཅག་ལགས), literally 'elder sister', for a woman. For example, to a man on the street who's about your age, but you don't know, you could say cho-la, gom-ba ka-bah du (ཇོ་ལགས དགོན་པ་ག་བར་འདུག), 'Hey Mister, where's the monastery?'. Other kinship terms include:

to someone ...	male	female
younger	bu (བུ) (lit: son)	bu-mo (བུ་མོ) (lit: daughter)
the same age	cho-la (ཇོ་ལགས) (lit: elder-brother)	ah-cha-la (ཨ་ཅག་ལགས) (lit: elder-sister)
older	pa-la (པ་ལགས) (lit: father)	ah-ma-la (ཨ་མ་ལགས) (lit: mother)
elderly	po-la (པོ་ལགས) (lit: grandfather)	mo-la (མོ་ལགས) (lit: grandmother)

body language

ལུས་ཀྱི་རྣམ་འགྱུར

In Tibet, people generally admire anyone who shows kindness, generosity and humility in their manner. For instance, if you're serving yourself at a meal, make sure you don't take the last of the food; leave enough for others.

When people meet and also when they farewell each other, they bow their heads slightly. When meeting, they'll also raise their right arm up from the elbow. When farewelling, the person staying may also extend their right hand with the palm facing upwards, as if showing the way for the person departing. Shaking hands has also become fairly common as a greeting.

meeting people

When closely related people meet after a long absence, or when they're due to part for a long time, they gently touch their foreheads together, while holding each other's hands and saying the relevant phrases. When meeting, they'll say ku-su de-po yin-pay (སྐུ་གཟུགས་བདེ་པོ་ཡིན་པས།), 'How are you?', and when departing they'll say châg-po nâng-ah (ཕྱག་པོ་གནང་ཨ།), 'Take care of yourself', to which the reply is thook-tel nâng mi-gö (ཐུགས་ཁྲལ་གནང་མི་དགོས།), 'You need not worry'.

When giving or receiving items, both hands are usually used. Alternatively, the right hand can be used to give or receive the item with the left hand bent towards the right elbow joint.

Other gestures you may see are head-scratching, which indicates doubt or nervousness, and shaking the index finger, which indicates warning. Sometimes, when listening to the words of a highly respected person, Tibetans may stick their tongue out slightly to show humbleness, respect and loyalty.

When visiting temples, you should take off your shoes, walk slowly and keep noise to a minimum. Hats should not be worn, nor should clothing which exposes the limbs (such as singlets and shorts).

kata culture

The ka-ta (ཁ་བཏགས།), a white ceremonial scarf, forms an indispensable part of Tibetan culture. It's an auspicious symbol of goodwill, friendship, harmony and love and, similar to flowers in the West, is used in many festivals and ceremonies, such as weddings, New Year and house-warmings. It's also used in greetings and goodbyes, and when people visit temples or lamas they offer ka-ta as a symbol of their faith and respect. Normally, the ka-ta is folded in half lengthwise and draped across both hands and is either placed around the neck of the recipient or given into their hands.

first meetings

When you first meet someone, use the relevant kinship term to address them (see page 109). Tibetans will be more comfortable giving their name once they've had a bit of a chat with you.

How are you?

kay-râng ku-su de-po yin-bay   ཁྱེད་རང་སྐུ་གཟུགས་བདེ་པོ་ཡིན་པས།

Fine. And you?

de-bo-yin. kay-râng-yâng   བདེ་པོ་ཡིན། ཁྱེད་རང་ཡང་སྐུ་གཟུགས་བདེ་པོ
ku-su de-po yin-bay   ཡིན་པས།

What's your name?

kay-râng-gi tsen-lâ kâ-ray-ray   ཁྱེད་རང་གི་མཚན་ལ་ག་རེ་རེད།

My name is ...

ngay-ming-la ... ray   ངའི་མིང་ལ ... རེད།

I'd like to introduce you to ...

ngay kay-râng-la ... ngo-tö shu-na ངས་ཁྱེད་རང་ལ ... ངོ་སྤྲོད་ཞུ་ན།

Pleased to meet you.

kay-râng jel-pa gâh-po choong   ཁྱེད་རང་མཇལ་པ་དགའ་པོ་བྱུང་།

making conversation

Asking someone where they're going (kay-râng ka-bah pay-kay, ཁྱེད་རང་ག་བར་ཕེབས་ས་གས) is a good way of opening casual conversation in Tibet.

Do you live here?

kay-râng-day shu-gi yö-bay   ཁྱེད་རང་འདིར་བཞུགས་ཀྱི་ཡོད་པས།

Where are you going?

kay-râng ka-bah pay-kay   ཁྱེད་རང་ག་བར་ཕེབས་སགས།

What are you doing?

kay-râng kâ-ray nâng-gi yö   ཁྱེད་རང་ག་རེ་གནང་གི་ཡོད།

This is my partner.

khong ngay-(tok-po/tok-mo) ray (m/f) ཁོང་ངའི་གྲོགས་པོ།/གྲོགས་མོ་རེད།

What do you think about ...?

kay-râng ... tog-la sâm-tsü kâ-ray-yö ཁྱེད་རང་ ... ཐོག་ལ་བསམ་ཚུལ་ག་རེད་ཡོད།

Can I take a photo (of you)?

(kay-râng) par-chig gyâb-na di-giy ray-bay (ཁྱེད་རང་)པར་ཅིག་རྒྱབ་ན་འགྲིག་གི་རེད་པས།

What's this called?

di-la kâ-ray sa འདི་ལ་ག་རེ་ཟ།

Beautiful, isn't it!

nying-je-po du-kah སྙིང་རྗེ་པོ་འདུག་ག

It's great here.

day pay-mi-si kyi-po du འདིར་དཔེ་མི་སྲིད་སྐྱིད་པོ་འདུག

We love it here.

ngân-tso day kyi-po du ང་ཚོ་འདིར་སྐྱིད་པོ་འདུག

What a cute baby!

pu-gu-di nying jay-pa-lah ཕྲུ་གུ་འདི་སྙིང་རྗེ་པ་ལ།

Are you waiting too?

kay-râng-yâng gook-tay yö-bay ཁྱེད་རང་ཡང་སྒུག་ཏེ་བསྡད་ཡོད་པས།

That's funny/strange.

te kyen-tsa-po ray དེ་ཁྱེན་མཚར་པོ་རེད།

Are you here on holiday?

kay-râng day goong-seng yin-bay ཁྱེད་རང་འདིར་གུང་གསེང་ཡིན་པས།

I'm here ...	nga day ... yin	ང་འདིར་ ... ཡིན།
for a holiday	goong-seng-chay	གུང་གསེང་ཆེད་
on business	tsong-lay-chay	ཚོང་ལས་ཆེད་
to study	lob-jong je-chay	སློབ་སྦྱོང་བྱེད་ཆེད་

How long are you here for?

kay-râng-day yün ring-lö day-ki-yin ཁྱེད་རང་འདིར་ཡུན་རིང་ལོས་བསྡད་ཀྱི་ཡིན།

I'm here for ... weeks/days.

nga day dün-ta/ དཔའ་འདིར་བདུན་ཕྲག/
nyin-ma ... day-ki-yin ཉིན་མ ... བསྡད་ཀྱི་ཡིན།

Do you like it here?

kay-râng-day kyi-po du-gay ཁྱེད་རང་འདིར་སྐྱིད་པོ་འདུག་གས།

Yes, a lot.

kyi-po shay-ta du སྐྱིད་པོ་ཞེ་དྲག་འདུག

We're here with our family.

ngân-tso-day nâng-mi ང་ཚོ་འདིར་ནང་མི
nyâm-tu leb-yö མཉམ་དུ་སླེབས་ཡོད།

I'm here with my boyfriend/girlfriend.

nga-day tok-po/tok-mo ང་འདིར་གྲོགས་པོ/གྲོགས་མོ
nyâm-tu leb-yö མཉམ་དུ་སླེབས་ཡོད།

Isn't the weather good today?

te-ring nâm-shi yâg-po du-gah དེ་རིང་གནམ་གཤིས་ཡག་པོ་འདུག་གཿ

Please sit here.

day shu-ro-nâng འདིར་བཞུགས་རོགས་གནང་།

Sure.	yin-da-yin	ཡིན་དང་ཡིན།
Just a minute.	teh-si gu-ah	ཐོག་ཙམ་སྒུག་ཨཱ།
I see.	ah-leh	ཨ་ལེ།
It's OK.	di-gi ray	འགྲིག་གི་རེད།
It's (not) important.	kay-chen-po (ma)-ray	གལ་ཆེན་པོ(མ)རེད།
It's (not) possible.	si-ki (ma)-ray	སྲིད་ཀྱི(མ)རེད།
Look!	mik ta-dâ	མིག་བལྟ་དང་།
Listen (to this)!	(di) nyön-da	(འདི)ཉོན་དང་།
I'm ready.	nga ta-dig-yin	ང་གྲ་འགྲིག་ཡིན།
Are you ready?	kay-râng ta-dig	ཁྱེད་རང་གྲ་འགྲིག
	yin-bay	ཡིན་པས།
Go away!	pah gyu	ཕར་རྒྱུགས།
Be quiet!	kah-ga shu	ཁ་རོགས་བཞུགས།
Never mind.	kay chay-kiy ma-ray	གའི་བྱེད་ཀྱི་མ་རེད།

meeting people

113

If your country isn't listed here, try pointing on a map.

Where are you from?

kay-râng loong-pa ka-nay yin   ཁྱེད་རང་ལུང་པ་ག་ནས་ཡིན།

I'm from ...	nga ...-nay yin	ང་ ...ནས་ཡིན།
We're from ...	ngân-tso ...-nay yin	ང་ཚོ་ ...ནས་ཡིན།
Africa	ah-fi-ri-ka	ཨ་ཕི་རི་ཀ
Asia	ay-shi-ya	ཨེ་ཤི་ཡ
Australia	o-ta-li-ya	ཨོ་སྟི་ལི་ཡ
Canada	ka-na-da	ཀེ་ན་ཌ
China	gyâ-nak	རྒྱ་ནག
England	in-ji loong-pa	དབྱིན་ཇི་ལུང་པ
Europe	yu-rop	ཡུ་རོབ
Finland	fin-land	ཕིན་ལན྄
France	fa-ren-si	ཕ་རན་སི
Germany	jar-man	འཇར་མན
Holland	ho-land	ཧོ་ལན྄
India	gya-ga	རྒྱ་གར
Ireland	ah-ri-len	ཨེ་རི་ལན྄
Israel	e-za-rel	ཨི་ཟ་རེལ
Italy	e-ta-lee	ཨི་ཏ་ལི
Japan	ree-bin	རི་བིན
the Middle East	shar-kyil gya-kab	ཤར་དཀྱིལ་རྒྱལ་ཁབ
New Zealand	nu-zee-land	ནེའུ་ཛི་ལན྄
Norway	naw-way	ནོར་ཝེ
Scotland	so-kot-land	སོ་ཀོཊ་ལན྄
South America	lho ah-mi-ri-ka	ལྷོ་ཨ་མི་རི་ཀ
Spain	se-pan	སེ་པན
Sweden	sü-den	སུད་ཏེན
Switzerland	sü-zee	སུད་སི
the USA	yu-es-ay/ah-mi-ri-ka	ཡུ་ཨེས་ཨེ /ཨ་མི་རི་ཀ
Wales	welz	ཝེལས

We come from a/the ...	ngân-tso ...-nay yin	རང་ཚོ་...ནས་ཡིན།
I live in/at the/a ...	nga ...-la dö-ki-yö	ང་...ལ་སྡོད་ཀྱི་ཡོད།
city	dong-kay	གྲོང་ཁྱེར།
countryside	dong-seb	གྲོང་གསེབ།
mountains	ri gâng	རི་སྒང༌།
seaside	tso-dâm	མཚོ་འགྲམ།
suburbs of ...	... dong-kay sa-kü	...གྲོང་ཁྱེར་ས་ཁུལ།
village	dong-seb	གྲོང་གསེབ།

cultural differences

ལུགས་སྲོལ་དང་རིག་གཞུང་མི་འདྲ་བ

How do you do this in your country?

kay-râng-gi loong-pay loog-sö-la
di kân-teh-si chay-gö-ray

ཁྱེད་རང་གི་ལུང་པའི་ལུགས་སྲོལ་ལ་འདི་གང་
འདྲ་བྱེད་དགོས་རེད།

Is this a local or national custom?

di sa-nay-ki loog-sö yin-na,
gyâ-kâb-ki loog-sö yin-na

འདི་ས་གནས་ཀྱི་ལུགས་སྲོལ་ཡིན་ན།
རྒྱལ་ཁབ་ཀྱི་ལུགས་སྲོལ་ཡིན་ན།

| local | sa-nay-ki | ས་གནས་ཀྱི། |
| national | gyâ-kâb-ki | རྒྱལ་ཁབ་ཀྱི། |

I don't want to offend you.

ngay kay-râng-la pok-tu
chay-sâm may

ངས་ཁྱེད་རང་ལ་ཕོག་ཐུག་བྱེད་བསམ་མེད།

**I'm sorry, it's not the custom
in my country.**

gong-ta te-da ngân-tsö
loong-pay loog-sö-la yö-ma-ray

དགོངས་དག་དེ་འདྲ་ངe་ཚོe་ལུང་པའི་ལུགས་
སྲོལ་ལ་ཡོད་མ་རེད།

the path to happiness

All Tibetan houses have an altar room and monks or nuns
are frequently invited to perform rituals or recite religious
books for the prosperity and happiness of the family. Outside each house, you'll find a Buddhist flag.

I'm not accustomed to this.

nga di-la gom-di may   ང་འདི་ལ་གོམས་འདྲིས་མེད།

I don't mind watching, but I'd prefer not to participate.

nga tay-mo ta-ya-tsâm ma-tok   ང་ལྟད་མོ་ལྟ་ཡག་ཙམ་ལས་གཤིབས་བྱེ་གཤིབས
thay-tog chay-dö may   བྱེད་འདོད་མེད།

I'll give it a go.

ngay ta-tsö chay-go   ངས་ལྟ་ཚོད་བྱེད་གོ

I'm sorry, it's	gong-ta di ngay	དགོངས་དག འདི་ངའི
against my ...	...-dâng tün-gee min-du	...དང་མཐུན་གྱི་མིན་འདུག
beliefs	ta-wa	ལྟ་བ
culture	rig-shoong	རིག་གཞུང
religion	chö-loog	ཆོས་ལུགས

age

རང་ལོ

How old are you?

kay-râng lo kâ-tsay yin   ཁྱེད་རང་ལོ་ག་ཚོད་ཡིན།

How old is your ...?	... lo kâ-tsay ray	... ལོ་ག་ཚོད་རེད།
son	kay-râng-gi bu	ཁྱེད་རང་གི་བུ
daughter	kay-râng-gi bu-mo	ཁྱེད་རང་གི་བུ་མོ

I'm ... years old.	nga lo ... yin	ང་ལོ ... ཡིན།
18	chö-gye	བཅོ་བརྒྱད
25	nyi-shu tsay-nga	ཉི་ཤུ་རྩ་ལྔ

(See **Numbers & Amounts**, page 37, for your age.)

occupations

The list opposite includes both local and Western occupations.

What do you do (for a living)?

kay-râng (tso-tâb-che) lay-kâ	ཁྱེད་རང་(འཚོ་ཐབས་ཆེད་)
kâ-ray chay-ki-yö	ལས་ཀ་ག་རེ་བྱེད་ཀྱི་ཡོད།

I'm a/an ...	nga ... yin	ང་ ... ཡིན།
actor	tâb tön-pa	འཁྲབ་སྟོན་པ
artist	ri-mo khen	རི་མོ་མཁན
businessperson	tsong-pa	ཚོང་པ
carpenter	shing-so-wa	ཤིང་བཟོ་བ
chef	ma-chen	མ་བྱན
doctor	ahm-chi	ཨེམ་རྗེ
driver	mo-ta tong-khen	མོ་ཊ་གཏོང་མཁན
engineer	so-tün chen-mo-wa	བཟོ་སྐྲུན་ཆེན་མོ་བ
factory worker	so-ta lay-ka chay-khen	བཟོ་གྲྭའི་ལས་ཀ་བྱེད་མཁན
farmer	shing-pâ	ཞིང་པ
journalist	tsâg-ba gya-khen	ཚགས་པར་རྒྱགས་མཁན
labourer	ngay-tsö gyu-khen	དལ་རྩོལ་རྒྱུ་མཁན
lawyer	tim tsö-pa	ཁྲིམས་རྩོད་པ
manual worker	ngay-tsö gyu-khen	དལ་རྩོལ་རྒྱུ་མཁན
mechanic	trü-lay pa	འཕྲུལ་ལས་པ
musician	ro-ja tong-khen	རོལ་ཆ་གཏོང་མཁན
nomad	dok-pa	འབྲོག་པ
nurse	men-khâng nay-yok	སྨན་ཁང་གི་ནད་གཡོག
office worker/ clerk	lay-koong lay-ka chay-khen; doong-yig	ལས་ཁུངས་ལས་ཀ་བྱེད་ མཁན་/དྲུང་ཡིག
scientist	tsen-rig pa	མཚན་རིག་པ
secretary	doong-yig	དྲུང་ཡིག
student	lob-toog	སློབ་ཕྲུག
tailor	tsen-po-wa	ཚེམ་པོ་བ
teacher	gay-gan	དགེ་རྒན
university lecturer	tsu-la lob-tay lek-chah shö-khen	གཙུག་ལག་སློབ་གྲྭའི་ ལེགས་བཤད་འདོན་མཁན
waiter	se-dim shâb-shu-wa	ཟས་འཐུངས་ཞབས་ཞུ་བ
writer	tsom-di-pa	རྩོམ་འབྲི་པ

I'm retired.

nga gen-yö yin   ང་རྒན་ཡོལ་ཡིན།

I'm unemployed.

ngah lay-ka may   ངར་ལས་ཀ་མེད།

What are you studying?

kay-râng lob-jong kâ-ray   ཁྱེད་རང་སློབ་སྦྱོང་ག་རེ་

nâng-gi yö   གནང་གི་ཡོལ།

I'm studying ...	nga ... lob-jong	ང་ ... སློབ་སྦྱོང་
	chay-ki yö	བྱེད་ཀྱི་ཡོལ།
art	ri-mo	རི་མོ
arts/humanities	gyu-tse rig-nay	རྒྱུ་རྩལ་རིག་གནས
Buddhism	nâng-chö	ནང་ཆོས
business	tsong-lay	ཚོང་ལས
engineering	so-tün rig-nay	བཟོ་སྐྲུན་རིག་གནས
English	in-ji kay-yig	དབྱིན་ཇི་སྐད་ཡིག
languages	kay-yig	སྐད་ཡིག
law	tim	ཁྲིམས
medicine	men	སྨན
science	tsen-rig	མཚན་རིག
teaching	gay-gan ö-jong	དགེ་རྒན་འོས་སྦྱོང་
Tibetan	bö-kay	བོད་སྐད

feelings

I'm ...	nga ...-gi du	ང་ ...གི་འདུག
Are you ...?	kay-râng ...-gi du-gay	ཁྱེད་རང་ ...གི་འདུག་གས།
afraid	tah	སྐྲག
angry	loong làng	ཟུང་ལང༌།
cold	khya	ཁྱག
depressed	sem-shu bay-ti châg	སེམས་ཤུགས་ཆུང་དེ་ཆགས།
hot	tsa-wa tsi	ཚ་བ་ཚིག
hungry	drö-kog tog	གྲོད་ཁོག་ལྟོགས།
sad	sem kyo	སེམས་སྐྱོ།
sleepy	nyi ku	གཉིད་ཁུག
sorry (regret)	gyö-pa kye	འགྱོད་པ་སྐྱེ།
thirsty	ka kom	ཁ་སྐོམ།
tired	kâ-lay ka	དཀའ་ལས་ཁ།
worried	sem-tel lâng	སེམས་འཁྲུལ་ལང༌།

I'm grateful.	kay-râng nga-la tâng kâ-tin chen-po yin	ཁྱེད་རང་ང་ལ་བཏང་ ཆེན་པོ་ཡིན།
I'm happy.	nga kyi-po du	ང་སྐྱིད་པོ་འདུག
I'm in a hurry.	nga te-wa yö	ང་འབལ་བ་ཡོད།
I'm keen to ...	nga ...-la dö-pa yö	ང་ ...ལ་འདོད་པ་ཡོད།
I'm sorry. (condolence)	nga lo-phâm yö	ང་བློ་ཕམ་ཡོད།
I'm well.	nga de-po yin	ང་བདེ་པོ་ཡིན།

breaking the language barrier

བོད་བརྗེ་མི་འཕྲོད་པའི་དཀའ་ངལ་སེལ་བ།

You'll find that English isn't widely spoken in Tibet, particularly in the more remote areas. Even in Lhasa the number of English speakers is relatively small.

Do you speak English?

kay-râng in-ji-kay shing-gi
yö-bay

ཁྱེད་རང་དབྱིན་ཇི་སྐད་
ཤེས་ཀྱི་ཡོད་པས།

Yes, I do.

la, yö

ལགས། ཡོད།

No, I don't.

la, may

ལགས། མེད།

Does anyone speak English?

in-ji-kay shay-khen yö ray-bay

དབྱིན་ཇི་སྐད་ཤེས་མཁན་ཡོད་རེད་པས།

I speak a little.

teh-si shin-gi yö

ཏོག་ཙམ་ཤེས་ཀྱི་ཡོད།

Do you understand?

ha ko song-ngay

ཧ་གོ་སོང་ངས།

I understand.

ha ko-song

ཧ་གོ་སོང་།

I don't understand.

ha ko ma-song

ཧ་གོ་མ་སོང་།

Could you speak more slowly please?

yâng-kya ka-lee ka-lee soong
nâng da

ཡང་སྐྱར་ག་ལེར་ག་ལེར་གསུང་གནང་དང་།

Could you repeat that?

te yâng-kya soong nâng-da

དེ་ཡང་སྐྱར་གསུང་གནང་དང་།

Please write it down.

ku-chi, shu-gü-tog ti nâng-da

སྐུ་མཁྱེན། ཤོག་བུའི་ཐོག་འབྲི་གནང་དང་།

How do you say ...?

... kân-te-si lâb gö ray

... གང་འདྲས་ལབ་དགོས་རེད།

What does ... mean?

...-gi tön-tâg kâ-ray ray

...གི་དོན་ཐག་ག་རེ་རེད།

What does this mean?

di tön-tâg kâ-ray ray

འདིའི་དོན་ཐག་ག་རེ་རེད།

What's this called?

di-la kâ-ray sa

འདི་ལ་ག་རེ་ཟ།

Just a moment, I'll try to find it in this book.

teh-si goo-ah, teb-di nâng yö-may ta-gi-yin

ཏེག་ཙམ་འགུག་ག་འ་དེབ་འདི་ནང་ ཡོད་མེད་བལྟ་གྱི་ཡིན།

Can you read this script for me please?

nga-la yi-ge-di lo-rog nâng-da

ང་ལ་ཡི་གེ་འདི་ཀློག་རོགས་གནང་དང་།

Can you show me (in this book)?

(teb di-nâng) mig tön-da

(དེབ་འདིའི་ནང་)མིག་སྟོན་དང་།

staying in touch

སྐུ་མཉམ་འབྲེལ་བ

Tomorrow is my last day here.

sa-nyin nga day dö-ya nyin ta-ma-te yin

སང་ཉིན་ང་འདིར་སྡོད་ཡ་ཉིན་མཐའ་མ་ འདེ་ཡིན།

Let's swap addresses.

ka-châng je-ray chay-na

ཁ་བྱང་བརྗེ་རེས་བྱེད་ན།

Do you have a pen and paper?

kay-râng-la nyu-gu dâng shu-gu yö-bay

ཁྱེད་རང་ལ་སྙུག་གུ་དང་ཤོག་གུ་ཡོད་པས།

What's your address?

kay-râng-gi ka-châng kâ-ray ray

ཁྱེད་རང་གི་ཁ་བྱང་ག་རེ་རེད།

What's your email address?

kay-râng-gi ee-mel ka-châng kâ-ray ray

ཁྱེད་རང་གི་ཨི་མེལ་ཁ་བྱང་ག་རེ་རེད།

Here's my address.

ngay ka-châng di-ray

ངའི་ཁ་བྱང་འདི་རེད།

If you ever visit (Scotland) you must come and visit us.

kay-râng gay-si (so-kot-land)-la pheb-na nga-tsö-sah ngay-pa-du pheb-nâng

ཁྱེད་རང་གལ་སྲིད་(སོ་ཀོཊ་ལེན་)ལ་ཕེབས་ན་ང་ཚོའི་སར་ངེས་པར་དུ་ཕེབས་གནང་།

If you come to (Birmingham) you've got a place to stay.

kay-râng gay-si (ba-min-gâm)-la pheb-na shoog-sa nga-tsö-sah yö

ཁྱེད་རང་གལ་སྲིད་(སྦར་མིང་འགམས་)ལ་ཕེབས་ན་བཞུགས་སར་ང་ཚོའི་སར་ཡོད།

Do you have an email address?

kay-râng-la ee-mel ka-châng yö-bay

ཁྱེད་རང་ལ་ཨི་མེལ་ཁ་བྱང་ཡོད་པས།

I'll send you copies of the photos.

ngay kay-râng-la par tâng yong-gi yin

ངས་ཁྱེད་རང་ལ་པར་གཏང་ཡོང་གི་ཡིན།

Don't forget to write!

nga-la yig-day nâng-ya ma-jay-ah

ང་ལ་ཡི་འབྲེལ་གནང་ཡག་མ་བརྗེད་ཨ།

It's been great meeting you.

kay-râng jay-wa ka-bo shay-ta choong

ཁྱེད་རང་མཇལ་བར་དགའ་པོ་ཞེ་དྲག་བྱུང་།

Keep in touch!

mu-tü-nay day-wa nâng-ah

སྐུ་མགྱུད་ནས་འབྲེལ་བ་གནང་ཨ།།

Tibetans may well refer to themselves as husband, kyo-ka (ཁྱོ་ག), literally meaning 'man', and wife, kye-man (སྐྱེས་དམན་), literally meaning 'woman', even if they're not married. For Tibetans, it's more appropriate for an unmarried foreign couple to introduce themselves as husband and wife, if they're in a serious relationship – otherwise tok-po (གྲོགས་པོ་), 'boyfriend', and tok-mo (གྲོགས་མོ་), 'girlfriend', are fine.

questions

བདྲི་རྩད་

Are you married?

kay-râng châng-sa
kyön tsa-bay

ཁྱེད་རང་ཆང་ས་
བརྒྱུན་ཚར་པས།

Is your husband/wife here?

kay-râng-gi kyo-ka/
kye-man day yö-bay

ཁྱེད་རང་གི་ཁྱོ་ག/སྐྱེས་དམན་འདིར་ཡོད་པས།

Do you have a boyfriend/girlfriend?

kay-râng-la tok-po/tok-mo
yö-bay

ཁྱེད་རང་ལ་གྲོགས་པོ/གྲོགས་མོ་ཡོད་པས།

How many children do you have?

kay-râng-la pu-gu kâ-tsay yö

ཁྱེད་རང་ལ་ཕྲུ་གུ་ག་ཚོད་ཡོད།

How many brothers/sisters do you have?

kay-râng-la pün-kya bu/bu-mo
kâ-tsay yö

ཁྱེད་རང་ལ་སྤུན་ཀྱག/བུ་མོ་ག་ཚོད་
ཡོད།

How old are they?

khong-tso lo kâ-tsay kâ-tsay ray

ཁོང་ཚོ་ལོ་ག་ཚོད་ག་ཚོད་རེད།

Do you live with your family?

kay-râng nâng-mi nyâm-tu   ཁྱེད་རང་ནང་མི་མཉམ་དུ་སྡོད་ཀྱི་ཡོད་པས།
dö-ki yö-bay

Do you get along with your family?

nâng-mi-dâng châm-bo yö-bay   ནང་མི་དང་འཆམ་པོ་ཡོད་པས།

replies

ལན་འདེབས།

I'm …	nga …	ང་ …
single	mi-hreng yin	མི་ཧྲེང་ཡིན།
married	châng-sa gyâb-tsah	འཆང་ས་བརྒྱབ་ཚར།
separated/	[kye-man/kyo-ka]-dâng	[སྐྱེ་དམན/དཀྱོག]
divorced	ka-ka châh song **(m/f)**	དགའ་ཁག་ཆགས་སོང་།

I'm a widower/widow.

ngay kye-man/kyo-ka dong-song   ངའི་སྐྱེ་དམན/ཁྱོ་ག་གྲོང་སོང་།

I have a girlfriend/boyfriend.

ngah tok-mo/tok-po yö   ངར་གྲོགས་མོ/གྲོགས་པོ་ཡོད།

We live together, but we're not married.

nga-nyi nyâm-tu dö-ki yö-te   ང་གཉིས་མཉམ་དུ་སྡོད་ཀྱི་ཡོད་དེ་
châng-sa gyâb-may   འཆང་ས་བརྒྱབ་མེད།

I don't have any children.

nga pu-gu chig-kyâng may   ང་ཕྲུ་གུ་གཅིག་ཀྱང་མེད།

I have a daughter/son.

nga-la pu-gu bu-mo-chig/bu-chig yö   ང་ལ་ཕྲུ་གུ་བུ་མོ་གཅིག/བུ་གཅིག་ཡོད།

I live with my family.

nga nâng-mi nyâm-tu dö-ki yö   ང་ནང་མི་མཉམ་དུ་སྡོད་ཀྱི་ཡོད།

family members

aunt	ah-nay/su-mo	ཨ་ནེ་/སྲུ་མོ
baby	pu-gu	ཕྲུ་གུ
boy	bu	བུ
brother	pün-kya bu	སྤུན་སྐྱ་བུ
children	pu-gu	ཕྲུ་གུ
dad	pa-la	པ་ལགས
daughter	bu-mo	བུ་མོ
daughter-in-law	bü kye-man	བུའི་སྐྱེས་དམན
family	nâng-mi	ནང་མི
family name	nâng-mi ming	ནང་མིའི་མིང་
father	pa-pha	པ་ཕ
father-in-law	sa-tsâng-gi pa-pha	བཟའ་ཚང་གི་པ་ཕ
girl	bu-mo	བུ་མོ
given name	bhö-ming	འབོད་མིང་
grandfather	po-po	སྤོ་སྤོ
grandmother	mo-mo	རྨོ་རྨོ
husband	kyo-ka	ཁྱོ་ག
mother	ah-ma	ཨ་མ
mother-in-law	sa-tsâng-gi ah-ma	བཟའ་ཚང་གི་ཨ་མ
mum	ah-ma	ཨ་མ
nickname	ming-tog	མིང་འདོགས
sister	pün-kya bu-mo	སྤུན་སྐྱ་བུ་མོ
son	bu	བུ
son-in-law	bu-mö kyo-ka	བུ་མོའི་ཁྱོ་ག
uncle	ah-shâng/ah-ku	ཨ་ཞང་/ཨ་ཁུ
wife	kye-man	སྐྱེས་དམན

help the aged

Younger people are expected to respect older people, and children are expected to support their aged parents.

parenting

When's the baby due?

pu-gu ka-dü kye-ren yö-ray

ཕྲུ་གུ་གང་དུས་སྐྱེ་རན་ཡོད་རེད།

What are you going to call the baby?

pu-gu-la ming kâ-ray ta-gi yin

ཕྲུ་གུ་ལ་མིང་ག་རེ་བཏགས་ཀྱི་ཡིན།

Is this your first child?

di kay-râng-gi pu-gu dâng-po re-bay

འདི་ཁྱེད་རང་གི་ཕྲུ་གུ་དང་པོ་རེད་པས།

How old are your children?

kay-râng-gi pu-gu-tso lo kâ-tsay kâ-tsay ray

ཁྱེད་རང་གི་ཕྲུ་གུ་ཚོ་ལོ་ག་ཚོད་ག་ཚོད་རེད།

I can't believe it! You look too young.

ngön-nay re-bay. kay-râng dân-ta-ahng shön-sha töh-po shay-ta du

དངོས་གནས་རེད་པས། ཁྱེད་རང་ད་ལྟ་ཡང་གཞོན་ཤ་ཏོད་པོ་ཤེད་ཏག་འདུག

Does he/she attend school?

kho/mo lob-ta doh-ki yö re-bay

ཁོ/མོ་སློབ་གྲྭ་འགྲོ་གི་ཡོད་རེད་པས།

Is it a private or state school?

te gay-pay/shoong-gi lob-ta re-bay

དེ་སྒེར་པའི/གཞུང་གི་སློབ་གྲྭ་རེད་པས།

Who looks after the children?

pu-gu sü ta-gi yö-ray

ཕྲུ་གུ་སུས་བལྟ་གི་ཡོད་རེད།

Do you have grandchildren?

kay-râng-la pu-gü pu-gu yö-bay

ཁྱེད་རང་ལ་ཕྲུ་གུའི་ཕྲུ་གུ་ཡོད་པས།

What's the baby's name?

pu-gü ming kâ-ray ray

ཕྲུ་གུའི་མིང་ག་རེ་རེད།

Is it a boy or a girl?

pu-gu bu ray, bu-mo ray

ཕྲུ་གུ་བུ་རེད། བུ་མོ་རེད།

126

Is he/she well-behaved?

kho/mo chö-lâm yâg-po yö-bay

ཁོ་/མོ་སྤྱོད་ལམ་ཡག་པོ་ཡོད་པས།

Does he/she let you sleep at night?

khö/mö kay-râng tsen-la
nyih khoog chu-gi du-gay

ཁོས་/མོས་ཁྱེད་རང་མཚན་ལ་གཉིད་
ཁུག་བཅུག་གི་འདུག་གས།

He's/She's very big for his/her age!

kho/mo rông-gi lo-tsay-la
pâg-bay soog-po chen-po
shay-ta du

ཁོ་/མོ་རང་གི་ལོ་ཚོད་ལ་དཔགས་པས་གཟུགས་
པོ་ཆེན་པོ་ཞེ་དྲག་འདུག

What a beautiful child!

pu-gu nying jay-wa-la

ཕྲུ་གུ་སྙིང་རྗེ་བ་ལ།

He/She looks like you.

kho/mo kay-râng dâng da-wo du

ཁོ་/མོ་ཁྱེད་རང་དང་འདྲ་པོ་འདུག

He/She has your eyes.

khö/mö mig kay-râng
mig-dâng da-wo du

ཁོའི་/མོའི་མིག་ཁྱེད་རང་མིག་དང་འདྲ་པོ་འདུག

Who does he/she look like, mum or dad?

kho/mo pa-pha-dâng
ah-ma-nyi su da-wo du

ཁོ་/མོ་པ་ཕ་དང་ཨ་མ་གཉིས་སུ་འདྲ་པོ་འདུག

talking with children

ཕྲུ་གུ་དང་སྐད་ཆ་འཆད་པ

What's your name?

kay-râng ming-la kâ-ray sa

ཁྱེད་རང་མིང་ལ་ག་རེ་ཟེར།

How old are you?

kay-râng lo kâ-tsay yin

ཁྱེད་རང་ལོ་ག་ཚོད་ཡིན།

When's your birthday?

kay-râng-gi kye-tsay ka-dü ray

ཁྱེད་རང་གི་སྐྱེ་ཚེས་ག་དུས་རེད།

Do you have brothers and sisters?

kay-râng-la pün-kya bu dâng
pün-kya bu-mo yö-bay

ཁྱེད་རང་ལ་སྤུན་ཀྱ་བུ་དང་སྤུན་
ཀྱ་བུ་མོ་ཡོད་པས།

Do you go to school or kindergarten?

kay-râng lob-ta do-gi
yö-na, bu-so-khâng do-gi
yö-na

ཁྱེད་རང་སློབ་གྲྭར་འགྲོ་གི་ཡོད་ན། བུ་གསོ་ཁང་
འགྲོ་གི་ཡོད་ན།

Is your teacher nice?

gay-gan-gi yag-po chay-kee
du-gay

དགེ་རྒན་གྱིས་ཡག་པོ་བྱེད་ཀྱི་འདུག་གས།

Do you like school?

lob-ta do-ya gah-po yö-bay

སློབ་གྲྭ་འགྲོ་ཡག་དགའ་པོ་ཡོད་པས།

Do you play sport?

tse-mo tsi-gi yö-bay

རྩེད་མོ་རྩེ་གྱི་ཡོད་པས།

What sport do you play?

tse-mo kâ-ray tsi-gi yö

རྩེད་མོ་ག་རེ་རྩེ་གྱི་ཡོད།

What do you do after school?

lob-da do-jay kâ-ray
chay-ki yö

སློབ་གྲྭ་གྲོལ་འཇུག་རྗེས་ག་རེ་བྱེད་ཀྱི་ཡོད།

Do you learn English?

in-ji-kay jong-gi yö-bay

དབྱིན་ཇི་སྐད་སྦྱོང་གི་ཡོད་པས།

We speak a different language in my country, so I don't understand you very well.

ngân-tsö loong-pâh kay
shen-da gya-gi yö-ray,
song-tsâng, ngay kay-râng-gi
kay-cha yâg-po ha go-ki
min-du

ང་ཚོའི་ལུང་པར་སྐད་གཞན་དག་རྒྱག་གི་ཡོད་
རེད། སོང་ཙང་། ངས་ཁྱེད་རང་གི་སྐད་ཆ་ཡག་པོ་
ཧ་གོ་གི་མིན་འདུག

I come from very far away.

nga loong-ba tâg ring-po
shig-nay yong-wa yin

ང་ལུང་པ་ཐག་རིང་པོ་ཞིག་ནས་ཡོང་བ་ཡིན།

Do you want to play a game?

ngah nyâm-du tse-mo tsi-gay

ང་མཉམ་དུ་རྩེད་མོ་ཞིག་རྩེ་གས།

What will we play?

kâ-ray tse-gâh

ག་རེ་རྩེ་ག

hobbies

ཁྱེར་བཏང་དགའ་མོས་བྱེད་ས

What do you do in your spare time?

kay-râng thoog day-pö-kâb
kâ-ray nâng-gi yö

ཁྱེད་རང་ཐུགས་དལ་པོའི་སྐབས་ག་རེ་
གནང་གི་ཡོད

Do you like ...?	kay-râng ...-la ka-bo yö-bay	ཁྱེད་རང་ ...་ལ་དགའ་པོ་ཡོད་པས
I like ...	nga ...-la ka-bo yö	ང་ ...་ལ་དགའ་པོ་ཡོད
I don't like ...	nga ...-la ka-bo may	ང་ ...་ལ་དགའ་པོ་མེད
cooking	kha-la so-ya	ཁ་ལག་བཟོ་ཡག
shopping	nyo-cha gya-ya	ཉོ་ཆ་རྒྱག་ཡག
reading	teb lo-ya	དེབ་ཀློག་ཡག
travelling	yu-ko tro-châm doh-ya	ཡུལ་སྐོར་སྤྲོ་ཚམ་འགྲོ་ཡག
talking	kay-cha-shö-ya	སྐད་ཆ་ཤོད་ཡག
watching football	kâng-bol ta-ya	རྐང་པོལ་བལྟ་ཡག
watching TV	dian-shi ta-ya; soog-tong loong-tin ta-ya	དེན་ཤི་བལྟ་ཡག/གཟུགས་མཐོང་རླུང་འཕྲིན་བལྟ་ཡག

I like ...	nga ... gya-ya ka-bo yö	ང་ ... རྒྱག་ཡག་ལ་དགའ་པོ་ཡོད
dancing	shâb-doh	ཞབས་བྲོ
discos	dis-ko	ཌིས་ཀོ
diving	chu-ting kay	ཆུ་གཏིང་རྒྱལ
hiking	kâng-dü	རྐང་འགུལ
meditation	gom	སྒོམ
photography	par	པར
swimming	kay	རྒྱལ
yoga	yo-ga-gom	ཡོ་ག་སྒོམ

I like ...	nga ... tsi-ya ka-bo yö	ང་ ... རྩེ་ཡག་དགའ་པོ་ཡོད།
aerobics/ athletics	lü-tsay	ལུས་རྩལ།
baseball	bas-bol	བེས་བོལ།
basketball	bis-ket-bol/sihn-bol	བིས་ཀེཏ་པོལ།/སིན་པོལ།
boxing	bok-sing	སྤོག་ཤིང་།
cricket	kri-ket	ཀིར་ཀེཏ།
football (soccer)	kâng-bol	རྐང་པོལ།
gymnastics	lü-tsay	ལུས་རྩལ།
hockey	hoc-key	ཧོག་ཀི།
judo	ju-doh	འཇུ་ཌོ།
martial arts	râng-soong dâg-tsay	རང་སྲུང་དག་རྩལ།
playing games	tsay-mo	རྩེད་མོ།
playing sport	tsay-mo/lü-tsay	རྩེད་མོ།/ལུས་རྩལ།
rugby	râg-bi po-lo	རག་སྦི་པོ་ལོ།
tennis	ten-nis	ཏེ་ནེ་སི།
Tai Chi	tai-chi	ཐའི་ཆི་ལུས་རྩལ།
volleyball	vo-lee-bol/dra-bol	ཕ་ལེའི་པོལ།/དྲ་པོལ།
weightlifting	ji-deg lü-tsay	ལྕིད་འདེགས་ལུས་རྩལ།

I like ...	nga ... tong-ya ka-bo yö	ང་ ... གཏོང་ཡག་དགའ་པོ་ཡོད།
cycling	kâng ga-ri	རྐང་འཁྲ་རིལ།
music	rö-ja	རོལ་ཆ།
rowing	dru	གྲུ།
skiing	gang-shü	གངས་ཤུད།

art

བྱུ་རྩུབ་རིག་གནས།

When's the gallery open?

dem-tön-khâng ka-dü
go chay-ki-ray

འགྲེམ་སྟོན་ཁང་ག་དུས་སྒོ་ཕྱེ་གྱི་རེད།

What kind of art are you interested in?

kay-râng lâg-tsay rig-nay
kân-day-la ying-yö

ཁྱེད་རང་ལག་རྩལ་རྩུབ་རིག་གནས་གང་
འདྲས་ལ་དབྱིངས་ཡོད།

I'm interested in ...   nga ...-la ying yö   ང་ ...འདྲིངས་ཡོད།
    painting   tsön-ti ri-mo   ཚོན་ཏྲི་རི་མོ
    performance art   tâb-tön   འཚབ་སྟོན
    sand mandalas   dü-tsön kyi-khoh   དྲུལ་ཚོན་དཀྱིལ་འཁོར
    sculpture   bu-kö   འབུར་ཁོས

altarpiece   chö-shom   མཆོད་གཤོམས
curator   dem-tö cha-lâg   འགྲེམ་སྟོན་ཅ་ལག་ཉམས
    nyâm-so chay-khen   གསོ་བྱེད་མཁན
gardens   doom-ra   སྒུམ་ར
photographer   pâh gya-khen   པར་རྒྱག་མཁན
sculptor   kö gya-khen   ཁོས་རྒྱག་མཁན
slide   sa-le-di log-nyen-pâh   སལེ་ཏི་ལྒོག་གཉན་པར
souvenir shop   den-ten cha-lâg   དྲན་རྟེན་ཅ་ལག་ཚོང་ཁང
    tsong khâng
statue   dâ-ku   འདྲ་སྐུ

talking about travel

ཡུལ་སྐོར་སྒྲོ་འཆམས་སྐོར་སྐད་ཆ་ཤོད་པ

Have you travelled much?

kay-râng loong-pa mâng-boh
dü-shü chay-nyong bay

ཁྱེད་རང་ལུང་པ་མང་པོ་འགྲུལ་བཞུད་
བྱེད་སྒོང་པས།

How long have you been travelling?

kay-râng dü-shü yün ring-lö
chay-pa yin

ཁྱེད་རང་འགྲུལ་བཞུད་ཡུན་རིང་ལོས་
བྱེད་པ་ཨིན།

I've been travelling for (two) months.

nga dü-shü da-wa (nyi)
chay-pa yin

ང་འགྲུལ་བཞུད་ཟླ་བ་(གཉིས)བྱས་པ་ཡིན།

Where have you been?

kay-râng ka-bah ka-bah chin-ba

ཁྱེད་རང་ག་བར་ག་བར་ཕྱིན་པ།

I've been to ...

nga ...-la chin yin

ང་ ...ལ་ཕྱིན་ཡིན།

What did you think of ...?

kay-râng-gi thong-tsü-la
... kân-day du

ཁྱེད་རང་གི་མཐོང་ཚུལ་ལ།
... གང་འདྲས་འདུག

I thought it was ...

	ngay sâm-pâh te ...-chi ray-sha	ངའི་བསམ་པར་ དེ ...ཅིག་རེད་ཤ།
boring	nyob-to	ཉོབ་ཏོ
great	pay yâg-po	དཔེ་ཡག་པོ
horrible	pay doog-châg	དཔེ་སྡུག་ཆགས
OK	dig-tsâm	འགྲིག་ཙམ
too expensive	doh-song chen-po	འགྲོ་སོང་ཆེན་པོ

There are too many tourists there.

pha-gay yu-kor toh-châm-pa
pay mâng-po du

ཕ་གིར་ཡུལ་སྐོར་སྤྲོ་འཆམ་པ་
དཔེ་མང་པོ་འདུག

Not many people speak (English).

(in-ji-kay) shin-khen
shay-ta min-du

(དབྱིན་ཇི་སྐད་) ཤེས་མཁན་ཞེ་དྲག
མིན་འདུག

I was ripped off in ...

ngah ...-la shen-ta-gi
go doong-choong

ང་ ...ལ་གཞན་དག་གི་མགོ་དྲུང་བྱུང་།

People are really friendly there.

mi-tso pay ka-bo nye-po
chay-ki du

མི་ཚོ་དཔེ་དགའ་པོ་ཉེ་པོ་བྱེད་ཀྱི་འདུག

What's there to do in ...?

...-la ka-ray ka-ray
chay-ya yö-ray

...ལ་ག་རེ་ག་རེ་བྱེད་ཡག་ཡོད་རེད།

There's a really good restaurant/hotel there.

sa-khâng/dön-khâng ngön-nay ཟ་ཁང་/མགྲོན་ཁང་དེ་ལ་གནས་ལ་
yâg-po-chi du ཡོ་ཆིག་འདུག

I'll write down the details for you.

ka-bah yö-may ngay shu-gü ག་བར་ཡོད་མེད་ངས་ཤོག་བུའི་སྟང་
gâng-la say-po-chay di-ko ལ་གསལ་པོ་བྱེད་བྲིས་ཀོ

The best time to go is in (December).

do-ya-ki dü-tsö yâg-shö འགྲོ་ཡག་གི་དུས་ཚོད་ཡག་ཤོས
(chin-da chu-nyi)-la ray (ཕྱི་ཟླ་བཅུ་གཉིས་)ལ་རེད་ཨག

Is it expensive?

doh-song chen-po re-bay འགྲོ་སོང་ཆེན་པོ་རེད་པས

Did you go alone?

kay-râng chig-bo chin-bay ཁྱེད་རང་གཅིག་པུ་ཕྱིན་པས

Is it safe for women travellers on their own?

kye-man chig-bo doh-na སྐྱེ་དམན་གཅིག་པོ་འགྲོ་ན་ཉེན་
nyen-ga yö ma-re-bay ཁ་ཡོད་མ་རེད་པས

Is it safe to hitchhike?

te-po ten-nay mo-tah dü-shü མཐེ་པོ་བསྟན་ནས་མོ་ཊར་འཁྱongwલ་བརྟེན་
chay-na nyen-ga yö ma-re-bay བྱེད་ན་ཉེན་ཁ་ཡོད་མ་རེད་པས

going out

ཕྱི་ལོགས་སུ་སྐྱིད་གཏོང་དུ་འགྲོ་བ

where to go

ག་བར་འགྲོ་ག

What's there to do in the evenings?

göng-da nâng-wa kyi-kyi དགོང་དག་སྦང་བ་སྐྱི་སྐྱིད་ག་རེ་གཏོང་
kâ-ray tong-ya yö-ray ཡག་ཡོད་རེད

Is there a local entertainment guide in English?

sa-nay-la tay-mo gâng ta-gyu
yö-may kyâb-ta-teb in-ji-tog
yö re-bay

ས་གནས་ལ་ལྟད་མོ་གང་བརྒྱུ
ཡོད་མེད་ཁྱབ་སྐྲགས་ནེབ་དབྱིན་ཇི་བོད
ཡོད་རེད་པས།

Are there any discos?

dis-ko tâb-sa yö re-bay

ཌིས་ཀོ་འཐབ་ས་ཡོད་རེད་པས།

How much is it to get in?

zü-la kâ-tsay tay-go-ray

འཛུལ་བླ་ག་ཚོད་སྤྲད་དགོས་རེད།

Are there places where you can hear local music?

yü-mee rö-ja nyen-sa yö re-bay

ཡུལ་མིའི་རོལ་ཆ་ཉན་ས་ཡོད་རེད་པས།

Where can I find out what's on?

nâng-wa kyi-kyi tong-ya
kâ-ray kâ-ray yö-may ka-nay
ha-go thoob-ki ray

སྣང་བ་སྐྱིད་ཀྱིད་གཏོང་ཡག་ག་རེ་ག་རེ་
ཡོད་མེད་ག་ནས་ཧ་གོ་ཐུབ་ཀྱི་རེད།

What's on tonight?

ta-ring gong-ta kâ-ray yö-ray

ད་རིང་དགོངས་དག་ག་རེ་ཡོད་རེད།

I feel like going (for a) ...	nga ... dro-nying dö-ki du	ང་ ... འགྲོ་སྙིང་འདོད་ཀྱི་འདུག
stroll	châm-châm	འཆམ་འཆམ
dancing	shay tâb-gah	གར་བཤབ་པ
coffee/drink	ka-bi toong-gâh; chig toong-gâh	ཁོ་ཕི་འཐུང་ག/ གཅིག་འཐུང་ག

I feel like going to a/the ...	nga ... dro-nying dö-ki du	ང་ ... འགྲོ་སྙིང་འདོད་ཀྱི་འདུག
bar/pub	châng-khâng	ཆང་ཁང་
cafe	cha-khâng	ཇ་ཁང་
cinema	log-nyen ta-sa	གློག་བརྙན་བལྟ་ས
concert	rö-yâng tro-tön ta-sa	རོལ་དབྱངས་རྟོགས་སྟོན་བལྟ་ས
monastery	gom-pa	དགོན་པ
nightclub	tsen-tsog tro-kyi tong-sa	མཚན་ཚོགས་རྟོ་སྐྱིད་གཏོང་ས

opera	dö-ga ta-sa	རྒྱལ་གར་བལྟ་ས
restaurant	sa-khâng	ཟ་ཁང
temple	lha-khâng	ལྷ་ཁང
theatre	tâb-tön-khâng	འཁྲབ་སྟོན་ཁང

invitations ‌ མགྲོན་འབོད

What are you doing this evening/weekend?

kay-râng [ta-ri gong-ta; ray-sa
pen-pa dâng nyin-ma]-la
kâ-ray nâng-gi yö

ཁྱེད་རང་[ད་རེས་དགོང་དག/རེས་གཟའ
སྤེན་པ་དང་ཉི་མ]་ལ་ག་རེ་གནང་གི་ཡོད

Do you want to go to a karaoke bar?
ga-la-wa châng-khâng-la doh-gay ‌ གར་ལས་ཆང་ཁང་ལ་འགྲོ་གས

Do you have to pay to enter?
zü-la tay-go re-bay ‌ འཛུལ་ལ་སྤྲད་དགོས་རེད་པས

No, it's free.
ma-ray, la tay-go ma-ray ‌ མ་རེད་ ལྒ་སྤྲད་དགོས་མ་རེད

Which song do you want to sing?
shay ga-gi tâng-dö yö ‌ གཞས་ག་གི་གཏང་འདོད་ཡོད

Do you like this song?
shay di-la ga-bo yö-bay ‌ གཞས་འདི་ལ་དགའ་པོ་ཡོད་པས

Do you want to sing this with me?
ngay nyâm-tu shay-di tâng-gay ‌ ངའི་མཉམ་ཏུ་གཞས་འདི་གཏང་གས

Who's this singer?
shay tong-khen-di su ray ‌ གཞས་གཏོང་མཁན་འདི་སུ་རེད

interests

135

Would you like to go out somewhere?

kay-râng chi-log chig-la
don-dhö yö-bay

ཁྱེད་རང་ཕྱི་ལོག་ཅིག་ལ་
འགྲོ་འདོད་ཡོད་པས།

Do you know a good restaurant (that's cheap)?

sa-khâng yâg-po
(gong kay-po)-chig ka-bah
yö-may ha-go-ki yö-bay

ཟ་ཁང་ལ་ཡག་པོ་(གོང་ཁེ་པོ་)ཅིག་ག་པར་
ཡོད་མེད་ཧ་གོ་གི་ཡོད་པས།

Would you like to go for a drink/meal?

chig toong-gâh/sa-gâh doh-gay

གཅིག་འཐུང་ག/ཟ་ག་འགྲོ་གས།

My shout. (I'll buy)

jin-dâk nga yin

སྦྱིན་བདག་ང་ཡིན།

Do you want to come to the ... concert with me?

ngay nyâm-tu ... rö-yâng
tro-tön ta-gâh doh-gay

ངའི་མཉམ་དུ་ ... རོལ།
དབྱངས་སྟོན་བལྟ་བར་འགྲོ་གས།

We're having a party.

ngân-tso thuk-tro tâng-gi yö

ང྅་ཚོ་ཐུགས་སྤྲོ་གཏང་གི་ཡོད།

Come along.

pheb nâng

ཕེབས་གནང་།

responding to invitations

བཀའ་ལན་སློག་པ

Sure!

la-se, yin-dâng yin

ལགས་སེ། ཡིན་དང་ཡིན།

Yes, I'd love to.

la-se, nga dö-pa yö

ལགས་སེ། ང་འདོད་པ་ཡོད།

Yes. Where shall we go?

la-se. ngân-tso ka-bah doh-ga

ལགས་སེ། ང་ཚོ་ག་པར་འགྲོ།

No, I'm afraid I can't.

la, yong thoob-sa ma-ray,
gong-gay may-pa-chi

ལགས། ཡོང་ཐུབ་ས་མ་རེད།
དགོངས་དག་མ་ལ་མེད་པ་ཅི

What about tomorrow?

sa-nyin chay-na gâng-day du · སང་ཉིན་བྱེད་ན་གང་འདྲ་འདུག

arranging to meet · དུས་བཀག་ནས་རྒྱགས།

What time shall we meet?

ngân-tso chu-tsö kâ-tsay thoog-pa chay-kah · ང་ཚོ་ཆུ་ཚོད་ག་ཚོད་ཐུག་པ་བྱེད་ཀ

Where will we meet?

ka-bah thoog-pa chay-gay · ག་བར་ཐུག་པ་བྱེད་གས།

Let's meet at (eight) o'clock at the ...

ngân-tso chu-tsö (gye-pa)-la ...-la thoog-pa chay-na · ང་ཚོ་ཆུ་ཚོད་(བརྒྱད་པ་)ལ ...ལ་ཐུག་པ་བྱེད་ན།

OK. I'll see you then.

la-ray. o-na je-yong · ལགས་རེད། འོ་ན་མཇལ་ཡོང་།

Agreed/OK!

mö-thün yö; di-gi ray · མོས་མཐུན་ཡོད་/འདི་གི་རེད།

I'll come over at (six) o'clock.

nga chu-tsö (doog-pa)-la yong-gi yin · ང་ཆུ་ཚོད་(དྲུག་པ་)ལ་ཡོང་གི་ཡིན།

I'll pick you up at (nine) o'clock.

ngay kay-râng chu-tsö (gu-pa) len-gâh yong-gi yin · ངས་ཁྱེད་རང་ཆུ་ཚོད་(དགུ་པ་)ལེན་གར་ཡོང་གི་ཡིན།

I'll try to make it (on time).

nga (dü-tsö tâg-tâg-la) leb thoob-pa chay-ki yin · ང་(དུས་ཚོད་ཏག་ཏག་ལ) སླེབས་ཐུབ་པ་བྱེད་ཀྱི་ཡིན།

If I'm not there by (nine), don't wait for me.

gay-si nga chu-tsö (gu-pa) གལ་སྲིད་ང་ཆུ་ཚོད་(དགུ་པ)གོང་
gong-la ma-joh-na ngah ལམ་འབྱོར་ན་རང་མ་བསྒུག་རོགས་གནང་།
ma-gu-ro nâng

I'll be along later. Where will you be?

nga je-la yong-gee yin. kay-râng ང་རྗེས་ལ་ཡོང་གི་ཡིན། ཁྱེད་རང་
ka-bah thoog thoob-ki ray ཁྱེད་རང་ག་བར་ཐུག་ཐུབ་ཀྱི་རེད།

See you later/tomorrow.

je-ma/sa-nyin jay-yong རྗེས་མ/སང་ཉིན་མཇལ་ཡོང་།

Sorry I'm late.

gong-da nga je-lü teb-song དགོངས་དག ང་རྗེས་ལུས་སེབས་སོང་།

Never mind.

kay chay-kiy ma-ray གལ་ཆེད་ཀྱི་མ་རེད།

རྒྱུད་རིང་སྐད་འགྲོས།

It's well worth travelling to the more remote areas of Tibet and exploring the country's natural diversity. The further away from the main towns you travel, however, the more you'll have to rely on Tibetan, as few people will understand English.

getting information

གནས་ཚུལ་ཤེས་པབས་བྱེད་པ།

Given the challenges of trekking in Tibet, many travellers wisely opt to hire a pack animal (usually a yak or a donkey) to carry their kit. It's best to swot up on your Tibetan before you enter into negotiations (see Bargaining, page 88), as there's generally haggling involved. It's worth it though – you'll have an easier trek and your yak driver will also serve as a guide, so you won't have to worry about getting lost.

Where can I find out about
hiking trails in the region?

sa-kü-day kâng-tâng-tog	ས་ཁུལ་འདིར་རྐང་པང་ཐོག
gyâng-ring châm-châm doh-ya	རྒྱང་རིང་ཆམ་ཆམ་འགྲོ་ཡག
lâm-gay-koh kay-cha di-sa	ལམ་གྱི་སྐོར་སྐད་ཆ་འདྲིས
ka-bah yö-ray	གབར་ཡོད་རེད།

I want to rent a ...	nga ...-chig la-gö-yö	ང་ ...གཅིག་ལ་དགོས་ཡོད།
donkey	boong-gu	བོང་གུ
horse	ta	རྟ
yak	yâk	གཡག

How much does it	... ray-ray-la la-ja	... རེ་རེ་ལ་གླ་ཆ
cost for each ...?	kâ-tsay ray	ག་ཚོད་རེད།
day	nyi-ma	ཉིནམ
week	dün-tâ	བདུན་ཕྲག

I need a ...	nga ...-chig gö	ང་ ...གཅིག་དགོས།
guide	lâm-gyü chay-khen	ལམ་རྒྱུད་བྱེད་མཁན།
pack animal	kay-ma	ཁལ་མ།
porter	do-bo kay-ngen	དོ་པོ་འཁྱེར་མཁན།

Is it safe to climb this mountain?

ri-di gâng-la zâg-na nyen-ga
yö ma-re-bay

རི་འདིའི་སྒང་ལ་འཛེག་ན་ཉེན་ཁ་ཡོད་མ་རེད་པས།

Is there a hut up there?

ya-gay khâng-pa yö re-bay

ཡ་གིར་ཁང་པ་ཡོད་རེད་པས།

Do I need a guide?

lâm-gyü chay-khen gö-ki
re-bay

ལམ་རྒྱུད་བྱེད་མཁན་དགོས་ཀྱི་རེད་པས།

Are there guided treks?

kâng-dü gyâb-nay doh-sa
de-po yö re-bay

རྐང་འགྲུལ་བརྒྱབ་ནས་འགྲོ་ས་
འདི་པོ་ཡོད་རེད་པས།

I'd like to talk to someone who knows this area.

sa-kü-te gyü-yö-khen mi-shig-la
kân-ti shu-dhö-yö

ས་ཁུལ་འདི་རྒྱུས་ཡོད་མཁན་མི་ཞིག་ལ་
བཀའ་འདི་ཞུ་འདོད་ཡོད།

How long is the trail?

kâng-lâm-te tâg ring-lö yö-ray

རྐང་ལམ་དེ་ཐག་རིང་ལོས་ཡོད་རེད།

Is the track (well-)marked?

lâm-ga-te kha-chog ka-ba
do-man tâg (say-bo) gyâb
yö re-bay

ལམ་ཀ་དེ་ཁ་ཕྱོགས་ག་བར་འགྲོ་མན་ཐགས་
(གསལ་པོ་)བརྒྱབ་ཡོད་རེད་པས།

How high is the climb?

yâh toh-lö za-ya yö-ray

ཡར་མཐོ་ལོས་འཛེག་ཡག་ཡོད་རེད།

Which is the shortest route?

lâm-chog tâg nye-shö ka-gi-ray

ལམ་ཕྱོགས་ཐག་ཉེ་ཤོས་ག་གི་རེད།

Which is the easiest route?

lâm-chog lay la-shö ka-gi-ray

ལམ་ཕྱོགས་ལས་ལ་ཤོས་ག་གི་རེད།

Is the path open?

lâm-ga go chay-yö re-bay

ལམ་ཀ་སྒོ་ཕྱེ་ཡོད་རེད་པས།

When does it get dark?

na-koong ka-dü cha-gi yö-ray ནག་ཁུང་ག་དུས་ཆགས་ཀྱི་ཡོད་རེད།

Is it very scenic?

yü-jong nying-je-po du-gay ཡུལ་ལྗོངས་སྙིང་རྗེ་པོ་འདུག་གས།

Where can I hire mountain gear?

ri za-gyü kho-chay ya-sa
ka-bah yö-ray རི་ར་འརོག་ལ་ཀུའི་མགོ་ཆས་གཡར་ས་
ག་བར་ཡོད་རེད།

Where can we buy supplies?

sa-chay nyo-sa ka-bah yö-ray བཟའ་ཆས་ཉོ་ས་གཡར་ཡོད་རེད།

Do you have any food suitable for trekking?

ri-loong-la kyâm-kyâm dro-tü
kye-ya ka-la yö-bay རི་ལུང་ལ་འབྱམས་འབྱམས་འགྲོ་དུས་འཁྱེར་
ཡག་ག་ལ་ཡོད་པས།

Do you have any dried fruit?

shing-toh kâm-bo yö-bay ཤིང་ཏོག་སྐམ་པོ་ཡོད་པས།

Once you get off the main roads in Tibet, there's very little in the way of accommodation and food. However, you may be able to buy grain and other items of food from villagers and they may even allow you to stay in their homes on some trekking routes.

What is the name of that ...?	... pha-gi ming-la kâ-ray ray	... ཕ་གིའི་མིང་ལ་ག་རེ་རེད།
bridge	sâm-pâ	ཟམ་པ
lake	tsho	མཚོ
river	tsâng-po	གཙང་པོ
village	loong-pa/dong-seb	ལུང་པ/གྲོང་གསེབ

Is this the trail/ road to ...?	di ... do-ya-gi lâm-ga re-bay	འདི ... འགྲོ་ཡག་གི་ལམ་ག་ རེད་པས།
Drigung	di-goong	འབྲི་གུང
Mt Kailash	gâng rim-po-che	གངས་རིན་པོ་ཆེ
Samye	sâm-ye	བསམ་ཡས
Tsetang	tse-tang	རྩེད་ཐང

Which way to ...?

... doh-ya-gi lâm-ga ka-gi-ray   ... འགྲོ་ཡག་གི་ལམ་ག་ག་གི་རེད།

Where have you come from?

kay-râng ka-nay yong-ba   ཁྱེད་རང་ག་ནས་ཡོང་པ།

How long did it take you?

gyün ring-lö goh-song   རྒྱུན་རིང་ལོས་འགོར་སོང་།

Where can we spend the night?

ngân-tso gong-da ka-bah day-go-ray   ང་ཚོ་དགོང་དག་ག་བར་བསྡད་དགོས་རེད།

Can I leave some things here for a while?

ngay cha-lâg ga-shay nay-kâb day shâg-na di-gi re-bay   ངའི་ཅ་ལག་འགའ་ཤས་གནས་སྐབས་ འདིར་བཞག་ན་འགྲིག་གི་རེད་པས།

Can we go through here?

dee bah-la do-na di-gi re-bay   འདིའི་བར་ལ་འགྲོ་ན་འགྲིག་གི་རེད་པས།

Is the water OK to drink?

chu-di toong lo-gi re-bay   ཆུ་འདི་འཐུང་ལོ་གི་རེད་པས།

What is the next village on the trail?

lâm-ga te-nay chin-na dâng-po   ལམ་ག་དེ་ནས་ཕྱིན་ན་དང་པོ་ལུང་པ་
loong-pa ka-ray leb-ki-ray   རེ་སླེབས་ཀྱི་རེད།

Will we reach (Samye) before dark?

sa ma-roop gong-la (sâm-ye)   ས་མ་རུབ་གོང་ལ་(བསམ་ཡས)སླེབས་ཀྱི་
leb-gi re-bay   རེད་པས།

I have to rest.

nga ngay-so gyâb gö-ki-du   ང་ངལ་གསོ་བརྒྱབ་དགོས་ཀྱི་འདུག

I need to go to the toilet. (urinate/defecate)

nga chim-ba/tsok-pa tâng-ga   ང་གཅིན་པ་/བཅོག་པ་བཏང་ག་
doh gö-ki-du   འགྲོ་དགོས་ཀྱི་འདུག

Are there any other areas to stay apart from here?

di mem-bay loong-pa shen-da   འདི་མིན་པའི་ལུང་པ་གཞན་དག་
dö-sa du-gay   ལ་སྡོད་ས་འདུག་གས།

Can we get accommodation at ...?

...-lâ nay-tsâng râ-gi re-bay   ...ལ་གནས་ཚང་རག་གི་རེད་པས།

How many ...	(sâm-ye) bah-tu ...	(བསམ་ཡས)བར་དུ་ ...
to (Samye)?	kâ-tsay go-gi-ray	ག་ཚོད་དགོས་ཀྱི་རེད།
hours	chu-tsö	ཆུ་ཚོད་
days	nyin-ma	ཉིན་མ་
kilometres	ki-lo-mi-tar	ཀི་ལོ་མི་ཏར་

Is the trail ...?	lâm-ga ... du-gay	ལམ་ག་ ... འདུག་གས།
bad	dhuk-cha	སྡུག་ཆགས་
good	yâg-po	ཡིག་པོ་
narrow	tog-po	དོགས་པོ་
safe	ten-po	བརྟན་པོ་
steep (uphill/ downhill)	(gyen/tu) sah-po	(གྱེན་/ཐུར་) ཟར་པོ་
wide	gya chem-po	རྒྱ་ཆེན་པོ་

trekking

143

Do we have to pay to sleep in your house?

kay-râng-gi khang-pah nay-la
tay-go re-bay
ཁྱེད་རང་གི་ཁང་པར་གནས་ལྭ་
སྟད་དགོས་རེད་པས།

Can we stay here tonight?

ngân-tso dho-gong day day-nâ
di-gi re-bay
ང་ཚོ་དགོང་འདིར་བསྡད་ན་འགྲིག་
གི་རེད་པས།

Please make a meal for us tonight.

dho-gong ngân-tsoh
kha-la-chi so nâng-dâ
དོ་དགོང་ང་ཚོ་ལ་ཁ་ལག་གཅིག་
བཟོ་གནང་དང་།

I'll pay you.

ngay kay-râng-la la-ja tay-go
ངས་ཁྱེད་རང་ལ་གླ་ཆ་སྤྲད་གོ།

Can we get food in that village/place?

loong-pa/sa-cha pha-gay
kha-la râ-gi re-bay
ལུང་པ/ས་ཆ་ཕ་གིར་
ཁ་ལག་རག་གི་རེད་པས།

Is there a restaurant?

sa-khâng du-gay
ཟ་ཁང་འདུག་གས།

Is there firewood and water here?

day chu-dâng may-shing du-gay
འདིར་ཆུ་དང་མེ་ཤིང་འདུག་གས།

Where is the leader?

go-tih ka-bah
འགོ་འཛིན་ག་བ།

Do you have any ... to sell?	... tsong-ya yö-bay	... བཙོང་ཡག་ ཡོད་པས།
meat	sha	ཤ
potatoes	sho-gok	ཞོག་ཁོག
rice	dray	འབྲས
roasted barley flour	tsâm-pa	ཙམ་པ
wholemeal flour	dro-shib	གྲོ་ཞིབ

Please lend me a ...	nga ...-chig ya-nâng-da	ང་ ...གཅིག་གཡར་གནང་དང་།
ladle	kyok	སྐྱོག
pot	nö-chay	སྣོད་ཆས

camping

Where's the nearest campsite?

gur gyâb-sa tâg nye-shö
ka-bah yö-ray

གུར་རྒྱབ་ས་ཐག་ཉེ་ཤོས་ག་བར་ཡོད་རེད།

Do you have any sites available?

gur gyâb-sa sa-cha
tong-pa yö-bay

གུར་རྒྱབ་ས་ས་ཆ་སྟོང་པ་ཡོད་པས།

How much is it	... ray-ray-la gong	... རེ་རེ་ལ་
per ...?	kâ-tsay ray	གོང་ག་ཚོད་རེད།
person	mi	མི་
tent	gur	གུར་
vehicle	mo-ta	མོ་ཊ།

I want to hire a tent.

nga gur-chig la-go-yö

ང་གུར་གཅིག་གླ་དགོས་ཡོད།

Where can I hire a tent?

gur la-sa ka-bah yö-ray

གུར་གླ་ས་ག་བར་ཡོད་རེད།

Is it waterproof?

chu thoob-ki re-bay

ཆུ་ཐུབ་ཀྱི་རེད་པས།

Are there shower facilities?

tor-chü soog-po tu-sa
yö re-bay

འཁྲུར་ཆུས་གཟུགས་པོ་འཁྲུས་ས་ཡོད་རེད་པས།

Am I allowed to camp here?

day gur gyâb-nay day
cho-gi re-bay

འདིར་གུར་བརྒྱབ་ནས་སྡོད་ཆོག་གི་
རེད་པས།

---

don't light up!

You shouldn't light campfires while on a trek – there's
scant firewood available in Tibet and what there is tends
to be in high demand by the locals.

weather

གནམ་གཤིས།

What's the weather like?

nâm-shi kân-day-du གནམ་གཤིས་གང་འདྲས་འདུག

The weather is	te-ring nâm-shi	དེ་རིང་གནམ་གཤིས་
... today.	... du	... འདུག
Will it be ...	sa-nyin nâm-shi ...	སང་ཉིན་གནམ་གཤིས་
tomorrow?	yö re-bay	... ཡོང་རེད་པས།
bad	dhuk-cha	སྡུག་ཆགས
cloudy	tin thib-	སྤྲིན་འཐིབས
cold	dâng-mo	གྲང་མོ
good	yâg-po	ལྱགཔོ
hot (very)	tsa-po (shay-ta)	ཚཔོ (ཞེ་དྲག)
warm	drö-po	དྲོད་པོ
windy	lhâg-pa tsa-po	ལྷགསཔ་ཚཔོ

It's humid (today).

(te-ring) sha-tsen chem-po du (དེ་རིང་)བཤའ་ཚོན་ཆེན་པོ་འདུག

It's raining (today).

(te-ring) chah-pa bâb-ki-ray (དེ་རིང་)འཆར་པ་བབ་ཀྱི་རེད།

It's snowing (today).

(te-ring) gâng bâb-ki-ray (དེ་རིང་)གངས་བབ་ཀྱི་རེད།

It's raining heavily.

chah-shoog chem-po bâb-ki-ray འཆར་ཤུགས་ཆེན་པོ་བབ་ཀྱི་རེད།

It's raining lightly.

chah-pa sib-sib bâb-ki-ray འཆར་པ་སིབ་སིབ་བབ་ཀྱི་རེད།

It's flooding.

chu-lo gya-ki-ray ཆུ་ལོག་རྒྱག་ཀྱི་རེད།

cloud	tin-pa	སྤྲིན་པ་
earth	sa	ས་
fog	moog-pa	སྨུག་པ་
frost	say/sil-wa/ba-mo	སད་/ཞིལ་བ་/བ་མོ་
ice	kyâg-pa	འཁྱགས་པ་
mud	dâm-pâg	འདམ་པག་
rain	chah-pa	ཆར་པ་
snow	gâng	གངས་
storm	loong-tsub dâng-wa	རླུང་འཚུབ་ལྡང་བ་
sun	nyi-ma	ཉི་མ་
thunderstorm	doo-kay gyâk-pa-dâng	འབྲུག་སྐད་རྒྱག་པ་དང་ཆར་
	cha-loong lâng-pa	རླུང་ལྡང་བ་

seasons

དུས་ཚིགས་

spring	chi-ka	དཔྱིད་ཀ་
summer	yar-ga	དབྱར་ག་
autumn	tön-ga	སྟོན་ག་
winter	gün-ga	དགུན་ག་
dry season	chah-chu may-pay dü-tsig	ཆར་ཆུ་མེད་པའི་དུས་ཚིགས་
monsoon season	chah-shö dü-tsig	ཆར་ཤོད་དུས་ཚིགས་
rainy season	chah-du	འཆར་དུས་

trekking

geographical terms

ས་ཁམས་དང་འབྲེལ་བའི་མིང་ཚིག

agriculture	shing-lay	ཞིང་ལས་
beach	tsho-khay chay-tâng	མཚོ་ཁའི་བྱེ་ཐང་
border	sa-tsâm	ས་མཚམས་
bridge	sâm-pa	ཟམ་པ་
cave	dâg-phuk	བྲག་ཕུག་
city	dong-kay	གྲོང་ཁྱེར་
desert	chay-tâng	བྱེ་ཐང་
earthquake	sa-yom	ས་འཡོམ་
farm	shing-ga	ཞིང་ག་
footpath	kâng-lâm	རྐང་ལམ་
forest	shing-nâg	ཤིང་ནགས་
gap; narrow pass	gâg dok-po	གགས་དོག་པོ་
grassy plains	tsa-kha sâng-pö-tâng	རྩ་ཁ་བཟང་པོའི་ཐང་
high plateau	sa thö tâng-shong	ས་མཐོའི་ཐང་གཤོངས་
hill	ri	རི་
hot spring	chu-tsen	ཆུ་ཚན་
island	tso-ling	མཚོ་གླིང་
jungle	shing-nâg	ཤིང་ནགས་
lake	tsho	མཚོ་
landslide	sa-rü	ས་རུད་
mountain	ri	རི་
mountain range	ri-gyü	རི་རྒྱུད་
national park	mi-mâng ling-ga	མི་དམངས་གླིང་ག་
ocean	gyâm-tsho	རྒྱ་མཚོ་
pass	la	ལ་
peak	tse-mo	རྩེ་མོ་
river	tsâng-po	གཙང་པོ་
scenery	yu-jong	ཡུལ་ལྗོངས་
sea	tsho	མཚོ་
valley	loong-shong	ལུང་གཤོངས་
village	dong-seb	གྲོང་གསེབ་
waterfall	bâb-chu	བབ་ཆུ་

fauna

What animal is that?

sem-chen pha-gi kâ-ray ray སེམས་ཅན་ཕ་གི་ག་རེ་རེད།

What's that animal called?

sem-chen pha-gee ming-la
kâ-ray-sa
སེམས་ཅན་ཕ་གིའི་མིང་ལ་ག་རེ་ཟ།

domestic creatures

ཁྱིམ་གསོས་སྲོག་ཚལ་

buffalo	ma-ye	མ་ཡེ་
calf	bay-hu	བེའུ་
cat	shi-mi	ཞི་མི་
chicken	cha-te	བྱ་ཏེ་
cow	ba-choog	བ་ཕྱུགས་
dog	kyi	ཁྱི་
domestic animal	go-choog	གོ་ཕྱུགས་
donkey	boong-gu	བོང་བུ་
duck	ngân-ba	ངང་པ་
goat	ra	ར་
hen	cha-mo	བྱ་མོ་
horse	ta	རྟ་
ox	lân-gok	གླང་གོག་
pig	phâg-pa	ཕག་པ་
rooster	cha-pho	བྱ་ཕོ་
sheep	loog	ལུག་

wildlife

 རི་སྐྱེས་སྲོག་ཆགས།

ant	tog-ma	གྲོག་མ།
antelope	tsö	གཙོད།
bee	dâng-bu	སྦྲང་བུ།
bird	cha/chi-hu	བྱ/བྱིའུ།
butterfly	chem chem ma; che-ma-leb	ཨེམ་ཆེམ་མ/ཕྱེ་མ་ལེབ།
camel	nga-mong	རྔ་མོང་།
cockroach	shom-bu	ཤོམ་བུ།
crocodile	chu-sin	ཆུ་སྲིན།
fish	nya	ཉ།
fly	drâng-bu	སྦྲང་བུ།
frog	bag-pa	སྦལ་པ།
leech	pay-pa; bu bay-bay	པད་པ/འབུ་སྦྲུས་སྦྲས།
lion	sen-gay	སེང་གེ།
lynx	yi	གཡི།
marmot	chi-wa	འཕྱི་བ།
monkey	pi-oo	སྤྲེའུ།
mosquito	duk-drâng	དུག་སྦྲང་།
mouse	tsi-tsi	ཙི་ཙི།
snail	moog-pay bu-mo	སྨུག་པའི་བུ་མོ།
snake	drül	སྦྲུལ།
spider	dhom-tâg	སྡོམ་ཐག
squirrel	say-mong	ས་མོང་།
toad	bag-pa chem-po-shig	སྦལ་པ་ཆེན་པོ་ཞིག
turtle	rü-bay	རུས་སྦལ།
wild animal	ri-dâg; nâg-nay sog-châg	རི་དྭགས/ནགས་གནས་སྲོག་ཆགས།
wild ass	kyâng	རྐྱང་།
yak (male)	yâk	གཡག
yak (female)	dri	འབྲི།
yak (wild)	drong	འབྲོང་།

flora & agriculture

ཀྱི་ཞིང་དང་ཞིང་ལས།

What tree/plant/flower is that?

shing-dong/tsi-shing/may-tog   ཞིང་སྟོང་/རྩི་ཞིང་/མེ་ཏོག་གཱ
pha-gi kâ-ray ray   ཕ་གི་རེ་རེད

What is it used for?

kâ-ray-la bay-chö yö-ray   ག་རེ་ལ་བེད་སྤྱོད་ཡོད་རེད

Can you eat the fruit?

shing-day-te sa lo-gi re-bay   ཞིང་འབྲས་དེ་ལོ་ལྒྱི་རེད་པས

cactus	lhu-shing	ལྷུ་ཞིང
eucalyptus	tsi-shing	རྩི་ཞིང
oak	bay-shing/bay-doh	བེ་ཞིང/བེ་དོ
palm	ta-lay-shing	ད་ལའི་ཞིང
coconut	bay-tay day-bu	བེདྲའི་འབྲས་བུ
date	kha-sur	ཁ་ཟུར
pine	tâng-shing	ཐང་ཞིང
scrub	shing-ten	ཞིང་ཐན
stick	gyuk-pa	རྒྱུག་པ
tree	shing-dong	ཞིང་སྟོང

herbs, flowers & crops

སྨན་རྩི་དང་མེ་ཏོག་ལོ་ཏོག

bougainvillea	til-shing ngo-doom-shig	འཐིལ་ཞིང་སྔོ་སྡུམ་ཞིག
corn	ah-shom; ma-mö lo-tog	ཨ་ཤོམ/མ་རྨོ་ལོ་ཏོག
crops	tön-tog	སྟོན་ཏོག
flower	may-tog	མེ་ཏོག
grapevine	gün-doom dong-po	རྒུན་འབྲུམ་སྟོང་པོ
harvest	tön-tog du-way-dü	སྟོན་ཏོག་བསྡུ་བའི་དུས
irrigation	shing-chu den-pa	ཞིང་ཆུ་འདེབས་པ
jasmine	may-tog kun-ta	མེ་ཏོག་ཀུན་ཏ
lavender	shing-pö	ཞིང་སྤོས
leaf	lo-ma	ལོ་མ
lemon tree	lim-bu dong-po	ལིམ་བུ་སྟོང་པོ
orchard	shing-dong doom-ra	ཞིང་སྟོང་སྡུམ་ར
orange tree	tsa-lu-may dong-po	ཚ་ལུམ་མེ་སྟོང་པོ

planting/sowing	tsi-shing zook-pa;	ཚི་ཤིང་འཛུགས་པ/
	sa-bön deb-pa	ས་བོན་འདེབས་པ
rice field/paddy	day-shing;	འབྲས་ཞིང/
	ma-ngay-pay day-shing	མ་འཛངས་པའི་འབྲས་ཞིང
rose	gya-say may-tog	རྒྱ་སེ་མེ་ཏོག
rosemary	gyun-jâng dong-toong	རྒྱུན་ལྗང་དོང་ཐུང
sunflower	nyi-ma may-tog	ཉི་མ་མེ་ཏོག
sugar cane	bur-shing	བུར་ཞིང
terraced land	kay-shing	སྐས་ཞིང
thyme	di-shim ngo-men-shig	དྲི་ཞིམ་སྔོ་སྨན་ཞིག
tobacco	doh-thâg	དོ་བ
vineyard	gün-doom shing-ra	རྒྱུན་འབྲུམ་ཞིང་ར

Sustainability ia an important part of the travel vernacular. In practical terms, this means assessing our impact on the environment and local cultures and economies – and acting to make that impact as positive as possible. Here are some basic phrases to get you on your way …

communication & cultural differences

I'd like to learn some of your local dialects.
nga yü-miy-kay jâng-dö-yö   ང་ཁྱུལ་མིའི་སྐད་སྦྱང་འདོད་ཡོད།

Would you like me to teach you some English?
ngay kay-râng-la in-ji-kay   ངས་ཁྱེད་རང་ལ་དབྱིན་ཇི་སྐད་
lâb gö-bay   བསླབ་དགོས་པས།

Is this a local or national custom?
di yü-miy loog-söl yin-na   འདི་ཁྱུལ་མིའི་ལུགས་སྲོལ་ཡིན་ནམ།
gya-kâb chi-yong-gi   རྒྱལ་ཁབ་སྤྱི་ཡོངས་ཀྱི་
loog-söl yin-na   ལུགས་སྲོལ་ཡིན་ནམ།

I respect your customs.
ngay kay-râng-gi   ངས་ཁྱེད་རང་གི
loog-söl-la tsi-kü shu-gi-yö   ལུགས་སྲོལ་ལ་རྩི་བཀུར་ཞུ་གི་ཡོད།

community benefit & involvement

What sorts of issues is this community facing?
chi-tsog-nâng yong-da   སྤྱི་ཚོགས་ནང་ཡོང་བཞིན་པའི་
do-nâng je-gö-pay   དོ་སྣང་བྱེད་དགོས་པའི་
nay-dön ka-ray yö-ray   གནས་དོན་ག་རེ་ཡོད་རེད།

commercial	tsong-lay-che sem-chen	ཚོང་ལས་ཆེ་སེམས་ཅན
hunting and poaching	kyi-ra gyâk-pa-dâng kog-sö je-pa	ཁྱི་ར་རྒྱག་པ་དང་ ཀོག་སོ་གས་བྱེད་པ
freedom of speech	ma-jö râng-wâng	སྨྲ་བརྗོད་རང་དབང་
health issues	töh-ten-tog	འཕྲོད་བསྟེན་ཐོག

indigenous language and culture	dö-may mi-rig-gi kay-yig-dâng rig-shoong	གདོད་མའི་མི་རིགས་ཀྱི་ སྐད་ཡིག་དང་རིག་གཞུང་
indigenous population	dö-may mi-rig-gi dâng-boh	གདོད་མའི་མི་རིགས་ཀྱི་ གྲངས་འབོར་
mining	râng-choong tay-ka dön-pa	རང་བྱུང་ གཏེར་ཁ་དོན་པ་
ownership and freedom of the media	sa-gö lay-khoong-ki wâng-ja-dâng râng-wâng	གསར་འགོད་ལས་ཁུངས་ཀྱི་ དབང་ཆ་དང་ རང་དབང་
protecting the environment	kor-yoog soong-kyob	འཁོར་ཡུག སྲུང་སྐྱོབ་
religious expression	chö-de râng-mö	ཆོས་ལུགས་རང་མོས་
threat to nomadic lifestyle	dok-pay tso-wa chö-dâng-la nyen-ka	འབྲོག་པའི་འཚོ་བ་ ཆོས་ལུགས་ལ་ཉེན་ཁ་
unemployment	lay-ka ma-tob-pay ka-ngal	ལས་ཀ་མ་ཐོབ་པའི་ དཀའ་ངལ་

I'd like to volunteer my skills.

nga dâng-lâng lay-ka jen-dö-yö ང་རང་གླས་ལས་ཀ་བྱེད་འདོད་ཡོད།

Are there any volunteer programs available in the area?

sa-kül-day dâng-lâng lay-ka ས་ཁུལ་འདིར་དང་གླང་ལས་ཀ་
ka-ray chay-ya yö-ray ག་རེ་བྱེད་ཡལ་ཡོད་རེད།

environment

Does your company have a green policy?

kay-râng-tsö lay-koong-la ཁྱེད་རང་ཚོའི་ལས་ཁུངས་ལ་
kor-yuk soong-kyob-che འཁོར་ལུག་སྲུང་སྐྱོབ་ཆེད་
si-jü yö re-bay སྲིད་ཇུས་ཡོད་རེད་པས།

Where can I recycle this?

di yâng-kyâh bay-chö འདི་ཡང་བསྐྱར་བེད་སྤྱོད་
tong-chay gay-nyig གཏོང་ཆེད་གང་ཉིག་
loog-nö ga-bah yö-ray བླུགས་སྣོད་ག་བར་ཡོད་རེད།

transport

Can we get there by public transport?

nga-tso pha-gay doh-ya-la chi-chö
tu-khoh tob-ki re-bay

ང་ཚོ་ཕ་གིར་འགྲོ་ཡ་ལ་སྤྱི་སྤྱོད་
འཁྲུལ་འཁོར་ཐོབ་ཀྱི་རེད་པས།

Can we get there by bicycle?

nga-tso kâng ga-ree-tog
pha-gay doh tob-kyi re-bay

ང་ཚོ་རྐང་སྒྲ་རི་འཁོར་
ཕ་གིར་འགྲོ་ཐུབ་ཀྱི་རེད་པས།

I'd prefer to walk there.

nga pha-gay gom-pa
gyâb-nay dohn-dö-yö

ང་ཕ་གིར་གོམ་པ་
བརྒྱབ་ནས་འགྲོ་འདོད་ཡོད།

accommodation

I'd like to stay at a locally-run hotel.

nga sa-nay yü-miy
dön-khâng-nâng den-dö yö

ང་ས་གནས་ཡུལ་མིའི་
འགྲོན་ཁང་ནང་བསྡད་འདོད་ཡོད།

Can I turn the air conditioning off and open the window?

dâng-log-say ge-koong
che-na dig-gi re-bay

གྲང་ལོག་བསལ་ སྒེ་ཁུང་
ཕྱེ་ན་འགྲིག་གི་རེད་པས།

There's no need to change my sheets.

ngay nye-che-re jay
gö-ya may

ངའི་ཉལ་ཆས་རེ་བརྗེ་
དགོས་ཡལ་མེད།

shopping

Where can I buy locally produced goods?

sa-nay râng-nay tön-pay
cha-lâg nyo-sa ga-bah yö-ray

ས་གནས་རང་ནས་བཟོས་པའི་
ཅ་ལག་ཉོ་ས་ག་བར་ཡོད་རེད།

Where can I buy locally produced souvenirs?

sa-nay râng-nay tön-pay
den-ten cha-lâg
nyo-sa ga-bah yö-ray

ས་གནས་རང་ནས་བཟོས་པའི་
དྲན་རྟེན་ཅ་ལག་
ཉོ་ས་ག་བར་ཡོད་རེད།

Is this made from ...?	diy gyub-ja ... re-bay	འདིའི་རྒྱུ་ཆ ... རེད་པས།
leopard bone	sig-ki rü-koh	གཟིག་གི་རུས་གོག
leopard skin	sig-pâg	གཟིག་ལྤགས

onyx	si	གཟི
tiger bone	tâg-gi rü-koh	སྟག་གི་དུས་གོག
tiger skin	tâg-pâg	སྟག་པགས
turquoise	yu	གཡུ

food

Do you sell …?	… tsong-ya yö-bay	… ཚོང་ཡག་ཡོད་པས
locally produced	sa-nay râng-nay	ས་གནས་རང་ནས
food	tön-pay sâb-chay	འཚོ་བའི་བཟའ་བཏང
organic produce	ze-joh may-pay	རྫས་སྦྱོར་མེད་པའི
	sâb-chay	བཟའ་བཏང

Can you tell me what traditional foods I should try?

loong-pay tön-mong ལུང་པའི་ཕུན་ཚོགས

ma-yim-pay kha-lah མ་ཡིན་པའི་ཁ་ལག

ga-ray sa na yâg-gi-ray ག་རེ་བཟའ་ན་ཡག་གི་རེད

sightseeing

Does your	kay-râng-tsö	ཁྱེད་རང་ཚོའི
company …?	lay-koong … yö re-bay	ལས་ཁུངས … ཡོད་རེད་པས
buy things	kho-che sa-nay	མགོ་ཚས་ས་གནས
from local	tsong-khâng-nay	ཚོང་ཁང་ནས
businesses	nyo-gi	ཉོ་གི
donate money	nyâm-tah-la nyül	ཉམས་ཐག་ལ་དངུལ
to charity	sha-teb bu-ki	ཞལ་འདེབས་འབུལ་གྱི
hire local guides	yü-miy	ཡུལ་མིའི
	nay-shen-pa la-wa	གནས་ཤེན་པ་ལ་བ

Does the guide	nay-shen-pay	གནས་ཤེན་པས
speak the …?	… shen-gi yö re-bay	… ཤེན་གྱི་ཡོད་རེད་པས
Amdo dialect	âmdo-kay	ཨ་མདོ་སྐད
Central dialect	wü-kay	དབུས་སྐད
Khâm dialect	khâm-kay	ཁམས་སྐད

Are cultural tours available?

rig-shoong shay-tog-chay རིག་གཞུང་ཤེས་རྟོགས་ཆེད

ta-koh doh-ya yö re-bay བལྟ་སྐོར་འགྲོ་ཡག་ཡོད་རེད་པས

FOOD

ཁ་ལག

In all of the main towns in Tibet, you'll find Tibetan, Muslim and Chinese restaurants. Tibetan cuisine centres around dumplings (mo-mo, ཅོག་ཅོག) and noodle soup (thuk-pa, ཐུག་པ་), and Chinese dishes often include either noodles (gyâ-thuk, རྒྱ་ཐུག) or stir-fried vegetable dishes (tsay, ཚལ). In Lhasa, some restaurants serve Western food.

meals

ཉིན་ཅི་པོ

Family members always eat together in Tibet. Usually they have a light breakfast and a big lunch and dinner. In addition, they drink a lot of butter tea (bö-ja; cha sü-ma, བོད་ཇ/ཅ་སྲུབས), which is more like a tea soup made of butter, milk and salty black tea.

breakfast	shog-cha; shog-kay kha-la	ཞོགཇ/ཞོག་སྐད་ཁ་ལག
lunch	nyin-goong kha-la	ཉིན་གུང་ཁ་ལག
dinner	gong-da kha-la	དགོང་དག་ཁ་ལག

breakfast

ཞོག་སྐད་ཁ་ལག

Most people have breakfast between 7 and 8 am. The typical breakfast for Tibetans is either pâg (སྤགས), a dough made of roasted barley flour (tsâm-pa, རྩམ་པ), or kyo-ma (སྐྱོ་མ), a porridge-type mixture made with tsâm-pa. Both are served with butter tea. Although eaten by Tibetans at home, these dishes are rarely offered at guesthouses or hotels.

157

bread	bâk-lay	བག་ལེབ
cereal	dru-say	འབྲུ་རས
... eggs	go-nga ...	སྒོང་ ...
hard-boiled	dhog-tsö	རྡོག་བཙོས
soft-boiled	chay-tsö	ཤུད་བཙོས
fried	ngö-pâ	བཟོས་པ
jam	jam; shing-day mar	ཇེམ/ཤིང་འབྲས་མར
omelette	gong-dre ngö-pâ; om-let	སྒོང་འབྲས་བཟོས་པ/ཨོམ་ལེད
rice porridge	day-thuk	འབྲས་ཐུག
toast	may-tâg bâk-lay	མེ་བཀགས་བག་ལེབ

chu-ra kâm-po   ཕྱུར་སྐམ་པོ   **dried cheese**
small cubes of hardened dried cheese are popular in Tibet.
They must be sucked at first, then chewed, and are often
used as a thirst-quencher.

de-sil   འབྲས་སིལ   **sweet rice pudding**
regarded as an auspicious food, it's usually served at festivals and ceremonies, but only in small quantities

khâb-say   ཁབ་ཟས   **deep-fried cookies**
always prepared for special occasions, such as weddings,
parties and New Year, as well as offered to guests

tsâm-pa   ཙམ་པ   **roasted barley flour**
a staple food in Tibet, but rarely served to guests or found
in restaurants. It's generally eaten as a snack or for breakfast – either on its own or with butter tea – but can also be
eaten as a main meal, served with vegetables and meat.

vegetarian & special meals

ཤ་མེད་དང་དམིགས་བསལ་ཁ་ལག

I'm vegetarian.
nga sha mi-sa-ken yin
ང་ཤ་མི་ཟ་མཁན་ཡིན།

I don't eat meat.
nga sha sa-gi may
ང་ཤ་ཟ་གྱི་མེད།

I don't eat chicken, fish or ham.
nga cha-sha-dâng, nya-sha, phâg-sha dü-ma sa-gi-may
ང་བྱ་ཤ་དང་ཉ་ཤ་ཕག་ཤ་འདུ་མ་ཟ་གྱི་མེད།

I can't eat dairy products.
ngah kar-chu-rig trö-ki may
ངར་དཀར་ཆུ་རིགས་འཕྲོད་ཀྱི་མེད།

Do you have any dishes without meat?
sha may-pay kha-la gay yö-bay
ཤ་མེད་པའི་ཁ་ལག་གང་ཡོད་པས།

Does this dish have meat?
kha-la di-la sha yö re-bay
ཁ་ལག་འདི་ལ་ཤ་ཡོད་རེད་པས།

Can I get this without meat?
di sha may-pa ra-gi re-bay
འདི་ཤ་མེད་པ་རག་གི་རེད་པས།

Does it contain eggs?
di-la go-nga yö re-bay
འདི་ལ་སྒོང་ང་ཡོད་རེད་པས།

I'm allergic to (peanuts).
ngah (ba-tâm) pho-gi-yö
ངར་(བྱུ་དྲམ་)ཕོག་གིས་ཀྱི་ཡོད།

eating out

ཟ་ཁང་ནང་ཁ་ལག་ཟ་བ

A table for ... please.
mi ...-la chog-tse-chig nang-ro
མི་...ལ་ཅོག་ཙེ་གཅིག་གནང་རོགས།

Can I see the menu please?
ngah kha-la-gi-tho tön nang-da
ངར་ཁ་ལག་གི་ཐོ་སྟོན་གནང་དང་།

159

Do you have a menu in English?

kha-la-gi-tho in-ji kay-tog yö-bay

ཁ་ལག་གི་ཐོ་དབྱིན་ཇི་སྐད་ཐོག་ཡོད་པས།

What's this/that?

diy/pha-gi kâ-ray ray

འདི/ཕ་གི་ག་རེ་རེད།

What do you recommend?

kay-râng chay-na kâ-ray yâ-gi-ray

ཁྱེད་རང་བྱེད་ན་ག་རེ་ཡག་གི་རེད།

I'll have what they're having.

khong-tsö chö-ya-te na-shin nga-la gö

ཁོང་ཚོས་མཆོད་ཡག་དེ་ན་བཞིན་ང་ལ་དགོས།

What's in that dish?

kha-la pha-gi-nâng kâ-ray yö-ray

ཁ་ལག་ཕ་གིའི་ནང་ག་རེ་ཡོད་རེད།

Please bring me ...

nga-la ...-chig tay-ro-nâng

ང་ལ་ ...ཅིག་སྟེར་རོགས་གནང་།

I'd like the set lunch, please.

nga-la nyin-goong sö-tön nâng-ro

ང་ལ་ཉིན་གུང་གསོལ་སྟོན་གནང་རོགས།

What does it include?

tay nyâm-tu kha-la kâ-ray kâ-ray sa-ya yö-ray

དེའི་མཉམ་ཏུ་ཁ་ལག་ག་རེ་ག་རེ་ཟ་ཡག་ཡོད་རེད།

Not too spicy, please.

men-na shay-ta ma-gyâ-ro-nâng

སྨན་སྣ་ཤེ་དྲགས་མ་རྒྱག་རོགས་གནང་།

Do I get it myself or do they bring it to us?

nga-râng râng-gi len-gah do-gö-ray, khong-tsö kye yong-gi-ray

ང་རང་རང་གིས་ལེན་གའི་འགྲོ་དགོས་རེད། ཁོང་ཚོས་འཁྱེར་ཡོང་གི་རེད།

Please bring a/an/the ... ...-chig nâng-da ...ཅིག་གནང་དང་།

bill	kha-la-gi zihn	ཁ་ལག་གི་འཛིན།
fork	kâng-ta	ཀང་ཏ།
glass of water	chu ga-la-si	ཆུ་གླ་ལསི།
with ice	kyâk-pa yö-pa	འཁྱགས་པ་ཡོད་པ།
without ice	kyâk-pa may-pa	འཁྱགས་པ་མེད་པ།
knife	di	གྲི།
plate	tha-pa	ཐབ།

Another ... please.

da-toong ... nang-da ད་དུང ... གནང་དང་།

Nothing more?

ta dig-song ད་འགྲིགས་སོང་།

Anything else?

shen-da-gay gö-bay གཞན་དག་གི་དགོས་པས།

No ice in my drink, please.

ngay toong-ya nyâm-tu ངའི་བཏུང་ཡག་དེ་མཉམ་དུ་འཁྱགས་པ་
kyâk-pa ma-loog-ro nâng མ་ལུགས་རོགས་གནང་།

Is service included in the bill?

ngü-tsi-nang lay-la tsi དངུལ་རྩིས་ནང་ལས་ལ་རྩ་ཆུ་ཡོད་
yö re-bay རེད་པས།

I love this dish.

nga kha-la di-la ka-bo yö ང་ཁ་ལག་འདི་ལ་དགའ་པོ་ཡོད།

We love the local cuisine.

ngân-tso sa-nay-ki ང་ཚོས་གནས་ཀྱི་ཁ་ལག་ལ་དགའ་པོ་ཡོད།
kha-la-la ka-bo yö

The meal was delicious!

kha-la shim-bu shay-ta choong ཁ་ལག་ཞིམ་པོ་ཞེ་དྲགས་བྱུང་།

typical dishes

bâk-thuk	བག་ཐུག
a variety of Tibetan soup (like ten-thuk but with hand made shell-shaped noodles)	
day-thuk	འབྲས་ཐུག
rice soup	
gya-thuk	རྒྱ་ཐུག
Tibetan noodle soup	
kö-den/châng-kö	སྐོལ་ལྡན/ཆང་འཁོལ
hot châng soup with tsâm-pa	
rhü cho-tse	རུས་ཅོ་ཙེ
meat dumplings in soup	
rü-tâng	རུ་ཐང
clear bone soup	
sog-thuk	སོག་ཐུག
Mongolian-style Tibetan soup	
ten-thuk	ཐེན་ཐུག
traditional Tibetan soup, with meat, vegetables and hand made noodles	
chí-may mo-mo	ཆི་སྨན་མོག་མོག
steamed yeast meat dumplings	
mo-mo	མོག་མོག
steamed meat dumplings	
mo-mo ngö-pa	མོག་མོག་བཙོས་པ
fried meat dumplings	
tsay mo-mo	ཚལ་མོག་མོག
vegetable dumplings	
cha-sha (ngö-pa/tâg-pa)	བྱ་ཤ (བཙོས་པ/བསྲེགས་པ)
chicken (fried/roasted)	
dâng-tsay	གྲང་ཚལ
salad	
day ngö-pa	འབྲས་བཙོས་པ
fried rice	

FOOD

162

do-fu dâng tsay དོ་ཕུ་དང་ཚལ
  sauteed bean curd with peppers/vegetables

phing-sha ཕིང་ཤ
  beef/chicken/pork with bean
  thread and red pepper (capsicum)

sham-day ཤ་འབྲས
  plain/fried rice with meat and
  bean thread/mokroe/vegetables

(cha-sha/phâg-sha/loog-sha/ (བྱ་ཤ/ཕག་ཤ/ལུག་ཤ/
yâk-sha/lâng-sha) tsay གཡག་ཤ/གླང་ཤ)དང་ཚལ
  (chicken/pork/lamb/yakmeat/
  beef) and stir-fried vegetables

tsib-sha རྩིབ་ཤ
  pork spare ribs

ahm-dho bâk-lay ཨམ་དོ་བག་ལེབ
  roasted pancake (bread)

bâk-cha ma-ku བག་ཚ་མར་ཁུ
  small tubes of wheat flour
  dough fried in ghee with molasses

lo-ko mo-mo ལོ་སྐོལ་མོག་མོག
  boiled bread

sha bâk-lay ཤ་བག་ལེབ
  fried pancake (bread) stuffed with meat

ting mo-mo སྟིང་མོག་མོག
  steamed bread

yu-shâng ཡུ་ཤང
  deep fried bread (puree)

sho dâng shing-toh ཞོ་དང་ཤིང་ཏོག
  fruit with yogurt

shing-toh dâng o-ti ཤིང་ཏོག་དང་འོ་སྲི
  fruit with cream

eating out

163

making your own meals

ཁ་ལག་རང་རང་གིས་བཟོ་བ

Where can I find the ...?	... nyo-sa ka-bah yö-ray	... ཉོས་ས་ག་བར་ཡོད་རེད།
I'd like some ...	nga ... gö	ང་ ... དགོས།
bread	bâk-lay	བག་ལེབ
butter	mâh	མར
cereal	dru-say	འབྲུ་རིགས
cheese	chu-ra	ཕྱུར་ར
chocolate	chok-let	ཅོག་ལེད
eggs	go-nga	སྒོང་ང
flour		
plain	may-da	མེ་ད
roasted barley	tsâm-pa	རྩམ་པ
wholemeal	dro-shib	གྲོ་ཞིབ

ghee	mâh-ku	མར་ཁུ
ham	phâg-sha dü-ma	ཕག་ཤ་བདུང་མ
honey	dâng-tsi	སྦྲང་རྩི
marmalade	tsa-lu-may jam	ཚ་ལུ་མའི་ཇེམ
milk	oh-ma	འོ་མ
molasses	bu-râm	བུ་རམ
noodles	gyâ-thuk	རྒྱ་ཐུག
olive oil	o-lib-noom	ཨོ་ལིབ་སྣུམ
pepper	ey-ma	གཡེར་མ
powdered milk	oh-tsâm	འོ་རྩམ
salt	tsha	ཚྭ
sugar	chay-ma ka-ra; chi-ni	བྱེ་མ་ཀ་ར/ཅི་ནི
vermicelli (bean thread noodles)	phing	ཕིང
yeast	chay-men	ཕབ་སྨན
yogurt	sho	ཞོ

at the market

འཕྲོ་ལ་སར་

How much is (a kilo of cheese)?

(chu-ra ki-lo-ray)-la gong
kâ-tsay ray

(ཕྱུར་གི་ལོ་རེ་)ལ་གོང་ག་ཚོད་རེད།

Do you have anything cheaper?

gong kay-wa gay yö-bay

གོང་ཆེ་བ་གང་ཡོད་པས།

What's the local speciality?

sa-nay-ki sa-chay mig-say
kâ-ray kâ-ray tsong-ya yö-ray

ས་གནས་ཀྱི་བཟའ་ཆས་དམིགས་བསལ་
ག་རེ་ག་རེ་འཚོང་ཡག་ཡོད་རེད།

Give me (half) a kilo please.

ngah ki-lo (chay-ka) nâng-da

ང་ར་གི་ལོ་(ཕྱེད་ག)གནང་དང་།

I'd like (six slices of ham).

ngah (phâg-sha dü-ma
lheb-lheb doog) nâng-da

ང་ར་(ཕག་ཤ་དུད་མ་ལྟེབ་ལྟེབ་དྲུག)
གནང་དང་།

Can I taste it?

toh-wa mik ta-na di-gi re-bay

ཏོག་ཤིག་བལྟ་ན་འགྲིག་གི་རེད་པས།

Do you have any ... to sell?

kay-râng-lâ ... tsong-ya yö-bay

ཁྱེད་རང་ལ་ ... འཚོང་ཡག་ཡོད་པས།

How much does the ... cost?

...-la gong kâ-tsay ray

...ལ་གོང་ག་ཚོད་རེད།

I'll buy ... kilos.

ngay ki-lo ... nyo-gi-yin

ངས་གི་ལོ་ ... ཉོ་གི་ཡིན།

---

taking a dip!

Impress the locals with your knowledge of this châng drinking ritual:

Raise your cup to eyelevel with your left hand. Dip in your right ring finger, then take it out and flick it. Repeat three times to show respect to heaven, earth and the gods.

meat & poultry

beef	lâng-sha	གྱང་ཤ
chicken	cha-sha	བྱ་ཤ
fish	nya-sha	ཉ་ཤ
goat meat	ra-sha	ར་ཤ
ham	phâg-sha dü-ma	ཕག་ཤ་དུས་མ
lamb	loog-sha	ལུག་ཤ
liver	chin-pa	མཆིན་པ
meat	sha	ཤ
boiled	sha tsö-bâ	ཤ་བཙོས་པ
dried	sha kâm-po	ཤ་སྐམ་པོ
roast	shâp-ta	ཤ་བརྒྱག
pork	phâg-sha	ཕག་ཤ
sausage	gyu-ma	རྒྱུ་མ
yak meat	yâk-sha	གཡག་ཤ

fruit & nuts

ཤིང་ཏོག

apple	ku-shu	ཀུ་ཤུ
apricot	ngâ-ri khâm-bu	མངའ་རིས་ཁམ་བུ
banana	kye-la	ཀེ་ལ
berry	say-hu	སེ་བུ
date	kha-su	ཁ་སུར
fruit	shing-tog	ཤིང་ཏོག
grape	chu gün-doom	རྒུན་འབྲུམ
lemon	lim-bu	ལིམ་བུ
mango	shing-tog-âhm	ཤིང་ཏོག་ཨམ
orange/tangerine	tsâ-lu-mâ	ཚ་ལུམ
peach	lo-soom khâm-bu	ལོ་གསུམ་ཁམ་བུ
peanut	ba-tâm	སྦ་དམ
pear	li	ལི
pomegranate	sin-dru	སེན་འབྲུ
rhubarb	chu-chu/chu-lo	རྩུ་རྩ/རྩུ་ལོ
walnut	tar-ka	སྟར་ཀ

vegetables

སྔོ་ཚལ།

bamboo shoots	nyug-tsa	སྙུག་ཚ།
beans	tray-ma	སྲན་མ།
cabbage (Chinese-style)	lo-koh pay-tsay	ལོ་ཁོག་པད་ཚལ།
capsicum (pepper)	ey-ma	གཡེར་མ།
carrot	gong lâ-bu	སྒོང་ལ་ཕུག
cauliflower	pool go-bi	ཕུལ་གོ་བིའི།
celery	jin-tsay	ཇིན་ཚལ།
cucumber	kâng-ra	གང་ར།
eggplant (aubergine)	chay-tsay	ཀེ་ཚལ།
onion	tsong	ཙོང་།
peas	tray-ma	སྲན་མ།
potato	sho-gok	ཞོག་ཁོག
radish	lâ-buk	ལ་ཕུག
pickled radish	sön lâ-buk	སོན་ལ་ཕུག
spinach	po-tsay	པོད་ཚལ།
spring onion	tsong ngön-po	ཙོང་སྔོན་པོ།
tomato	to-ma-to	ཏོ་མ་ཏོ།
turnip	nyoong-mâ	ཉུང་མ།

grains & pulses

འབྲུ་རིགས།

barley	nay/dru	ནས། / འབྲུ།
popped barley	nay-yö	ནས་ཡོས།
buckwheat (sweet)	gya-da	རྒྱ་བྲ།
corn	ah-shom;	ཨ་ཤོམ། /
	ma-mö lo-tog	མ་མོས་ལོ་ཏོག
millet	mön-châg	མོན་ཆག
plain flour	may-da	མེ་དྲ།
rice	day	འབྲས།
popped rice	day-yö	འབྲས་ཡོས།
wholemeal flour	dro-shib/ah-ta	གྲོ་ཞིབ། / ཨ་ཏ།

vegetables

167

spices & condiments

སྤྱིན་སྣ་རིགས།

chilli (ground)	si-pan (shib-shib)	ཤི་པན་(ཞིབ་ཞིབ་)
chilli (with water)	si-pan mah-du	ཤི་པན་དམར་བདུར་
coriander	so-nam pay-zom	བསོད་ནམས་པད་འཛོམ་
garlic	gok-pa	སྒོག་པ་
ginger	ga-moog	སྨེ་སྨུག་
pepper	ey-ma	གཡེར་མ་
salt	tsha	ཚ་
soy sauce	jâng-yü	བྱང་ཡུལ་
turmeric	ga-say	གསེ་
vinegar	tsuh	ཚུར་

drinks

བཏུང་བ

nonalcoholic

ཆང་རག་མིན་པའི་བཏུང་བ

coffee	cha ka-bi; tsig-cha	ཇ་གོ་ཕི་/ཚིག་ཇ་
black	cha ka-bi oh-ma may-pa	ཇ་གོ་ཕི་འོ་མ་མེད་པ་
juice	shin-tog khu-wa	ཤིང་ཏོག་ཁུ་བ་
orange	tsâ-lu-may khu-wa	ཚ་ལུ་མའི་ཁུ་བ་
milk	oh-ma	འོ་མ་
soda	chu nga-mo	ཆུ་མངར་མོ་
orange	tsâ-lu-may chu nga-mo	ཚ་ལུ་མའི་ཆུ་མངར་མོ་
tea	cha	ཇ་
black	cha-tâng	ཇ་ཐང་
butter	bö-ja; cha sü-ma	བོད་ཇ་/ཇ་སྲུབ་མ་
Chinese-style	chin-drâng	ཅིན་ཐང་
with sugar	cha nga-mo	ཇ་མངར་མོ་
water	chu	ཆུ་
boiled	chu khö-ma	ཆུ་འཁོལ་མ་
mineral	bu-tog-chu	བུལ་ཏོག་ཆུ་

alcoholic

ཆང་རིགས།

Home-brewed chång (ཆང་), made from fermented barley, wheat, rice and millet, is very popular in Tibet.

beer (home-brew)	chång	ཆང་
beer (bottled)	bee-yar	བི་ཡར/ཤེལ་ཆང་
Chinese brandy	gya-mee ah-råk	རྒྱ་མིའི་ཨ་རག
liquor	ah-råk	ཨ་རག
wine	gün-doom chång-råk	རྒུན་འབྲུམ་ཆང་རག

in the bar

ཆང་ཁང་ནང་།

Excuse me!
ku-chi **(inf)**; gong-ge may-pa-chi **(pol)**

སྐུ་མཁྱེན། /དགོངས་འགལ་མེད་པ་ཞུ།

I'm next.
ta ngay ray-mö ray

ད་ངའི་རེ་མོས་རེད།

I'll buy you a drink.
toong-ya-chig ngay nyo-go

འཐུང་ཡག་ཅིག་ངས་ཉོ་གི་ཡིན།

What would you like?
kay-rång kâ-ray gö

ཁྱེད་རང་ག་རེ་དགོས།

I'll have ...
nga ... gö

ང་ ... དགོས།

---

the lesser of two evils

chång toong-na go-na, ma-toong-na nying-na

ཆང་བཏུང་ན་མགོ་ན། མ་བཏུང་ན་སྙིང་ན།

If you drink chång, you'll get a headache; if you don't, you'll get heartache.

No ice please.

kyâk-pa ma-loog-ro nâng

བཁྱགས་པ་མ་ལུག་རོགས་གནང་།

You can get the next one.

je-ma-te ngâg cho-gi ray

རྗེས་མ་དེ་མངག་ཆོག་གི་རེད།

Same again, please.

yâng-kya te na-shin-chig nâng-da

ཡང་བསྐྱར་དེ་ན་བཞིན་གཅིག་གནང་དང་།

How much is that?

te-la gong kâ-tsay ray

དེ་ལ་གོང་ག་ཚད་རེད།

general

 སྤྱིར་བཏང་

Help!	rog nâng-da	རོགས་གནང་དང་།
Stop!	kha kâg-dâng	ཁ་བཀག་དང་།
Go away!	phâh gyook	ཕར་རྒྱུགས།
Thief!	ku-ma du	རྐུ་མ་འདུག
Fire!	may bâh-gee	མེ་འབར་གྱི།
Watch out!	sâb sâb nâng	གཟབ་གཟབ་གནང་།
Wait!	gu nâng-da	སྒུག་གནང་དང་།
Don't move!	gü-kyog ma-tâng	འགུལ་སྐྱོད་མ་གཏང་།

Does anyone speak English?

in-ji-kay shay-khen yö ray-bay དབྱིན་ཇི་སྐད་ཤེས་མཁན་ཡོད་རེད་པས།

It's an emergency.

za dâg-po ray ཉེན་དུགས་པོ་རེད།

There's been an accident!

phâ-gay kye-ngen choong sha ཕ་གིར་སྐྱེན་ངན་བྱུང་ཤག

Please help me.

ngah ro nâng-dâ ང་ལ་རོགས་གནང་དང་།

Could I please use the telephone?

kha-pah bay-chö chay-na di-gi re-bay ཁ་པར་བེད་སྤྱོད་བྱེད་ན་འགྲིགས་གི་རེད་པས།

I'm lost.

nga lâm-ga la-sha ང་ལམ་ཀ་བརྫགས་ཤག

Where are the toilets?

sâng-chö ka-bah yö-ray གསང་སྤྱོད་ཀ་པར་ཡོད་རེད།

police & crimes

སྐོར་སྲུང་དང་

Call the police!
  kor-soong-wa kay tong-da སྐོར་སྲུང་བ་སྐད་གཏོང་དང་།

I'll get the police!
  ngay kor-soong-wa kay tâng-go ངས་སྐོར་སྲུང་བ་སྐད་གཏང་གོ

Where's the police station?
  kor-soong-way le-koong སྐོར་སྲུང་བའི་ལས་ཁུངས་གང་པར་ཡོད་རེད།
  ka-bah yö-ray

We want to report an offence.
  ngân-tsö chay-nyen nye-sâng ང་ཚོས་བྱས་ཉེས་སྙན་ཤེས་ནུ་གྱི་ཨིན།
  shu-gi yin

I've been raped.
  nga-la tsen-wâng-tog ང་ལ་བཙན་དབང་ཐོག་ཆགས་པས་སྲུང་སོང་།
  châg-pa chay-song

I've been assaulted.
  ngah gö-zing chay-choong ངར་རྐོལ་འཛིངས་བྱས་བྱུང་།

I've been robbed.
  nga ku-may chom-song ང་རྐུ་མས་བཅོམས་སོང་།

My ... was/were stolen.	ngay ... ku-ma shoh-song	ངའི ... རྐུ་མ་ཤོར་སོང་།
I've lost my ...	ngay ... lâg-song	ངའི ... བརྒྱགས་སོང་།
backpack	gya-phay	རྒྱབ་ཁད་
bags	bag-la/jo-la	འབེགལ/འཇོལ
handbag	lâg-kye bag-la	ལག་འཁྱེར་འབེགལ
money	ngü	དངུལ་
papers	yig-cha	ཡིག་ཆ
passport	pa-se-pot; chi-kyö lâg-teb	པ་སེ་པོཊ/ ཕྱི་བསྐྱོད་ལག་དེབ
travellers cheques	drü-shü ngü-zin	བགྲུལ་བཞུད་དངུལ་འཛིན
wallet	bâh-koog	སྒྲུ་ཁུག

SAFE TRAVEL

172

My possessions are insured.

ngay cha-lâg-la in-shu-ren gan-gya sö-yö

ངའི་ཅ་ལག་ལ་ཨིན་ཤུ་རན་འགན་འགྱ་བསོ་ཡོད།

I'm sorry; I apologise.

gong-da

དགོངས་དག

I didn't realise I was doing anything wrong.

ngay nön-trü chay yö-pa ha-ko-ma-song

ངས་ནོར་འཁྲུལ་བྱས་ཡོད་པ་ཧ་གོ་མ་སོང་།

I didn't do it.

ngay chay-gyu ma-choong

ངས་བྱེད་རྒྱུ་མ་བྱུང་།

We're innocent.

ngân-tsoh nâg-nye may

ང་ཚོར་ནག་ཉེས་མེད།

We're foreigners.

ngân-tso chi-gye-wa yin

ང་ཚོ་ཕྱི་རྒྱལ་བ་ཡིན།

I want to contact my embassy/consulate.

ngân-tsö shoong-tsab/dön-chö khâng-la day-wa chay-gö-yö

ང་ཚོའི་གཞུང་ཚབ། / དོན་གཅོད་ཁང་ལ་འབྲེལ་བ་བྱེད་དགོས་ཡོད།

Can I call someone?

ngay chig-la kha-pah tâng-ga

ངས་གཅིག་ལ་ཁ་པར་གཏང་ག

Can I have a lawyer who speaks English?

ngah in-ji-kay shin-khen tim-tsö-pa-chi râg thoob-ki re-bay

ངར་དབྱིན་ཇི་སྐད་ཤེས་མཁན་ཁྲིམས་རྩོད་པ་གཅིག་རག་ཐུབ་ཀྱི་རེད་པས།

emergencies

173

Is there a fine we can pay to clear this?

nye-chay-di ngü tay-nay
ja-ya yö re-bay

ཉེས་ཆད་འདི་དངུལ་སྤྲད་ནས་འཛལ་
ལ་ཡོང་རེད་པས།

Can we pay an on-the-spot fine?

nye-chay ngü-bâb da-ta-râng
tay-na di-gi re-bay

ཉེས་ཆད་དངུལ་འབབ་ད་ལྟ་རང་
སྤྲད་ན་འགྲིག་གི་རེད་པས།

I understand.

ha go-song

ཧ་གོ་སོང་།

I don't understand.

ha go-ma-song

ཧ་གོ་མ་སོང་།

I know my rights.

ngay nga-râng-gi thob-tâng
ha go-gi-yö

ངས་ང་རང་གི་ཐོབ་ཐང་ཧ་གོ་གི་ཡོད།

arrested	zin-soong chay-pa	འཛིན་བཟུང་བྱས་པ།
cell	tsön-khâng nâng-gi khâng-choong	བཙོན་ཁང་ནང་གི་ཁང་ཆུང་
consulate	dön-chö-khâng	དོན་གཅོད་ཁང་
embassy	shoong-tsâb-khâng	གཞུང་ཚབ་ཁང་
fine	nye-chay	ཉེས་ཆད་
guilty	nâg-nye yö-pa	ནག་ཉེས་ཡོད་པ།
not guilty	nâg-nye may-pa	ནག་ཉེས་མེད་པ།
lawyer	tim-tsö-pa	ཁྲིམས་རྩོད་པ།
police officer	kor-soong-wa	སྐོར་སྲུང་བ།
police station	kor-soong lay-koong	སྐོར་སྲུང་ལས་ཁུངས།
prison	tsön-khâng	བཙོན་ཁང་
trial	tim-chö	ཁྲིམས་གཅོད་

What am I accused of?	ngah nâg-nye kâ-ray gay yö-ray	ང་ལ་ཉེས་ག་རེ་བཀལ་ཡོད་རེད།
You'll be charged with ...	kay-râng-la ... nye-chay gay-gi-ray	ཁྱེད་རང་ལ ... ཉེས་ཆད་བཀལ་གྱི་རེད།
He'll/She'll be charged with ...	kho/mo-la ... nye-chay gay-gi-ray	ཁོ/མོ་ལ ... ཉེས་ཆད་བཀལ་གྱི་རེད།
anti-government activity	shoong-la ngo-lo-gi lay-gü tsâm-pa	གཞུང་ལ་ངོ་ལོག་གི་ལས་འགུལ་བརྩམས་པ
assault	gö-zing chay-pa	རྐྱེན་འཛིངས་བྱེད་པ
disturbing the peace	shi-de toog-pa	ཞི་བདེ་དཀྲུགས་པ
possession (of illegal substances)	(trim-gay-gi ngö-zay) kye-wa	(ཁྲིམས་འགལ་གྱི་དངོས་ཟས)བཀྱེར་བ
illegal entry	trim-gay-gi gya-kâb-nâng zü-ba	ཁྲིམས་འགལ་གྱིས་རྒྱལ་ཁབ་ནང་འཛུལ་བ
murder	mi sö-pa	མི་གསོད་པ
not having a visa	vi-za may-pa	ཝི་ཟ་མེད་པ
overstaying your/his/her visa	kay-râng-gi/ khö/mö vi-zay dü-tsö-lay gay-te dhö-pa	ཁྱེད་རང་གི/ ཁོའི/མོའི ཝི་ཟའི་དུས་ཚོད་ལས་འགལ་ཏེ་སྡོད་པ
rape	tsen-yem chay-pa	བཙན་གཡེམ་བྱེད་པ
robbery/theft	tog-chom chay-pa; ku-ma kü-pa	འཕྲོག་བཅོམ་བྱེད་པ/ རྐུ་མ་རྐུས་པ
shoplifting	tsong-so jâb-kü chay-pa	ཚོང་ཚོའི་འཇབ་རྐུ་བྱེད་པ
traffic violation	lâm-gay-trim gay-wa	ལམ་འགྲོའི་ཁྲིམས་འགལ་བ
working without a permit	chog-chen may-pah lay-ga chay-pa	ཆོག་འཆན་མེད་པར་ལས་ཀ་བྱེད་པ

medical emergencies

འཕྲོད་བསྟེན་

Call a doctor!

ahm-chi kay tong-da

ཨེམ་ཆི་སྐད་གཏོང་དང་།

Call an ambulance!

nay-pa or-khen mo-ta
kay tong-da

ནད་པ་འཕེར་མཁན་མོ་ཊ་སྐད་གཏོང་དང་།

I'm ill.

nga na-gi-du

ང་ན་གི་འདུག

My friend is ill.

ngay rog-pa na-gi-du

ངའི་རོགས་པ་ན་གི་འདུག

I have medical insurance.

nga-la trö-ten-chay in-shu-ren
gan-gya sö-yö

ང་ལ་འཕྲོད་བསྟེན་ཆེད་ཨིན་ཤུ་རན་བགན་རྒྱ་བཟོས་ཡོད།

**My blood group is (A/B/O/AB)
positive/negative.**

ngay tâg-rig (e/bi/o/e-bi)
po-si-ti-yu/ne-ge-ti-yu ray

ངའི་ཁྲག་རིགས་(ཨེ་/བི་/ཨོ་/ཨེ་བི་)
པོ་སི་ཏི་ཡུ་/ནེ་གེ་ཏི་ཡུ་རེད།

Contact number (next of kin).

de-thoog chay-sa
(pün-tâg-nye-shö)
kha-pah ahng-dâng

འབྲེལ་ཐུག་བྱེད་ས་(སྤུན་ཐག་ཉེ་ཤོས་)
ཁ་པར་ཨང་གྲངས།

Should you require medical attention in any of Tibet's main towns, you'll generally have a choice of Tibetan or Western medicine. Doctors are well trained, but it's unlikely they'll speak English. At Tibetan hospitals (men-tsi-khâng, སྨན་རྩིས་ཁང་, or bö-bay men-khâng, བོད་པའི་སྨན་ཁང་), where Tibetan medicine is practised, staff generally speak Tibetan. At People's or Chinese hospitals, (mi-mâng men-khâng, མི་དམངས་སྨན་ཁང་, or gyâ-mee men-khâng, རྒྱ་མིའི་སྨན་ཁང་), where Western medicine is practised, staff speak either Chinese or Tibetan (more commonly Chinese).

Outside of the main towns, there's little choice of medical care and it tends to be of a lower standard.

at the doctor

ཡིམ་ཇི་འི་མར

I'm sick.

nga na-gi-du   ང་ན་གི་འདུག

My friend is sick.

ngay rog-pa na-gi-du   ངའི་རོགས་པ་ན་གི་འདུག

Is there a doctor who speaks English?

in-ji-kay shin-khen ahm-chi   དབྱིན་ཇི་སྐད་ཤེས་མཁན་ཡེམ་ཇི་ཡོད་རེད་པས།
yö re-bay

Could the doctor come here?

ahm-chi-la day pheb thoob-ki   ཡེམ་ཇི་ལགས་འདིར་ཕེབས་ཐུབ་ཀྱི་རེད་པས།
re-bay

I need a doctor.

nga ahm-chi-chig ten gö yö   ང་ཡེམ་ཇི་ཅིག་བསྟེན་དགོས་ཡོད།

kay-râng kâ-ray na-gi-du
ཁྱེད་རང་ག་རེ་ན་གྱི་འདུག
  What's the matter?

na-tsa tâng-gi du-gay
ན་ཚ་གཏོང་གི་འདུག་གས
  Do you feel any pain?

na-tsa ka-bah tâng-gi-du
ན་ཚ་ག་བར་གཏོང་གི་འདུག
  Where does it hurt?

tsha-wa ba-gi du-gay
ཚ་བ་འབར་གྱི་འདུག་གས
  Do you have a temperature?

kay-râng na-nay gyün
ring-lö chin-song
ཁྱེད་རང་ན་ནས་རྒྱུན་
རིང་པོར་ཕྱིན་སོང་
  How long have you been ill?

din-ta ngön-ma na nyong-ngay
འདི་འདྲ་སྔོན་མ་ན་མྱོང་ངས
  Have you had this before?

kay-râng men sa-gi yö-bay
ཁྱེད་རང་སྨན་ཟ་གྱི་ཡོད་པས
  Are you on medication?

tha-ma ten-gi yö-bay
ཐ་མག་འཐེན་གྱི་ཡོད་པས
  Do you smoke?

châng-râg toong-gi yö-bay
ཆང་རག་འཐུང་གི་ཡོད་པས
  Do you drink?

si-men sa-gi yö-bay
གཟི་སྨན་ཟ་གི་ཡོད་པས
  Do you take drugs?

kay-râng-gi lü-la phog-khen-ri
gay yö-bay
ཁྱེད་རང་གི་ལུས་ལ་འཕོག་མཁན་
རི་གས་ག་རེ་ཡོད་པས
  Are you allergic to anything?

ngay kay-râng-gi	དས་ཁྱེད་རང་གི	I'll take your/a ...
... ta-gi-yin	... ལྟ་གི་ཡིན	
tâg	ཁྲག	blood sample
tâg-shay chay-chung	ཁྲག་ཤེད་ཆེ་ཆུང	blood pressure
tsa	རྩ	pulse
châp-chen	ཆབ་ཆེན	stool sample
tsha-wa	ཚ་བ	temperature
chin-pâ/châp-sâng	གཅིན་པ/ཆབ་སང	urine sample

kha dhong-dâ		ཁ་གདོང་དང་།
Open your mouth.		
oog shoog-chay ya ten-dâ		དབུགས་ཤུགས་ཆེ་པར་ཐེན་དང་།
Take a deep breath.		
lo gyön-da		ལོ་བརྒྱུན་དང་།
Please cough.		
ngay kâp gyâ-gi-yin		ངས་ཁབ་རྒྱ་གི་ཡིན།
I'll give you an injection.		
ngay men tay-gi-yin		ངས་སྨན་སྟེར་གི་ཡིན།
I'll give you medicine.		
kay-râng-gi na-tsa		ཁྱེད་རང་གི་ན་ཚ་ཚབ་ཆུག་ཁགས་
dhuk-cha min-du		མིན་འདུག
Your illness is not serious.		

Where's the	... tâg nye-shö	... བག་ཉེ་ཤོས་ག
nearest ...?	ka-bah yö-ray	པར་ཡོད་རེད།
chemist	men tsong-khâng	སྨན་ཚོང་ཁང་
dentist	so men-khâng	སོ་སྨན་ཁང་
doctor	ahm-chi	ཨེམ་རྗེ་
hospital	men-khâng	སྨན་ཁང་

symptoms & conditions

ནད་རྟགས།

I've been ill for ... days.

nga na-nay nyi-ma ... chin-song ང་ནས་ནས་ཉིན་མ ... ཕྱིན་སོང་།

I've been vomiting.

nga kyoog-pa kyu-gi-du ང་སྐྱུགས་པ་སྐྱུག་གི་འདུག

I can't sleep.

nga nyi ku-gi min-du ང་གཉིད་ཁུག་གི་མིན་འདུག

I feel ...	nga ...-gi	ང་ ...གི།
dizzy	gu-yu kho	མགོ་ཡུར་འཁོར་
nauseous	kyong-may lâng	སྐྱུག་མེར་ལང་
shivery	dâr	འདིར་

I feel feverish.	ngah tsha-wa gye-sha	ངར་ཚ་བ་རྒྱས་ཤག
I feel weak.	ngay tob-shay	འདི་སྟོབས་ཤེད་ཉམས་ཤག
	nyâm-sha	

I'm having trouble breathing.

nga oog tong-ya kâg-po
chay-ki-du

ང་དབུགས་གཏོང་ཡ་ལ་གལ་པོ་བྱེད་ཀྱི་འདུག

It hurts here.

day na-tsa gya-gi

འདིར་ན་ཚ་རྒྱག་གི་ཤག

I have (a/an) ...	ngah ... yö	ངར་ ...ཡོད།
I've had (a/an) ...	nga ... na-nyong	ང་ ...ན་མྱོང་།
allergy	phog-nay	ཕོག་ནད་
cancer	can-sah; ten-nay na-tsa	གེན་སར་/སྐྲན་ནད་ནཚ་
chickenpox	sib-bi na-tsa	ཤིབ་བི་ནཚ་
diabetes	chay-ma ka-ray na-tsa	བྱེ་མ་ཀ་རའི་ནཚ་
glandular fever	men-bü tsay-nay	སྨེན་བུའི་ཚད་ནད་
hay fever	mig-na-nay chu	མིག་སྣ་ནས་ནས་འཛག་
	zâg-pay phog-nay	པའི་ཕོག་ནད་
heart condition	nying-khâm ma-de-wa	སྙིང་ཁམས་མ་བདེ་བ་
hepatitis	chim-ba na-tsa	མཆིན་པ་ནཚ་
indigestion	say-ju ma-thoob-pay nay	ཟས་འཇུ་མ་ཐུབ་པའི་ནད་
infection	gö-nay/rim-nay	འགོས་ནད་/རིམས་ནད་
malaria	ma-le-ri-ya rim-nay	མ་ལེ་རི་ཡ་རིམས་ནད་

migraine	go-se gya-gyu	མགོ་གཟེར་རྒྱུག
	na-tsa-shig	རྒྱུ་ན་ཚ་ཞིག
rheumatism	doom-nay	གྲུམ་ནད
typhoid	ta-ye-pho gö-nay	གཱ་ཡེ་ཕོ་འགོས་ནད
venereal disease	tig-joh-lay choong-way	འབྲིག་སྦྱོར་ལས་འབྱུང
	gö-nay	བའི་འགོས་ནད

I have (a/an) ...	ngah ...-sha	ང་...ཤག
I've had ...	ngah ... nyong	ང་...མྱོང
anaemia	trâg-shay nyâm	ཁྲག་ཤེད་ཉམས
blister	chu-gâng dön	ཆུ་སྒུར་རྡོན
boil	nyem-bu dön	གཉེན་འབུར་རྡོན
conjunctivitis	mig-nâng nyen-ga bâh	མིག་ནང་གཉེན་ག་འབར
cramp (in calf)	nya gyur	ཉ་འགྱུར
dehydration	lü-nâng shâ-lön kâm	ལུས་ནང་ཤ་རློན་སྐམས
food poisoning	say-doog phog	ཟས་དུག་ཕོག
frostbite	khyâg-bö teb	འཁྱག་བོས་ཐེབས
gastroenteritis	pho-wa-dâng	ཕོ་བ་དང་རྒྱུ་མ་སྒྲངས
	gyu-ma trâng	
inflammation	lü-la nyen-ga bâh	ལུས་ལ་གཉེན་ག་འབར
lice	shig	ཤིག
lump	boor-tog dön	འབུར་རྡོག་རྡོན
rash	tho-mâh sib-sib	ཐོར་དམར་སིབ་སིབ་རྡོན
sore throat	mik-pay-nâng ma châg	མིད་པའི་ནང་མ་ཆགས
sprain	tsig chü	ཚིགས་འཆུས
sunburn	nyib-ta teb	ཉི་བཀྲག་འཐེབས
swollen foot	kâng-ba trâng	རྐང་པ་སྒྲངས
urinary infection	chin-lâm-la	གཅིན་ལམ་ལ་འགོས
	gö-nay-chi phog	ནད་ཅིག་ཕོག

health

181

I have (a/an) ...	nga ...-gi	ང་ ...གིས།
I've had ...	ngah ... nyong	ང་ ... མྱོང་།
altitude sickness	lâ-du na	ལ་དུག་ན།
bronchitis	lo-yü tsa-nay na	གློ་ཡུའི་ཚ་ནད་ན།
cold	châm-ba na	ཆམ་པ་ན།
cystic fibrosis	sis-tik fa-ye bor-sis-shay	སིས་ཊིག་ཕ་ཡེ་བོར་སིས་ཤེ།
	mi-gyü-nay yong-way	མིས་རྒྱུད་ནས་ཡོང་བའི།
	men-bü nay-chig na	ཨེན་བུའི་ནད་ཅིག
dysentery	di-sen-ti-ri na-tsa	ཌི་སེན་ཊི་རི་ན་ཚ་ཤིག
	drö-kog mâ-shay gya	དགྲང་ཁོག་མ་ཤེས་རྒྱ།
fever	tsha-wa na	ཚ་བ་ན།
flu	châm-rim	ཆམ་རིམས་དུག་པོ་ཞིག་ན།
	dâg-po-shi na	
headache	go na	མགོ་ན།
itch	sâb-ra lâng	ཟབ་ར་ལང་།
pain	na-soog gya	ན་ཟུག་རྒྱ།
stomachache	drö-kog na	གྲོད་ཁོག་ན།
sunstroke	tsa-doog na	ཚ་དུག་ན།
toothache	so na	སོ་ན།
travel sickness	dim-drü-la tan-nay	འགྲིམ་འགྲུལ་ལ་བརྟེན།
	go-yom-dâng	ནས་མགོ་ཡོམ།
	kyook-may lâng	དང་སྐྱུག་མེར་ལང་།

I'm constipated.

nga tsog-pa bâb-kee min-du ང་བཙོག་པ་འབབ་ཀྱི་མིན་འདུག

I have diarrhoea.

nga drö-kog shay-gi ང་གྲོད་ཁོག་བཤལ་གྱིས།

I have a cut.

ngah ma sö-song ངར་རྨ་བཟོས་སོང་།

My foot's swollen.

ngay kâng-pa bö-sha ངའི་རྐང་པ་སྦོས་ཤག

I have a temperature.

ngah tsha-wa gye-sha ངར་ཚ་བ་རྒྱས་ཤག

I have worms.

ngay khog-pay nâng bu du ངའི་ཁོག་པའི་ནང་འབུ་འདུག

I feel better/worse.

nga dâg-tu/dhuk-tu chin-sha

ང་དྲག་ཏུ་/སྡུག་ཏུ་ཕྱིན་ཤག

This is my usual medicine.

di ngay dü-gyün sa-ya men ray

འདི་རའི་དུས་རྒྱུན་ཟ་ཡ་སྨན་རེད།

I don't want a blood transfusion.

ngah tâg tay mi-gö

ང་ཁྲག་སྟེར་མི་དགོས།

Can I have a receipt for my insurance?

in-shu-ren gan-gyay-chay choong-zin-chi nâng thoob-ki re-bay

ཨིན་ཤུ་རན་གན་རྒྱ་ཆེད་ཆུང་འཛིན་ཅིག་གནང་ཐུབ་ཀྱི་རེད་པས།

women's health

བུད་མེད་ཀྱི་འཕྲོད་བསྟེན

I'd like to see a female doctor.

nga kye-man ahm-chi-chig ten-dö yö

ང་སྐྱེ་དམན་ཨེམ་ཆི་ཞིག་བསྟེན་འདོད་ཡོད།

I want to see a gynaecologist.

nga mo-nay ahm-chi kay-pa-chi ten-dö yö

ང་མོ་ནད་ཨེམ་ཆི་མཁས་པ་ཅིག་བསྟེན་འདོད་ཡོད།

I'm pregnant.

nga-la pu-gu kye-ya-yö

ང་ར་ཕྲུ་གུ་སྐྱེ་ལ་ཡོད།

I think I'm pregnant.

ngah pu-gu châg yö-sa-ray

ང་ར་ཕྲུ་གུ་ཆགས་ཡོད་ས་རེད།

the doctor may say	
kay-rrâng-la pu-gu kye-ya yö-bay	ཁྱེད་རང་ལ་ཕྲུ་གུ་ སྐྱེ་ལག་ཡོད་པས།
Are you pregnant?	
kay-rrâng dha-tsen bâb-ki du-gay	ཁྱེད་རང་ཟླ་མཚན་ བབས་ཀྱི་འདུག་གས།
Are you menstruating?	

I'm on the Pill.

nga kye-gok-men sa-gi-yö　　　ང་སྐྱེ་འགོག་སྨན་ཟ་གི་ཡོད།

I haven't had my period for ... months.

nga-la dha-tsen ma-bâb-nay　　ང་ལ་ཟླ་མཚན་མ་བབས་ནས
da-wa ... chin-song　　　　　ཟླ་བ་ ... ཕྱིན་སོང་།

I'd like to get the morning-after pill.

nga chu-tsö so-doog tsâm-ring　　ང་ཆུ་ཚོད་སོ་དྲུག་ཙམ་རིང་སྐྱེ་འགོག་ཁྲབ
kye-gok thoob-ya men nyon-dö yö　ཡག་སྨན་ཉོ་འདོད་ཡོད།

I'd like to use contraception.

nga kye-gok bay-chö　　　　ང་སྐྱེ་འགོག་བེད་སྤྱོད
tong-ya dö-pa yö　　　　　གཏོང་ཡག་འདོད་པ་ཡོད།

I'd like to have a pregnancy test.

nga pu-gu châg yö-may　　　ང་ར་ཕྲུག་ཁམས་ཡོད་མེད
tâg-chay chay-dö yö　　　　བརྟག་དཔྱད་བྱེད་འདོད་ཡོད།

abortion	pu-gu ngel-nay dön-pa	ཕྲུ་གུ་མངལ་ནས་དོན་པ
cystitis	chin-nö gâng-bu-nâng	གཅིན་ནོ་སྒོང་བུར་ནང་
	nyen-ga châg-pa	གཉེན་ཁ་ཆགས་པ
diaphragm	ngel-ka-la jog-ya	མངལ་ཁ་ལ་འཇོག་ཡག་སྐྱེ
	kye-gok lâg-ja-shig	འགོག་ལག་ཆ་ཞིག
mammogram	log-pah-shig	བློ་པར་ཞིག
maternity	pu-gu kay-say men-khâng	ཕྲུ་གུ་སྐྱེ་སའི་སྨན་ཁང་
hospital		
menstruation	dha-tsen/dha-trâg	ཟླ་མཚན/ཟླ་ཁྲག
miscarriage	pu-gu nge-nay shor-wa	ཕྲུ་གུ་མངལ་ནས་ཤོར་བ
pap smear	chay-shay-tog tâg-chay	ཚེ་ཞེས་ཐོག་བརྟག་དཔྱད
	chay-ya zay	བྱེད་ཡག་ཟས
period pain	dha-tsen bâb-kâb na-soog	ཟླ་མཚན་འབབ་སྐབས་ན་ཟུག
the Pill	kye-gok-men	སྐྱེ་འགོག་སྨན
pregnancy	pu-gu châg-man	ཕྲུ་གུ་ཆགས་མན་བཟོ
test kit	ta-ya yo-chay	ཡག་ཡོ་ཆས
thrush	thor-kya sib-sib dön-pay	ཐོར་སྐྱ་སིབ་སིབ་དོན
	gö-nay-chig	པའི་འགོག་ནད་ཅིག
ultrasound	öl-dra-sa-wong-shay	འོལ་ཊ་ས་ཝོང་ཤེས་ཞེས་གཏོ་བོར
	tso-o kog-pay-nâng pu-gu	ཕྱོགས་པའི་ནང་ཕྲུག་བར་མ
	châg yö-may ta-ya log-pah	ཆགས་ཡོད་པར་ལྟ་ཡག་ཆ་ཞིག
	trü-cha-shig	

special health needs

I'm ...	nga ... chog-chog yin	ང་...ཚོག་ཚོག་ཡིན།
anaemic	trâg-shay nyâm	ཁྲག་ཤེད་ཉམས།
asthmatic	oog-tsâng-nay na	དབུགས་ཚང་ནད་ན།
diabetic	chay-ma ka-ray na-tsa na	གྱི་མ་ཀ་རའི་ན་ཚན།
epileptic	sa-dib na	གཟའ་སྒྲིབ་ན།

I'm allergic to ...	... nga-la phog-gi yö	...ང་ལ་འཕོག་གི་ཡོད།
antibiotics	nay-bu gok-men an-ti ba-ye o-tik	ནད་འབུ་འགོག་སྨན། ཨེན་ཏི་བ་ཡེའི་ཨོ་ཏིག
aspirin	nyen-jom-men es-pi-rin	མཉེན་འཇོམས། སྨན་ཨེ་སི་པི་རིན།
bees	dâng-bu	སྦྲང་བུ།
dairy products	kar-chu	དཀར་ཆུ།
penicillin	nyen-jom-men pe-ni-si-lin	མཉེན་འཇོམས། སྨན་པི་ནི་སི་ལིན།
pollen	may-tog-gi sen-drü-dü	མེ་ཏོག་གི་ཟེའི་འབྲུའི་རྡུལ།

I have a skin allergy.

ngay sha pâg-pa-la nyen-ga lâng chog-chog yin

ངའི་ཤ་པགས་པ་ལ་མཉེན། གའང་ཚོག་ཚོག་ཡིན།

I have high/low blood pressure.

ngay tâg-shay tho-po/ma-po ray

ངའི་ཁྲག་ཤེད་མཐོ་པོ་/དམའ་པོ་རེད།

I have a heart condition.

ngay nying-kâm de-po-may

ངའི་སྙིང་ཁམས་བདེ་པོ་མེད།

I've been vaccinated.

ngah nay-rim ngön-gok-gi men-khâb gyâb-tsa yin

ང་ར་རིམས་ནད་སྔོན་འགོག་གི་སྨན་ཁབ་བརྒྱབ་ཚར་ཡིན།

Is that a new syringe you're using?

kay-râng-gi bay-chö chay-ya men-khâb-te sa-pa re-bay

ཁྱེད་རང་གི་བེད་སྤྱོད་བྱེད་ཡག སྨན་ཁབ་དེ་གསར་པ་རེད་པས།

I have my own syringe.

nga-râng râng-gi men-khâb yö

ང་རང་རང་གི་སྨན་ཁབ་ཡོད།

I'm on medication for ...

> nga men sa-nay nyin-ma
> ... chin-song

ང་སྨན་ཟ་ནས་ཉིན་མ ... ཕྱིན་སོང་།

I'm on a special diet.

> nga trö-ten-chay kha-la sa-tsö
> kay-pa chay-ki yö

ང་འཕྲོད་བསྟེན་ཆེད་ཁ་ལག་ཟ་ཚོད་མགས་པ་བྱེད་ཀྱི་ཡོད།

I need a new pair of glasses.

> ngah mik-shay
> sa-pa-shig go-ki du

ངར་མིག་ཤེལ་གསར་པ་ཞིག་དགོས་ཀྱི་འདུག

parts of the body

My ... hurts.

> ngay ... na-soog gya-gi

ངའི ... ན་ཟུག་རྒྱག་གི་ཡིས།

I have a pain in my ...

> ngay ...-la na-soog gya-gi

ངའི ...ལ་ན་ཟུག་རྒྱག་གི་ཡིས།

I can't move my ...

> ngay ... gü-kyok gya
> thoob-ki min-du

ངའི ... འགུལ་བསྐྱོད་རྒྱག་ཐུབ་ཀྱི་མིན་འདུག

ankle	kâng-tsig	ཀང་ཚིགས
appendix	gyu-lhâg	རྒྱུ་ལྷག
arm	lâg-pa	ལག་པ

back	gyâb	ཀྱབ
bladder	chin-nö gâng-bu	གཅིན་སྣོད་ལྒང་བུ
blood	tâg	ཁྲག
body	soog-po	གཟུགས་པོ
bone	rü-gok	རུས་གོག
chest	bang-go	བྲང་ཁོག
chin	ma-lay/og-ma	མ་ལེ/འོག་མ
ear	ahm-chog	ཨམ་ཆོ
elbow	dru-mo	གྲུ་མོ
eye	mig	མིག
face	dong	གདོང
finger	zu-gu	མཛུབ་གུ
foot	kâng-pa	རྐང་པ
hand	lâg-pa	ལག་པ
head	goh	མགོ
heart	nying	སྙིང
hip	chi-go	དཔྱི་མགོ
jaw	dâm-pa	འགྲམ་པ
kidney	kay-ma	མཁལ་མ
knee	pü-mo	པུས་མོ
leg	kâng-pa	རྐང་པ
liver	chin-pa	མཆིན་པ
lungs	lo-wa	གློ་བ
mouth	kha	ཁ
muscle	sha-gyü	ཤ་རྒྱུ
nose	na-khoog	སྣ་ཁུག
ribs	tsib-ma	རྩིབ་མ
shoulder	poong-pa/trâg-pa	དཔུང་པ/ཕྲག་པ
skin	sha pâg-pa	ཤ་པགས་པ
spine	gay-tsig	སྒལ་ཚིགས
stomach	drö-kog	གྲོད་ཁོག
teeth	so	སོ
throat	mik-pa	མིད་པ
tongue	chay	ལྕེ
tonsils	chay-tsay men-bu	ལྕེ་རྩེའི་རྨེན་བུ
vein	tâg-tsa	ཁྲག་རྩ

སྨན་ཚོང་ཁང་

Is there an (all-night) chemist nearby?

day (tsen-gâng) go-chay-khen men tsong-khâng yö re-bay

འདིར་(མཚན་གང་) གྲོ་ཕྱུ་མཁན་སྨན་ ཚོང་ཁང་ཡོད་རེད་པས།

Do I need a prescription for ...?

... nyo-wa-la ahm-chi men-tho go-gi re-bay

... ཉོ་བའ་ལ་ཨེམ་ཆིའི་སྨན་བྱོ་ དགོས་ཀྱི་རེད་པས།

I have a prescription.

ngah men-tho yö

ངར་སྨན་བྱོ་ཡོད།

How many should I take a day?

nyin-ma re-ray-la teng kâ-tsay sa-gö-ray

ཉིན་མ་རེ་རེ་ལ་ཐེང་ ག་ཚོད་ཟ་དགོས་རེད།

Take this ... a day.	di nyin-mâ re-ray-la teng ... chö-nâng	འདི་ཉིན་མ་རེ་རེ་ལ་ ... ཐེང་གནང་།
twice	nyi-ray	གཉིས་རེ་
three times	soom-ray	གསུམ་རེ་
four times	shi-ray	བཞི་རེ་

Take ... pill(s)	teng re-ray ri-bu ...	ཐེང་རེ་རེར་རི་ལབུ་ ...
each time	(kha-la nyâm-tu)	(ཁ་ལག་མཉམ་དུ་)
(with food).	chö-gö	མཆོད་དགོས།
one	re-ray	རེ་རེ་
two	nyi-ray	གཉིས་རེ་
three	soom-ray	གསུམ་རེ་

Can I drive on this medication?

men-di sa-shin-khâb mo-ta tâng-na di-gi re-bay

སྨན་འདི་ཟ་བཞིན་ཁབ་སྣ་བས་མོ་ག་བཏང་ ན་འགྲིག་གི་རེད་པས།

Will it make me drowsy?

tey nyi doh chu-ki ma-re-bay

དེའི་གཉིད་ལྡོ་བཅུག་གི་མ་རེད་པས།

| antibiotics | nay-bu gok-men an-ti ba-ye o-tik | ནད་འབུ་འགོག་སྨན་ཨེན་ཊི་ བྱེ་ཨོ་ཊིག |

anti-diarrhoeal drug	drö-gok shay-gok men	གྲོད་གོག་བཤལ་གོག་སྨན
antiseptic	nyen-ka gok-chay men	མཉེན་ཀ་འགོག་བྱེད་སྨན
aspirin	nyen-jom-men as-pi-rin	མཉེན་འཇོམས་སྨན་ཨེས་པི་རིན
bandage	ma-ti/ma-ray	མ་དཏི/མ་རས
Band-Aid	ko-yö	ཀོ་ཡོལ
cold/flu medicine	châm-bay-men	ཆམ་པའི་སྨན
condoms	lig-shoob	རིག་ཤུབས
contraceptives	kye-go gok-men	སྐྱེ་སྒོ་འགོག་སྨན
cotton balls	tin-bay du-gu	སྲིན་བལ་གྱི་གུ
cough medicine	lo-men	གློ་སྨན
eye medicine	mik-men	མིག་སྨན
gauze	sâng-ray	སང་རས
iodine	nyen-chog ba-tsha ah-ey-o-din	མཉེན་གཙོག་པ་ཚ་ཨེ་ཡ་ཨོ་དིན
laxatives	tsog-pa bâb chu-ya-men lek-sa-tiv	བཙོག་པ་འབབ་བཅུག་ཡག་སྨན་ལེགས་ཨ་ཏིའུ
painkillers	nay-soog cha-ya-men	ནད་གཟུག་གཅོག་ཡག་སྨན
sleeping pills	nyi-men	གཉིད་སྨན
throat medicine	mik-pay-men	མིད་པའི་སྨན
vitamins	tob-kye-men	སྟོབས་བསྐྱེད་སྨན
worm medicine	bu-men	འབུ་སྨན

See the **Shopping** chapter, page 85, for general toiletries.

at the dentist

སོ་ཨེམ་ཇི་ཟར

I have a toothache.

nga so na-gi ནས་སོ་ན་གིས

I have a cavity.

ngah so kog-tong yö ངར་སོ་ཁོག་སྟོང་ཡོད

I've lost a filling.

ngay so-koong-nâng gyong-zay may-pa châg-sha ངའི་སོ་ཁུང་ནང་གྱོང་ཟས་མེད་པ་ཆགས་ཤག

health

I've broken my tooth.

   ngay so châg-sha   ངའི་སོ་ཆག་ཤག

My gums hurt.

   ngay so-nyil-nâng soog gya-gi ངའི་སོ་རྙིལ་ནང་ཟུག་རྒྱག་གིས

I don't want it extracted.

   nga so chi-log dön-dö may   ང་སོ་ཕྱིར་འདོན་འདོད་མེད

Please give me an anaesthetic.

   nga-la bee-men gya nâng-dâng ང་ལ་སྦྱིར་སྨན་རྒྱག་གནང་དང་

Ouch!   âh-tsa-tsa   ཨ་ཚ་ཚ

A

able, to be (can)	thoob-pa • nü-pa	ཐུབ་པ • ནུས་པ

Can I take a photo (of you)?
(kay-râng) par-chig gyâb-na
di-giy ray-bay
(ཁྱེད་རང་) པར་ཅིག་རྒྱབ་ན
འགྲིག་གི་རེད་པས།

Can you show me (on the map)?
(sâp-ta di-nâng) tön nâng-da
(ས་བཀྲ་འདི་ནང་) སྟོན་གནང་དང་།

aboard	du-sing dâng nâm-du sog nâng shoog-pa	གྲུ་གཟིངས་དང་གནམ་གྲུ སོགས་ནང་ཞུགས་པ
abortion	pu-gu ngay-nay chi dön-pa	ཕྲུག་མངལ་ནས་ཕྱིར་འདོན་པ
above	gâng-la	གང་ལ
abroad	chi-gye	ཕྱི་རྒྱལ
to accept	ngö-len chay-pa	ངོས་ལེན་བྱེད་པ
accident (collision)	dhong-tu gyâb-pa	གདོང་ཐུག་རྒྱབ་པ
accommodation	dhö-nay	སྡོད་གནས
across	tay-la	འདོན་ལ
activist	hoor-tsön-chen	ཧུར་བརྩོན་ཅན
adaptor	log-shoog cho-ya	ལོག་ཤུགས་གཏོང་ཡག་ལ་ཁ
addiction	kya-lâng sho-wa	སྐྱག་ལང་ཤོར་བ
address	ka-châng	ཁ་བྱང
to admire	tö-pa	བསྟོད་པ
admission	nâng zü	ནང་འཛུལ
to admit	ngö len-pa	ངོས་ལེན་པ
adult	na-so lön-pa	ན་སོ་ལོན་པ
advantage	kay-pen	ཁེ་ཕན
advice	lâb-ja	བསླབ་བྱ
aeroplane	nâm-du	གནམ་གྲུ
afraid, to be	shay-nâng kye-wa	ཞེད་སྣང་སྐྱེ་བ
after	je-la	རྗེས་ལ
(in the) afternoon	chi-toh(-la)	ཕྱི་དྲོ་(ལ)
this afternoon	te-ring chi-toh	དེ་རིང་ཕྱི་དྲོ
again	yâng-kya	ཡང་སྐྱར
against	khâ-te-tu	ཁ་གཏད་དུ
age	lo	ལོ
aggressive	tsen-po wâng-yö	བཙན་པོ་དབང་ཡོད

(a while) ago	(dü gay) ngön-tu	(དུས་འགའི་) སྔོན་ཏུ་
(half an hour) ago	(chu-tsö chay-ka) ngön-tu	(ཆུ་ཚོད་ཕྱེད་ཀ་) སྔོན་ཏུ་
(three days) ago	(nyin soom) ngön-tu	(ཉིན་གསུམ་) སྔོན་ཏུ་
to agree	mö-thün chay-pa	མོས་མཐུན་བྱེད་པ་

I don't agree.
nga mö-thün may   ང་མོས་མཐུན་མེད་

Agreed!
mö-thün yö   མོས་མཐུན་ཡོད་

agriculture	shing-lay	ཞིང་ལས་
ahead	dün-la	མདུན་ལ་
aid (help)	rog-râm	རོགས་རམ་
air	loong	རླུང་
air-conditioned	dâng-log	གྲང་ལོག་
air mail	nâm-dâg	གནམ་སྒྲུག་
airport	nâm-tâng	གནམ་ཐང་
airport tax	nâm-tâng tel	གནམ་ཐང་ཁྲལ་
alarm clock	lâng-da tong-ya chu-tsö	ལང་འཛུ་གཏོང་ཡག་ཆུ་ཚོད་
all	tshâng-ma	ཚང་མ་
allergy	phog-nay	ཕོགས་ནད་
to allow	chay chog-pa	བྱེད་ཆོག་པ་

It's allowed.
cho-gi ray   ཆོག་གི་རེད་

It's not allowed.
cho-gi ma-ray   ཆོག་གི་མ་རེད་

almost	phay-chay	ཕལ་ཆེར་
alone	chig-po	གཅིག་པོ་
already	tsar-wa	ཚར་བ་
also	yâng	ཡང་
altitude	gyâm-tsö ngö-nay	རྒྱ་མཚོའི་ངོས་ནས་འབུར་
	tsi-pay tho-tsay	བའི་མཐོ་ཚད་
always	tâg-pah	རྟག་པར་
amateur	lay-sho-la ka-lay	ལས་ཤོ་ལ་ཁ་དཀར་ལས་
	gya-khen	རྒྱག་མཁན་
ambassador	shoong-tsâp	གཞུང་ཚབ་
among	nâng-nay	ནང་ནས་
anarchist	si-shoong may-pay ring-loog	སྲིད་གཞུང་མེད་པའི་རིང་ལུགས་
ancient	na nga-mo	གནའ་སྔ་མོ་
and	dâng	དང་
angry	loong lâng-po	རྫུང་ལང་པོ་

animals	dü-do • sem-chen	དུད་འགྲོ • སེམས་ཅན
annual	lo-ray	ལོ་རེ
answer	len	ལན
ant	(bu) tog-ma	(འབུ)གྲོག་མ
antibiotics	nay-bu gok-men	ནད་འབུ་འགོག་སྨན
	an-ti ba-ye ot-ik	ཨེན་ཏི་བཱ་ཡེ་ཨོཏིཀ
antiques	na-nga-mö	གནའ་རྙིང་མོའི
antiseptic	nyen-ka gok-chay-men	སྙན་ཀ་འགོག་བྱེད་སྨན
any	kâ-ray yi-nay	གང་རེ་ཡིན་ནས
apartment	dö-khâng cha-tsâng-chi	སྡོད་ཁང་ཚ་ཚང་གཅིག
appointment	dü-kâg thoog-tay	དུས་བཀག་ཐུག་འཕྲད
archaeological	na ngo-la tâg-pay	གནའ་རྙིང་ལ་བཏག་པའི
	rig-nay	རིག་གནས
archaeological	ahr-lay cha-gö-pa	འར་ལས་ཆ་འགོད་པ
architecture	ahr-lay lâg-tsay	འར་ལས་ལག་རྩལ
to argue	tsö-pa gyâk-pa	རྩོད་པ་རྒྱག་པ
arm	lâg-nga • lâg-pa	ལག་ང • ལག་པ
to arrive	lep-pa • jor-wa	སླེབས་པ • འབྱོར་བ
art	lâg-tsay	ལག་རྩལ
art gallery	lâg-tsay dem-tön-khâng	ལག་རྩལ་འགྲེམས་སྟོན་ཁང
artist	ri-mo kay-pa • gyu-tsay-wa	རི་མོ་མཁས་པ • རྒྱུ་རྩལ་བ
artwork	ri-mo • lâg-sö	རི་མོ • ལག་བཟོས
ashtray	tha-ma dâb-sa-nö	ཐ་མག་འདབ་ས་སྣོད
to ask (for something)	ray-kü shu-wa	རེ་སྐུལ་ཞུ་བ
to ask (a question)	di pa	འདྲི་པ
aspirin	nyen-jom-men es-pi-rin	སྙན་འཇོམས་སྨན་ཨེས་པི་རིན
asthmatic	oog-tsâng-nay na chog-cho	འུག་ཚང་ནད་ཅན་ན་ཚོག་ཚོག
atmosphere	ba-nâng loong	བར་སྣང་རླུང
aunt	su-mo	སུ་མོ
autumn (fall)	tön-ga	སྟོན་ག
awful	shay-nâng-chen	ཞེ་སྣང་ཅན

B

baby	pu-gu	ཕུ་གུ
baby food	pu-gü kha-la	ཕུ་གུའི་ཁ་ལག
baby powder	pu-gü soog-poh	ཕུ་གུའི་གཟུགས་པོའི་
	chu-ya po-tah	ཕྱི་པའི་ཕྱེ་མ་གུར
babysitter	pu-gu ta-khen • bu-zi	ཕུ་གུ་བལྟ་མཁན • བུ་ཟི
back (body)	gyâb	རྒྱབ
at the back (behind)	gyâb-la	རྒྱབ་ལ
backpack	gya-phay	རྒྱ་འཕེད
bad	dhuk-cha	སྡུག་ཆགས
bag	bag-la • jo-la	འབེག་ལག • ཇོ་ལ
baggage	tog-tay	དོ་པོ་
baggage claim	tog-tay len-sa	དོ་པོ་ལེན་ས
bakery	bâg-leb tsong-khâng	བག་ལེབ་ཚོང་ཁང
balcony	tsom-chen	ཚོམས་ཆེན

ball (sport)	po-lo	པོ་ལོ་
bank	ngü-khâng	དངུལ་ཁང་
banknotes	ngü-shog	དངུལ་ཤོག
bar	châng-khâng	ཆང་ཁང་
bath	soog-po tru-wa	གཟུགས་པོ་འཁྲུབ་
bathing suit	chu-kay gyön-chay	ཆུ་ཁུག་གྱོན་ཆས་
bathroom	trü-khâng	ཁྲུས་ཁང་
battery	log-shu-men • bay-ti-ri	གློག་ཤུགས་སྨན་ • བེ་ཊི་རི་
to be	yin/ray • yö/du • yö-ray	ཡིན་/རེད་ • ཡོད་/འདུག • ཡོད་རེད་
beach	tsho-khay chay-tâng	མཚོ་ཁའི་བྱེ་ཐང་
beautiful	nying je-po	སྙིང་རྗེ་པོ་
because	gâng-yin say-na	གང་ཡིན་ཟེར་ན་
bed	nye-ti	ཉལ་ཁྲི་
bedroom	nye-khâng	ཉལ་ཁང་
before	ngön-la	སྔོན་ལ་
beggar	trâng-po	སྤྲང་པོ་
to begin	gon-zoog	འགོ་འཛུགས་
behind	gyâb-la	རྒྱབ་ལ་
below	wog-la	འོག་ལ་
beside	tih-la	འཐིབས་ལ་
best	yâg-shö	ཡག་ཤོས་
bet	gyen jog-pa	རྒྱན་འཇོག་པ་
better	yâg-pa	ཡག་པ་
bicycle	kâng-ga-ri	རྐང་སྒྲེལ་རི་
big	chen-po	ཆེན་པོ་
bill (account)	ngü-tsi	དངུལ་རྩིས་
binoculars	gyâng-shay	རྒྱང་ཤེལ་
biography	nâm-tar	རྣམ་ཐར་
bird	chi-hu	བྱིའུ་
birth certificate	kye-tse lâg-kay	སྐྱེ་ཚེས་ལག་ཁྱེར་
birthday	kye-kah-nyin	སྐྱེས་སྐར་ཉིན་
bite	so gyâb-pa	སོ་བརྒྱབ་པ་
black	nâg-po	ནག་པོ་
B&W (film)	(phing-sho) tshön-ta may-pa	(ཕིང་ཤོ) ཚོན་མདོག་མེད་པ་
blanket	nye-chay • kâm-ba-li	ཉལ་ཆས་ • ཀམ་བ་ལི་
to bleed	tâg zâg-pa	ཁྲག་འཛག་པ་
to bless	jin-gi lâb-pa	བྱིན་གྱིས་བརླབས་པ་
blind	long-wa • shar-wa	ལོང་བ་ • ཤར་བ་
blood	tâg	ཁྲག
blood group	tâg-rig	ཁྲག་རིགས་
blood pressure	tâg-shay	ཁྲག་ཤེད་
blood test	tâg-chay	ཁྲག་བཤེར་དཔྱད་
blue	ngön-po	སྔོན་པོ་
to board (ship etc)	nâng shoog-pa	ནང་ཞུགས་པ་
boarding pass	dhö-say pa-say	སྡོད་སེའི་པ་སེ་
boat	dru • dru-zing	གྲུ་ • གྲུ་གཟིངས་
body	soog-po • lü	གཟུགས་པོ་ • ལུས་

Bon appetit!
shay-la nye-bo nâng
བཞེས་ལག་མངར་པོ་གནང་།

Bon voyage!
toh-bo-chay peb-nâng
སྐྱོད་བྱུང་ཞེབས་གནང་།

bone	rü-gok	རུས་གོག
book	teb	དེབ
to book	ngön-ngâg chay-pa	སྔོན་ཚགས་བྱེད་པ
bookshop	teb tsong-khâng	དེབ་ཚོང་ཁང
boots	lhâm-gok yün-ring •	ལྷམ་གོག་ཡུན་རིང •
	ju-ta yu-ring	འཇུར་ཏ་ཡུ་རིང
border	sa-tsâm	ས་མཚམས
bored	nyob-pa	ཉོབ་པ
boring	nyob-to	ཉོབ་ཏོ
to borrow	yâr-wa	གཡར་བ
both	nyi-ga	གཉིས་ཀ
bottle	shay-tâm	ཤེལ་དམ
bottle opener	shay-tâm kha che-yâk	ཤེལ་དམ་ཁ་ཕྱེ་ཡག
(at the) bottom	thih(-la)	མཐིལ(ལ)
box	gâm	སྒམ
boy	bu	བུ
boyfriend	tok-po	གྲོགས་པོ
branch	ye-ga • yen-la	ཡལ་ག • ཡན་ལག
brave	pah-o	དཔའ་བོ
bread	bâk-lay	བག་ལེབ
to break	chog-pa	གཅོག་པ
breakfast	shog-cha •	ཞོགས་ཇ •
	shog-kay kha-la	ཞོགས་ཀའི་ཁ་ལག
to breathe	oog tong-wa	དབུགས་གཏོང་བ
bribe	kog-ngan	ཀོག་ངན
to bribe	kog-ngan tö-pa	ཀོག་ངན་སྤྲོད་པ
bridge	sâm-pa	ཟམ་པ
brilliant	kay-tu phâg-pa	ཤེད་དུ་འཕགས་པ
to bring	kay yong-wa	འཁྱེར་ཡོང་བ
broken	châg-pa	ཆག་པ
brother	pün-kya-bu	སྤུན་སྐྱ་བུ
brown	moog-po	སྨུག་པོ
bruise	moog-tig	སྨུག་ཏིག
Buddhist	nâng-pa	ནང་པ
bug	de-shig	འབུ་ཞིག
to build	soh-wa	བཟོ་བ
building	khâng-pa	ཁང་པ
bus (city)	(dong-kay)	(གྲོང་ཁྱེར་)
	chi-chö lâng-kho	སྤྱི་སྤྱོད་རླངས་འཁོར་
bus (intercity)	(dong-kay nâng-ku)	(གྲོང་ཁྱེར་ནང་ཁུལ་)
	do-khen	འགྲོ་མཁན
	chi-chö lâng-kho	སྤྱི་སྤྱོད་རླངས་འཁོར་

bus station	chi-chö lång-kho	བསྐོར་སྐུད་དགོས།
	bâb-tsoog	འབབ་ཚུགས།
bus stop	chi-chö lång-kho kâg-sa	བསྐོར་སྐུད་དགོས་བཀག་ས།
business	tsong	ཚོང་
businessperson	tsong-pa	ཚོང་པ་
busy	tay-wa	བྲེལ་བ་
but	yin-ma-yâng • yin-nay	ཡིན་མ་ཡང་
butterfly	chay-ma-leb	བྱེ་མ་ལེབ་
buttons	teb-ji	ཏེབ་ཇི་
to buy	nyo-wa	ཉོ་བ་

I'd like to buy ...
nga ... nyon-dhö yö ང་ ... ཉོན་འདོད་ཡོད།

Where can I buy a ticket?
ti-ka-si nyo-sa ka-bah yö-ray ཊི་ཀ་སི་ཉོ་ས་ག་བར་ཡོད་རེད།

C

cafe	cha (tsong-)khâng	ཇ་(ཚོང་)ཁང་
calendar	lo-tho	ལོ་ཐོ་
camera	par-chay	པར་ཆས་
camera operator	par gya-khen	པར་རྒྱག་མཁན་
camera shop	par (tsong-)khâng	པར་(ཚོང་)ཁང་
to camp	gur gyâb-nay dö-pa	གུར་བརྒྱབ་ནས་སྡོད་པ་

Can we camp here?
day gur gyâb-nay
de-na di-gi re-bay
འདིར་གུར་བརྒྱབ་ནས་བསྡད་
ན་འགྲིག་གི་རེད་པས།

| campsite | gur gyâb-sa sa-cha | གུར་བརྒྱབ་ས་ས་ཆ་ |
| can (to be able) | thoob-pa • nü-pa | ཐུབ་པ་ • ནུས་པ་ |

We can do it.
nga-tsö thoob-ki ray ང་ཚོས་ཐུབ་ཀྱི་རེད།

I can't do it.
ngay thoob-sa ma-ray ངས་ཐུབ་ས་མ་རེད།

can (aluminium)	châg-tin	ལྕགས་ཏིན་
can opener	châg-tin kha che-yak	ལྕགས་ཏིན་ཁ་ཕྱེ་ཡག
to cancel	chi-ten chay-pa	ཕྱིར་འཐེན་བྱེད་པ་
candle	yân-lah	ཡང་ལ་

car	mo-ta	མོ་ཊ
car owner's title	mo-ta dâg-pö ming	མོ་ཊ་བདག་པོའི་མིང
car registration	mo-tay teb-kye	མོ་ཊའི་དེབ་སྐྱེལ
to care (about)	sâb-sâb chay	གཟབ་གཟབ་བྱེད
to care (for someone)	tse-doong chay-pa	བརྩེ་གདུང་བྱེད་པ

caring	tse-doong-chen	བརྩེ་གདུང་ཅན
to carry	kay-wa	འཁྱེར་བ
carton	sho-gâm	ཤོག་སྒམ
cashier	ngü-nya	དངུལ་གཉེར
cassette	teb-tâg	སྒྲ་འཕྲིན
castle	khâr-zong	མཁར་རྫོང
cat	shi-mi	ཞི་མི
cathedral	ye-shu lha-khâng	ཡེ་ཤུ་ལྷ་ཁང
cave	dâg-phuk	བྲག་ཕུག
CD	si-di	སི་ཌི
to celebrate	ten-del chay	རྟེན་འབྲེལ་བྱེད
centimetre	sin-ti-mi-tar	སེན་ཊི་མི་ཊར
ceramic	za-sö	རྫ་བཟོས
certificate	lâg-kay	ལག་ཁྱེར
chair	koob-kyâg	ཀུབ་ཀྱག
chance (opportunity)	go-kâb	གོ་སྐབས
to change	je-wa • gyur-wa	བརྗེ་བ • འགྱུར་བ
change (coins)	ngü sil-ma je-wa	དངུལ་སིལ་མ་བརྗེ་བ
changing rooms	khâng-pa je-wa	ཁང་པ་བརྗེ་བ
charming	sem goog-pa	སེམས་འགུགས་པ
to chat up	kay-cha shö-pa	སྐད་ཆ་བཤད་པ
cheap	kay-po	ཁེ་པོ
to cheat	go-kor tong-wa	མགོ་སྐོར་གཏོང་བ

to check	shib-shay chay-pa	ཞིབ་བཤེར་བྱེད་པ
checkpoint	gâ-go	བཀག་སྒོ
cheese	chu-ra	ཕྱུར་ར
chemist	men tsong-khâng	སྨན་ཚོང་ཁང
chest	bâng-go	བྲང་ཁོག
chewing gum	gyik chi-ri	འཆིག་ཕྱི་རིལ
chicken	cha-te	བྱ་ཕྲུག

child/children	pu-gu	ཕྲུ་གུ
childminding	pu-gu ta-khen	ཕྲུ་གུ་ལྟ་མཁན་
chocolate	chok-let	ཅོག་ལེཊ་
to choose	dem-pa	འདེམས་པ་
Christian	yig-shu	ཡེ་ཤུ་
church	lha-khâng	ལྷ་ཁང་
cigarettes	tha-ma	ཐ་མག་
cigarette papers	tha-ma shu-gu	ཐ་མག་ཤོག་གུ་
cinema	lo-nyen	གློག་བརྙན་
citizenship	mi-say	མི་སེར་
city	dong-kay	གྲོང་ཁྱེར་
city centre	dong-kay-kyil	གྲོང་ཁྱེར་དཀྱིལ་
civil rights	mi-say thob-tâng	མི་སེར་ཐོབ་ཐང་
class	de-rim	གྲལ་རིམ་
clean	tsâng-ma	གཙང་མ་
client	tsong-shah	ཚོང་ཤག་
cliff	yang sah-po	གཡང་གཤགས་པོ་
to climb	zeg-pa	འཛེགས་པ་
clock	chu-tsö	ཆུ་ཚོད་
closed	go gyâb-pa	སྒོ་བརྒྱབས་པ་
clothing	du-log	དུག་ལོག་
clothing store	du-log tsong-khâng	དུག་ལོག་ཚོང་ཁང་
cloud	tin-pa	སྤྲིན་པ་
cloudy	tin thib-pa	སྤྲིན་བཏིབས་པ་
coins	pay-sha sil-ma	དངུལ་ཤག་སིལ་མ་
cold (n)	châm-pa	ཆམ་པ་
to have a cold	châm-pa gyâ-pa	ཆམ་པ་བརྒྱབ་པ་
cold (adj)	dâng-mo	གྲང་མོ་
cold water	chu dâng-mo	ཆུ་གྲང་མོ་

It's cold.
dâng-mo du   གྲང་མོ་འདུག

---

colleague	lay-rog	ལས་རོགས་
college	tho-lob	མཐོ་སློབ་
colour	tsön-dog	ཚོན་མདོག་
comb	gyook-shay	སྐྲ་ཤད་
to come	yong-wa	ཡོང་བ་
comfortable	kyi-po • de-po	སྐྱིད་པོ་ • བདེ་པོ་
communion	thun-mong-gi long-chö	ཐུན་མོང་གི་ལོངས་སྤྱོད་
communist	goong-ten ring-loog	གུང་བྲན་རིང་ལུགས་
companion	rog-pa	རོགས་པ་
company	so-tsong khâng	བཟོ་ཚོང་ཁང་
compass	chog-tön khor-lo	ཕྱོགས་སྟོན་འཁོར་ལོ་
computer	câm-pu-tah	གམ་པུ་ཊར་
computer games	câm-pu-tah tse-mo	གམ་པུ་ཊར་རྩེད་མོ་
concert	ro-yâng to-tön	རོལ་དབྱངས་སྒྲོ་སྟོན་

| confession (religious) | shag-pa | བཤགས་པ |
| to confirm (a booking) | ra-tö | ར་འཕྲོད |

Congratulations!
ta-shi de-lek བཀྲ་ཤིས་བདེ་ལེགས

conservative	lay-pa nying-pa	ལས་པ་རྙིང་པ
to be constipated	tsog-pa mi-bâb-pa	བཙོག་པ་མི་འབབ་པ
construction work	so-lay	བཟོ་ལས
consulate	dön-chö	དོན་གཅོད
contraception	kye-go gok-pa	སྐྱེ་སྒོ་འགོག་པ
contraceptives	kye-go gok-chay	སྐྱེ་སྒོ་འགོག་བྱེད
contract	gan-gya	གན་རྒྱ
convent	tsong-du kong-wa	ཚོགས་འདུ་ཁོང་པ
to cook	kha-la so-wa	ཁ་ལག་བཟོ་བ
cool (colloquial)	tsâb-tsoob may-pa	འཚབ་འཚུབ་མེད་པ
corner	sur	ཟུར
corrupt	lhay sho-wa	ལྷད་ཤོར་བ
to cost	gong gyâb-pa	གོང་རྒྱགས

How much does it cost to go to ...?
... doh-wa-la gong kâ-tsay ... འགྲོ་བ་ལ་གོང་ག་ཚོད
nay-ki ray གནས་ཀྱི་རེད

It costs a lot.
gong chen-po nay-ki ray གོང་ཆེན་པོ་གནས་ཀྱི་རེད

cotton	tin-bay	སྲིན་བལ
country	dong-seb	གྲོང་གསེབ
countryside	dong-seb-kü	གྲོང་གསེབ་ཁུལ
cough	lo	ལོ
to count	dâng-ga tsi-pa	གྲངས་ཀ་རྩི་པ
court (legal)	tim-khâng	ཁྲིམས་ཁང
cow	ba-choog	བ་ཕྱུགས
crafts	lâg-shay	ལག་ཤེས
crafty	yo-gyu tsa-po	གཡོ་རྒྱུ་ཚ་པོ
crag	dâg-rong	བྲག་རོང
crazy	nyön-pa	སྨྱོན་པ
credit card	bu-lön shog-jâng	བུ་ལོན་ཤོག་བྱང

Do you accept credit cards?
bu-lön shog-jâng-tog བུ་ལོན་ཤོག་བྱང་ཐོག
rim-pa tay-na di-gi re-bay སྤྲོད་ན་འགྲིག་གི་རེད་པས

cross (angry)	loong lâng-wa	ཁོང་ཁྲོ་བ
cup	ka-yö	དཀར་ཡོལ
current affairs	sân-gyur	གསར་འགྱུར
customs	gom-söl	གོམས་སྲོལ
to cut	toob-pa	གཏུབ་པ
to cycle	kâng ga-ri shön-pa	རྐང་སྒར་རི་ལ་འཛུལ་བ
cyclist	kâng ga-ri tong-khen	རྐང་སྒར་རི་ལ་གཏོང་མཁན

D

dad	pa-la	པ་ལགས
daily	nyin-tah	ཉིན་ལྟར
dairy products	kar-chu	དཀར་ཆུ
to dance	shay tâb-pa	གཞས་བཏབ་པ
dangerous	nyan-ga	ཉེན་ག
dark	nâ-goong	ནག་གྲུང
date (appointment)	dü-kâg	དུས་བཀག
date (time)	tshe-pa	ཚེས་པ
date of birth	kye-tse	སྐྱེ་ཚེས
to date (someone)	dü-kâg gya-pa	དུས་བཀག་རྒྱགས
daughter	bu-mo	བུ་མོ
dawn	nâm lâng-dü	ནམ་ལངས་དུས
day	nyin-ma	ཉིན
day after tomorrow	nâng-nyin	གནངས་ཉིན
day before yesterday	kay nyin-mo	ཁེ་ཉིན་མོ
in (six) days	nyin (doog) nâng	ཉིན་（དྲུག）ནང
dead	shi-wa	ཤི་བ
deaf	wön-ba	འོན་བ
to deal	de-wa chay-pa	འབྲེལ་བ་བྱེད་པ
death	chi-wa	འཆི་བ
to decide	tâg-chö chay-pa	ཐག་ཆོད་བྱེད་པ
deep	ting	གཏིང
deforestation	shing-na may-pa so-wa	ཤིང་ནགས་མེད་པ་བཟོ་བ
delay	gyâng-wa	འགྱངས་བ
delirious	sem-toog chem-po	སེམས་འཁྲུགས་ཆེན་པོ
democracy	mâng-tso ring-loog	དམངས་གཙོ་རིང་ལུགས
demonstration	ngâm-tön	ངམ་སྟོན
dental floss	so-trü dar-kü	སོ་འཕྲུད་དར་སྐུད
dentist	so ahm-chi	སོ་ཨེམ་ཆི
to deny	kay-len mi-chay-pa	ཁས་ལེན་མི་བྱེད་པ
deodorant	lü-di gok-men	ལུས་དྲི་འགོག་སྨན་དྲི་ཡོ་དོ་རེན
	di-yo do-ren	
to depart (leave)	chi thön-pa	ཕྱིར་ཐོན་པ
department store	de-tsen tsong-khâng	སྡེ་ཚན་ཚོང་ཁང
departure	thön-yak	ཐོན་ཡག
descendant	mi-gyü	མི་རྒྱུད
desert	chay-tâng	བྱེ་ཐང
design	cha-shi ding-wa	འཆར་གཞི་འདིང་བ
destination	leb-sa	སླེབས་ས

to destroy	tor-shi tong-wa	གཏོར་བཤིག་གཏོང་བ
detail	shib-ta	ཞིབ་ཕྲ
diabetic	chay-ma ka-ray na-tsa	བྱེ་མ་ཀ་རའི་ནཚ
diaper (nappy)	pu-gü chu-den	པུ་གུའི་ཆུ་གདན
diarrhoea	nyàng-shay	རྙིང་ཤལ
diary	nyin-to gö-teb	ཉིན་ཐོ
dice/die	sho	ཤོ
dictionary	tshing-dzö	ཚིག་མཛོད
different	mi-da-wa	མི་འདྲ་བ
difficult	khâg-po	ཁག་པོ
dinner	gong-da kha-la	དགོང་དག་ཁ་ལག
direct	ka-thoog	ཁ་ཐུག
director	wu-zin	དབུ་འཛིན
dirty	tsog-ba-chen	བཙོག་པ་ཅན
disabled	wàng-po kyön-chen	དབང་པོ་སྐྱོན་ཅན
disadvantage	kyön	སྐྱོན
discount	gong châg-pa	གོང་ཆག་པ
to discover	tsay-wa	འཚལ་བ
discrimination	ten-kye • yen-je	འབྱེད་འབྱིར་ • དབྱེ་འབྱེད
disease	nay	ནད
diving	chu-ting do-wa	ཆུ་གཏིང་འགྲོ
dizzy	goh-yu kho-wa	མགོ་ཡུ་འཁོར་བ
to do	chay-ya	བྱེད་ཡག

What are you doing?
kâ-ray chay-ki yö
ག་རེ་བྱེད་ཀྱི་ཡོད

I didn't do it.
ngay chay-gyu ma-choong
ངས་བྱེད་རྒྱུ་མ་བྱུང

doctor	ahm-chi	ཨམ་ཆི
dog	kyi	ཁྱི
dole (unemployment benefits)	lay-may-phog	ལས་མེད་ཕོགས
door	go	སྒོ
dope (drugs)	si-men • nye-tha	བསི་སྨན་ • ཉེ་ཐག
double	nyi-tsâg • nyi-dâb	ཉིས་ཚག་ • ཉིས་ལྡབ
double bed	mi-nyi shong-say nye-ti	མི་གཉིས་ཤོང་སའི་ཉལ་ཁྲི
double room	mi-nyi dö-say khâng-mi	མི་གཉིས་སྡོད་སའི་ཁང་མིག
downhill	too	ཐུར
dozen	dar-tsen	བདར་ཚན
drama	tâb-shoong • dhö-gar	འཁྲབ་གཞུང་ • བྲོ་གར
dramatic	dhö-ga tâb-pa tar	བྲོ་གར་འཁྲབ་པ་ལྟར
to dream	mi-lâm tong-wa	རྨི་ལམ་གཏོང་བ
dress	mo-chay	མོ་ཆས
drink	toong-ya	འཐུང་ཡག

201

to drink	toong-wa	འཐུང་བ
to drive	mo-ta tong-wa	མོ་ཊ་གཏོང་བ
drivers licence	mo-ta tong-ya lâg-kay	མོ་ཊ་གཏོང་ཡག་ལག་ཁྱེར
drug(s)	si-men	བསི་སྨན
drug addiction	si-men sa-ya	བསི་སྨན་ཟ་ཡ་ལས་སྐུལ་ལྭང་ཤོར་བ
	kya-lâng sho-wa	
drums	nga	རྔ
to be drunk	ra si-wa	ར་བཟི་བ
to dry (clothes)	(du-log) kâm-po so-wa	(དུག་ལོག)སྐམ་པོ་བཟོ་བ
dummy (pacifier)	jib-ru	འཇིབ་རུ

E

each	re-re	རེ་རེ
ear	ahm-chog	ཨམ་ཅོག
early	nga-po	སྔ་པོ
earrings	ahm-cho-gyen	ཨམ་ཅོག་རྒྱན

It's early.
nga-po ray-sha སྔ་པོ་རེད་ཤག

---

ears	ahm-chog	ཨམ་ཅོག
Earth	sa	ས
earth (soil)	sa	ས
earthquake	sa-yom	ས་ཡོམ
east	shâr	ཤར
easy	lay-la-po	ལས་སླ་པོ
to eat	sa-wa	ཟ་བ
economy	pay-jor	དཔལ་འབྱོར
education	shay-yön • lob-jong	ཤེས་ཡོན • སློབ་སྦྱོང
elections	wö-dem	འོས་འདེམས
electricity	log	གློག
elevator (lift)	log ken-za	གློག་སྐས་འཛེགས
embarrassed	ka kyeng-pa	ཁ་སྐྱེངས་པ
embassy	shoong-tsab	གཞུང་ཚབ
emergency	za-dâg	ཟ་དྲག
employee	lay-chay-pa	ལས་བྱེད་པ
employer	lay-ka trö-khen	ལས་ཀ་སྤྲོད་མཁན
empty	tong-pa	སྟོང་པ
end	ta-joog	མཇུག་འཇུག
to end	ta-joog dil-wa	མཇུག་འཇུག་སྒྲིལ་བ
endangered	tsa-tong do-way nyen-ga	རྩ་སྟོང་འགྲོ་བའི་ཉེན
species	leb-pay sem-chen	ཁ་སྤྲོ་བའི་སེམས་ཅན
engine	trü-kho ah-ma	འཕྲུལ་འཁོར་ཨ་མ
English	in-ji	དབྱིན་ཇི

to enjoy (oneself)	(rang-râng) kyi-po tong-wa	(རང་རང་)སྐྱིད་པོ་གཏོང་བ
enough	dig-pa	འགྲིགས་པ

Enough!		འགྲིགས་སོང
dig-song		

to enter	zü-pa	འཛུལ་བ
entertaining	nâng-wa kyi-kyi	སྣང་བ་སྐྱིད་སྐྱིད
envelope	yi-gok	ཡིག་སྒྲོམ
environment	khor-yoog	ཁོར་ཡུག
epileptic	sa-dib	གནས་གྲིབ
equal opportunity	thob-tâng da-nyâm	ཐོབ་ཐང་འདྲ་མཉམ
equality	da-nyâm	འདྲ་མཉམ
equipment	lâg-cha	ལག་ཆ
European	eu-rop-mi	ཡུ་རོབ་མི
euthanasia	jâm-sö • jâm-shi	འཇམ་གསོད • འཇམ་ཤི
evening	gong-da	དགོང་དག
every day	nyin-tar	ཉིན་ལྟར
example	pay	དཔེ

For example ...		དཔེ་བཞག་ན ...
pay sha-na ...		

excellent	pay-mi-si yâk-po	དཔེ་མི་སྲིད་ཡག་པོ
exchange	je-len	བརྗེ་ལེན
to exchange	je-len gya-pa	བརྗེ་ལེན་རྒྱག་པ
exchange rate	ngü-je-gong	དངུལ་བརྗེ་གོང
excluded	khong-nay bü-pa	ཁོངས་ནས་འབུད་པ

Excuse me.		དགོངས་དག
gong-da		

to exhibit	dem-tön chay-pa	འགྲེམས་སྟོན་བྱེད་པ
exhibition	dem-tön	འགྲེམས་སྟོན
exit	dön-sa	དོན་ས
expensive	gong chen-po	གོང་ཆེན་པོ
to express (one's view)	tön-pa	སྟོན་པ
express mail	nyur-kye-dâg	མྱུར་སྐྱེལ་སྦྲག
eye	mig	མིག

F

face	dong	གདོང་
face cloth (flannel)	dong chi-ray	གདོང་ཕྱིས་རས་
factory	so-ta	བཟོ་གྲྭ་
factory worker	so-ta lay-ka chay-khen	བཟོ་གྲྭ་ལས་ཀ་བྱེད་མཁན་
fall (autumn)	tön-ga	སྟོན་ཁ་
family	mi-tshång	མི་ཚང་
famous	kay-ta chem-po	སྐད་གྲགས་ཆེན་པོ་
fan (hand-held)	loong-yâb	རླུང་གཡབ་
fan (machine)	loong-khoh	རླུང་འཁོར་
fans (of a team)	ga-po chay-khen	དགའ་པོ་བྱེད་མཁན་
far	ta ring-po	ཐག་རིང་པོ་
farm	shing-ga	ཞིང་ག་
farmer	shing-pa	ཞིང་པ་
fast	gyok-po	མགྱོགས་པོ་
fat	gyâk-pa	རྒྱགས་པ་
father	pa-pha	པ་ཕ་
fault (someone's)	non-trü	ནོར་འཁྲུལ་
faulty	kyön sho-wa	སྐྱོན་ཤོར་བ་
fear	shay-nâng	ཞེད་སྣང་
to feel	tsor-wa • nyong-wa	ཚོར་བ་ • མྱོང་བ་
feelings	tsor-wa	ཚོར་བ་
fence	châg-ri	ལྕགས་རི་
fencing	ti-tse tse-wa	གྲི་རྩེད་རྩེ་བ་
festival	dü-chen	དུས་ཆེན་

It's foggy.
moog-pa tig-sha

སྨུག་པ་འཐིབས་ཤག

---

fever	tsha-wa	ཚ་བ་
few	nyoong-shay	ཉུང་ཤས་
fiance(e)	long-chång sin-pay na-ma • mâg-pa	ལོང་ཆང་ཟིན་པའི་ མནའ་མ་ • མགཔ་
fiction	tog-sö	རྟོག་བཟོ་
field	shing-ga	ཞིང་ག་
fight	gyâk-re	རྒྱག་རེས་
to fight	gyâk-re gyâk-pa	རྒྱག་རེས་རྒྱག་པ་
to fill	gyong-wa	སྐྱོང་བ་
film (camera)	phing-sho	ཕིང་ཤོག
film (cinema)	log-nyen	གློག་བརྙན་
filtered	tsâg gyâk-pa	འཚག་རྒྱག་པ་
to find	tsay-wa	བཙལ་བ་
fine (money)	chay-pa	ཆད་པ་
finger	zu-gu	མཛུབ་གུ་
fire	may	མེ་

firewood	may-shing	ཤིང་སྲེག
first	tâng-po	དང་པོ
first-aid kit	ka-toog bay-chö chay-ya men-chö yo-chay	ཁ་ཕུག་བདེ་སྐྱོང་བྱེད་ཡག སྨན་བཅོས་ཡོ་ཆས
fish (alive)	nya	ཉ
fish (as food)	nya-sha	ཉ་ཤ
fish shop	nya thong-khâng	ཉ་འཚོང་ཁང
flag	dar-chog	དར་ལྕོག
flannel (face cloth)	dong chi-ray	གདོང་ཕྱི་རས
flat (land etc)	sa thay-thay	ས་མཉམ་མཉམ
flea	kyi-shig	ཁྱི་ཤིག
flashlight (torch)	log-shu	གློག་ཤུ
flight	nâm-du do-ya	གནམ་གྲུ་འགྲོ་ཡག
floor	shay-la • pâng-chay	ཞལ་ལ • བང་གཅལ
floor (storey)	khâng-tog	ཁང་ཐོག
flour (wholemeal)	dro-shib	གྲོ་ཞིབ
flower	may-tog	མེ་ཏོག
fly	dâng-bu	སྦྲང་བུ

to follow	je-su dâng-wa	རྗེས་སུ་འབྲང་བ
food	kha-la	ཁ་ལག
foot	kâng-pa	རྐང་པ
football (soccer)	kâng-pol	རྐང་པོལ
footpath	kâng-lâm	རྐང་ལམ
foreign	chi-gye	ཕྱི་རྒྱལ
forest	shing-nâg	ཤིང་ནགས
forever	tâg-tu	རྟག་ཏུ
to forget	jay-pa	བརྗེད་པ

I forget.
ngay jay-sha   ངས་བརྗེད་ཤག

Forget about it; Don't worry!
kay chay-kiy ma-ray •   གང་བྱེད་ཀྱི་མ་རེད •
sem-tel ma-chay   སེམས་འཚབ་མ་བྱེད

---

to forgive	nying-je tâ-wa	སྙིང་རྗེ་བཏང་བ
fortnight	dün-ta nyi-re	བདུན་ཕྲག་གཉིས་རེ
fortune teller	ngön-shay shö-ken	མངོན་ཤེས་ཤོད་མཁན
free (not bound)	râng-wâng thob-pa	རང་དབང་འཐོབ་པ
free (of charge)	rin may-pa	རིན་མེད་པ
to freeze	kyâg choog-pa	འཁྱག་བཅུག་པ
friend	tok-po/tok-mo **(m/f)**	གྲོགས་པོ/གྲོགས་མོ
in front of	dün-lâ	མདུན་ལ
frozen foods	kyâk-teb kha-la	འཁྱགས་འབེབས་ཁ་ལག
full	kheng-pa	ཁེངས་པ
fun	nâng-wa kyi-kyi	སྣང་བ་སྐྱིད་སྐྱིད
for fun	nâng-wa kyi-kyi-chay	སྣང་བ་སྐྱིད་སྐྱིད་ཆེད

to have fun	ten-shig long-wa	བདེན་པའི་སྐྱོང་བ
to make fun of	gö long-ya	གོད་སྐྱོང་ཡག
funeral	ku-phoong kyel-wa	སྐུ་སྤུང་སྐྱེལ་བ
furnished	nâng-chay zom-pa	ནང་ཆའི་འཛོམས་པ
future	ma-wong-pa	མ་འོང་པ

G

game	tsay-mo	རྩེད་མོ
(games, sport)		
garage	za-re zo-re loog-sa	ཟ་རེ་ཟོ་རེ་ལུགས་ས་ཁང་པ
	khâng-pa	
garbage	gay-nyig	གད་སྙིགས
gardens	doom-ra	སྡུམ་ར
gas cylinder	gas gâm	གས་སྒམ
gate	go	སྒོ
general	chi-tâng	སྤྱིར་བཏང
gift	lâg-tâg	ལག་རྟགས
girl	bu-mo	བུ་མོ
girlfriend	tok-mo	གྲོགས་མོ
to give	trö-pa · te-wa	སྤྲོད་པ · སྟེར་བ

Could you give me ...?
ngah ... tay-da   ངར་ ... སྒྲད་དང

---

glass	ge-la-si	གྲ་ལ་སི
to go	doh-wa	འགྲོ་བ
to go out with	nyâm-tu chi-lo doh-wa	མཉམ་དུ་ཕྱི་ལོག་འགྲོ་བ

Let's go.
ta doh   ད་འགྲོ

We'd like to go to ...
ngân-tso ...-la don-dhö yö   ང་ཚོ ...ལར་འགྲོ་འདོད་ཡོད

Go straight ahead.
ka-toog do-shi   ཁ་ཐུག་འགྲོ་ཤིག

---

goal	mik-yü	དམིགས་ཡུལ
goalkeeper	go kâg-khen	སྒོ་བཀག་མཁན
goat	ra	ར
God	kön-chok	དཀོན་མཆོག
of gold	say-gi	གསེར་གྱི
good	yâg-po	ཡག་པོ

Good afternoon.		
chi-to de-lek		ཕྱི་དྲོ་བདེ་ལེགས།
Good evening.		
gong-to de-lek		དགོང་དྲོ་བདེ་ལེགས།
Good morning.		
nga-to de-lek		སྔ་དྲོ་བདེ་ལེགས།
Good night.		
sim-ja nâng-go		གཟིམ་འཇགས་གནང་གོ

government	shoong	གཞུང་
gram	ga-râm	སྒྲ་རམ་
grandchild	pu-gü pu-gu	ཕུ་གུ་ཕྲུ་གུ
grandfather	po-po	པོ་པོ་
grandmother	mo-mo	མོ་མོ་
grapes	gün-doom	རྒུན་འབྲུམ་
grass	tsa	རྩྭ་
grave	du-trö	དུར་ཁྲོད་
great	chen-po	ཆེན་པོ་

Great!	
yâk-po choong-sha	ཡག་པོ་བྱུང་ཤ

green	jâng-gu	ལྗང་གུ
greengrocer	ngo-tse tsong-khâng	སྔོ་ཚེ་ཚོང་ཁང་
grey	kya-wo	སྐྱ་བོ་
to guess	tsö-pâg chay-pa	ཚོད་དཔག་བྱེད་པ་
guide (person)	lâm-tön-pa	ལམ་སྟོན་པ་
guidebook	lâm-tön-teb	ལམ་སྟོན་དེབ་
guide dog	long-wa ti-khen-kyi	ལོང་བ་འཁྲིད་མཁན་གྱི་
guided trek	kâng-lâm do de-po	རྐང་ལམ་འགྲོ་བདེ་པོ་
guitar	da-nyan • pi-wâng	སྒྲ་སྙན • པི་ཝང་
gym	lü-tse	ལུས་རྩལ་
gymnastics	lü-tse-gi	ལུས་རྩལ་གྱི

H

hair	ta	སྐྲ་
hairbrush	ta-shay phâg-se	སྐྲ་ཤད་ཕག་སེ་
half	chay-ka	ཕྱེད་ཀ་
half a litre	li-tar chay-ka	ལི་ཊར་ཕྱེད་ཀ་
to hallucinate	trü-nâng shâ-wa	འཁྲུལ་སྣང་ཤར་བ་
ham	phâg-sha dü-ma	ཕག་ཤ་བསྡུས་མ་
hammer	tho-wa	ཐོ་བ་

hand	lâg-pa	ལག་པ།
handbag	lâg-kay bag-la	ལག་འཁྱེར་འབེགས་ལ།
handicrafts	lâg-shay	ལག་ཤེས།
handmade	lâg-sö	ལག་བཟོས།
handsome	zay-po	མཛེས་པོ།
happy	kyi-po	སྐྱིད་པོ།

Happy Birthday!
kye-kah-nyin ta-shi de-lek
སྐྱེས་སྐར་ཉིན་བཀྲ་ཤིས་བདེ་ལེགས།

harbour	dru-ka	གྲུ་ཁ།
hard (not soft)	teg-po	མཁྲེགས་པོ།
harness	ta-chay	རྟ་ཆས།
harassment	nye-chö	གཉའ་ཚོས།
to have	yö-pa	ཡོད་པ།

Do you have ...?
kay-râng-la ... yö-bay
ཁྱེད་རང་ལ ... ཡོད་པས།

I have ...
nga-la ... yö
ང་ལ ... ཡོད།

he	kho	ཁོ།
head	go	མགོ།
headache	go-na	མགོ་ནད།
health	trö-ten	འཕྲོད་བསྟེན།
to hear	ahm-chog go-wa	ཨམ་ཅོག་གོ་བ།
heart	nying	སྙིང་།
heat	tsha-wa	ཚ་བ།
heater	tsha-log	ཚ་ལོག
heavy	ji-kog	ལྗིད་ཏིག

Hello.
ta-shi de-lek
བཀྲ་ཤིས་བདེ་ལེགས།

Hello! (answering telephone)
ha-lo
ཧ་ལོ།

| helmet | châg sha-mo | ལྕགས་ཞྭ་མོ། |
| to help | rog nâng-wa | རོགས་གནང་བ། |

Help!
rog nâng-da
རོགས་གནང་དང་།

herbs	men-tsa	སྨན་རྩ
herbalist	men-tsa kay-pa	སྨན་རྩ་མཁས་པ
here	day	འདིར
heroin	nye-tha hi-ro-yen	ཉལ་ཐ་ཧི་རོ་ཡེན
heroin addict	nye-tha hi-ro-yen-la	ཉལ་ཐ་ཧི་རོ་ཡེན་ལ་སྒྲུག་ཡོང
	kyâg-lâng shoh tsa-khen	དེད་ཆར་ཚར་མཁན
high (altitude)	tho-po	མཐོ་པོ
high school	tho-rim lob-ta	མཐོ་རིམ་སློབ་གྲྭ
to hike	kâng-drö gyâk-pa	རྐང་འགྲོས་རྒྱག་པ
hiking boots	kâng-drö gyâk-dü	རྐང་འགྲོས་རྒྱག་དུས
	gyön-ya lhâm-ko	གྱོན་ཡག་ལྷམ་ཀོ
hiking routes	kâng-drö lâm	རྐང་འགྲོས་ལམ
hill	ri	རི
Hindu	hin-du	ཧིན་དུ
to hire	yâr-wa	གཡར་བ
to hitchhike	drü-pa tay-po ten-nay	འགྲུལ་པ་མཐེལ་པོ་བསྟན་ནས
	mo-ta-nâng do-wa	མོ་ཊ་ནང་འགྲོ
holiday (vacation)	goong-seng	གུང་གསེང
homeless	kyim-may	ཁྱིམ་མེད
homosexual	phö pho-la châg-pa chay-pa	ཕོ་ཕོ་ལ་ཆགས་པ་བྱེད་པ
honey	dâng-tsi	སྦྲང་རྩི
horrible	dhuk-cha	སྡུག་ཆགས
horse	ta	རྟ
horse riding	ta shön-pa	རྟ་བཞོན་པ
hospital	men-khâng	སྨན་ཁང
private hospital	gay-gi men-khâng	སྒེར་གྱི་སྨན་ཁང
hot	tsha-po	ཚ་པོ
hot water	chu tsha-po	ཆུ་ཚ་པོ

| It's hot. | | |
| tsha-po du | ཚ་པོ་འདུག |

to be hot	tsha-wa	ཚ་བ
house	khâng-pa	ཁང་པ
housework	nâng-lay	ནང་ལས
how	kân-te-si	གང་འདྲས་ཤེ

How do I get to ...?	
...la kân-te-si do-gö-ray	...ལ་གང་འདྲས་ཤེ་འགྲོ་དགོས་རེད
How do you say ...?	
... kân-te-si lâb-gö-ray	... གང་འདྲས་ལབ་དགོ་རེད

hug	tse-way thâm-pa	བརྩེ་བས་འཐམ་པ
human rights	do-wa-mee thob-tâng	འགྲོ་བ་མིའི་ཐོབ་ཐང
hundred	gya • gya tâm-pa	བརྒྱ/བརྒྱ་ཐམ་པ

to be hungry	drö-kog tog-pa	བྲོད་ཁོག་རྟོགཔ་
in a hurry	tay-way ngâng	ཐེལ་འཕྱི་རང་
husband	kyo-ga	ཁྱོ་ག་

I

ice	kyâg-pa	འཁྱགཔ་
ice axe	kyâg-pa cho-ya ta-re	འཁྱགཔ་གཅོད་ཡག་ལྟ་སྟེ་
ice cream	kyâg-pa ngâ-mo	འཁྱགཔ་མངར་མོ་
identification	ngo-trö	ངོ་སྤྲོད་
identification card	ngo-trö lâg-kay	ངོ་སྤྲོད་ལག་ཁྱེར་
idiot	len-ta-chen	གླེན་རྟ་ཅན་
if	kay-te	གལ་ཏེ་
ill	na-wa	ན་བ་
immigration	chi-gye-la shi châg-pa	ཕྱི་རྒྱལ་ལ་གཞིས་ཆགས་པ་
important	kay-chen-po	གལ་ཆེན་པོ་

It's important.
kay-chen-po ray གལ་ཆེན་པོ་རེད་

It's not important.
kay-chen-po ma-ray གལ་ཆེན་པོ་མ་རེད་

included	nâng-tshü	ནང་ཚུད་
incomprehensible	lö pog mi-thoob-pa	བློ་རྡོགས་མི་ཐུབ་པོ་
indicator	dâ tong-ya	བརྡ་གཏོང་ཡག་
indigestion	kha-la mi-ju-wa	ཁ་ལག་མི་འཇུ་བ་
industry	so-dra	བཟོ་གྲྭ་
inequality	da-nyâm may-pa	འདྲ་མཉམ་མེད་པ་
to inject	men-khâb gyâk-pa	སྨན་ཁབ་རྒྱགཔ་
injection	men-khâb	སྨན་ཁབ་
injury	may-kyön	རྨས་སྐྱོན་
inside	nâng-lâ	ནང་ལ་
instructor	lob-tön-pa	སློབ་སྟོནཔ་
insurance	in-shu-ren gan-gya	ཨིན་ཤུ་རེན་འགན་རྒྱ་
intense	shoog-ta chem-po	ཤུགས་དྲག་ཆེམ་པོ་
interesting	nâng-wa dro-po	སྣང་བ་དགའ་པོ་
international	gya-chee	རྒྱལ་སྤྱི་
interview	ngo-toog di-len shu-wa	ངོ་ཐུག་འདྲི་ལེན་ཞུ་བ་
island	tso-ling	མཚོ་གླིང་
itch	sâb-ra lâng-wa	ཟ་ར་ལང་བ་
itinerary	drü-shü dü-tsö re-mik	འགྲུལ་བཞུད་དུས་ཚོད་རེའུ་མིག་

J

jail	tsön-khâng	བཙོན་ཁང་
jealous	tâg-tog	ཕྲག་དོག་
jeans	jeen	ཇིན་

jeep	mo-ta jeep	མོ་ཊ་འཇིབ
jewellery	gyen-jâ	རྒྱན་ཆ
job	lay-ka	ལས་ཀ
joke	gö toh-po	བཞད་གདོང
to joke	gö long-wa	བཞད་གད་ལོང་བ
journalist	sar-gö-pa	གསར་འགོད་པ
journey	drü-kyö	འགྲུལ་སྐྱོད
judge	tim-pön	ཁྲིམས་དཔོན
juice	shing-toh khu-wa	ཤིང་ཏོག་ཁུ་བ
to jump	chong-wa	མཆོང་བ
jumper (sweater)	ba-len • o-mo-sü tö-toong	སྤུ་ལེན • ཨུ་མོའི་སྤུའི་སྟོད་ཐུང
justice	dâng-dhen	དྲང་བདེན

K

key	di-mig	ལྡེ་མིག
kick	dhog-gya	རྡོག་རྒྱག
to kill	sö-pa	བསད་པ
kilogram	ki-lo-ga-râm	ཀེ་ལོ་གྲམ
kilometre	ki-lo-mi-tar	ཀེ་ལོ་མི་ཏར
kind	sem sâng-po	སེམས་བཟང་པོ
kindergarten	chi-so-khâng	ཕྱི་སོ་ཁང
king	gyal-po	རྒྱལ་པོ
kiss	kha-kye • woh	ཁ་སྐྱེ • ཨོ
to kiss	kha kye-wa • woh chay-pa	ཁ་སྐྱེ་བ • ཨོ་བྱེད་པ
kitchen	thâb-tsang	ཐབ་ཚང
kitten	shim-toog	ཞིམ་ཐུག
knapsack	phay-kok	ཕད་ཀོག
knee	pü-mo	པུས་མོ
knife	ti	གྲི
to know	ha go-wa	ཧ་གོ་བ

I don't know.	
ha go-ki-may	ཧ་གོ་གི་མེད

L

lace	ju-toh	འཇུར་སྒྲོག
lake	tsho	མཚོ
lamp	shu-mah	བུས་མར
land	sa-cha	ས་ཆ
language	kay-yig	སྐད་ཡིག
large	chen-po	ཆེན་པོ
last	tha-ma	མཐའ་མ
last month	da-wa ngön-ma	ཟླ་བ་སྔོན་མ
last night	ka-sa gong-ta	ཁ་ས་དགོང་དག
last week	dün-ta ngön-ma	བདུན་ཕྲག་སྔོན་མ
last year	lo ngön-ma	ལོ་སྔོན་མ

late	chi-po	ཕྱི་པོ
laugh	gay-mo shor-wa	གད་མོ་ཤོར་བ
laundry	tu-log trü-khâng	དག་ལོག་འཁྲུད་ཁང་
law	tim	ཁྲིམས
lawyer	tim-tsö-pa	ཁྲིམས་རྩོད་པ
lazy	nyob-to • lay-lo-chen	ཉོབ་ཏོ • ལས་ལོ་ཅན
leader	go-ti	འགོ་འཁྲིད
to learn	châng-wa	སྦྱང་བ
leather	ko-wa	ཀོ་བ
leather goods	gyu-cha ko-wa	རྒྱུ་ཆ་ཀོ་བ
to be left (behind/over)	gyâb-la shâg-pa • shâg-pa	རྒྱབ་ལ་བཞག་པ • བཞག་པ
left (not right)	yön	གཡོན
left-wing	yön-chog sho-kak	གཡོན་ཕྱོགས་ཤོ་ཁག
leg	kâng-pa	རྐང་པ
legalisation	tim-tün	ཁྲིམས་མཐུན
legislation	cha-tim	བཅའ་ཁྲིམས
lens	par-shay	པར་ཤེལ
lesbian	mö mo-la châg-pa	མོས་མོ་ལ་ཆགས་པ་བྱེད་མཁན
	chay-khen	
less	nyoong-wa	ཉུང་བ
letter	yi-ge	ཡི་གེ
liar	kyâg-zün shö-khen	སྐྱག་རྫུན་ཤོད་མཁན
library	pan-zö-khâng	དཔེ་མཛོད་ཁང་
lice	shig	ཤིག
to lie	kyâg-zün shö-pa	སྐྱག་རྫུན་ཤོད་པ
life	tse • sog	ཚེ • སྲོག
lift (elevator)	log ken-za	གློག་སྐས་འཛེགས
light (bright)	kar-cha	དཀར་ཆ
light (weight)	yang-po	ཡང་པོ
light (sun/lamp)	wö	འོད
light (clear)	tsön-shi tâng-po	མཚོན་གཞི་དྭངས་པོ
light bulb	log shay-tog	གློག་ཤེལ་ཏོག
lighter	may-par-yak	མེ་སྤར་ཡག
to like	ga-po chay	དགའ་པོ་བྱེད
line	thig	ཐིག
lips	chu-toh	མཆུ་ཏོ
lipstick	chu-toh choog-ya tsö	མཆུ་ཏོ་བྱུག་ཡག་ཚོས
to listen	ahm-chog nyen-pa	ཨམ་ཅོག་ཉན་པ
little (small)	choong-choong	ཆུང་ཆུང
a little (amount)	nyoong-nyoong	ཉུང་ཉུང
to live (somewhere)	dhö-pa	སྡོད་པ

Long live ...!
... ku-tse ten-pa-sho

... སྐུ་ཚེ་བརྟན་པར་ཤོག

---

local	sa-nay	ས་གནས
local city bus	dong-kay nâng-kü	གྲོང་ཁྱེར་ནང་ཁུལ་འགྲོ་མཁན་
	do-khen chi-chö lâng-kho	སྤྱི་སྤྱོད་རླངས་འཁོར

location	sa-chog	ས་ཆོགས
lock	gon-châg	སྒོ་ལྕགས
to lock	gon-châg gyâk-pa	སྒོ་ལྕགས་རྒྱག་པ
long	ring-po	རིང་པོ
long distance	sa-tâg ring-po	ས་ཐག་རིང་པོ
long-distance bus	sa-tâg ring-po do-khen chi-chö lâng-kho	ས་ཐག་རིང་པོ་འགྲོ་མཁན་སྤྱི་སྤྱོད་ལྡང་འཁོར
to look	mik ta-wa	མིག་ལྟ་བ
to look after	je-la mik ta-wa	རྗེས་ལ་མིག་ལྟ་བ
to look for	la mik-ta-wa	ལ་མིག་ལྟ་བ
loose change	see-ma	སིལ་མ
to lose	lâg-pa	རླགས
loser	phâm-khen	ཕམ་མཁན
loss	gyong	གྱོང

Get lost!
phah gyook-shi

ཕར་རྒྱུགས་ཤིག

a lot	mâng-po	མང་པོ
loud	kay-shoog chen-po	སྐད་ཤུགས་ཆེན་པོ
to love	ga-po chay	དགའ་པོ་བྱེད
lover	ga-po chay-khen	དགའ་པོ་བྱེད་མཁན
low	mah-po	དམའ་པོ
loyal	sha-shen-chen	ཞ་ཞེན་ཅན
luck	lâm-do • loong-ta	ལམ་འགྲོ • རླུང་རྟ
lucky	loong-ta tho-po	རླུང་རྟ་མཐོ་པོ
luggage	tog-tay	དོ་པོ་ཆས
luggage lockers	tog-tay gon-châg	དོ་པོ་ཆས་སྒོ་ལྕགས
left luggage	tog-tay shâg-pa	དོ་པོ་ཆས་བཞག་པ
lump	boor-tog	འབུར་ཐོག
lunch	nyin-goong kha-la	ཉིན་གུང་ཁ་ལ
lunchtime	nyin-goong kha-la dü-tsö	ཉིན་གུང་ཁ་ལ་དུས་ཚོད
luxury	ha-châng kyi-po	ཧ་ཅང་སྐྱིད་པོ

M

machine	trü-khor	འཕྲུལ་འཁོར
mad	nyön-pa	སྨྱོན་པ
made (of)	sö-pay	བཟོས་པའི
magazine	dü-teb	དུས་དེབ
magician	jâ-du tön-khen • gyu-ma-khen	ཇ་འདུ་སྟོན་མཁན • སྒྱུ་མ་མཁན
mail	dâg	དྭགས
mailbox	dâg-gâm	དྭགས་སྒམ
main road	lâm-chen	ལམ་ཆེན
main square	mi-mâng zom-sa te-wa	མི་དམངས་འཛོམས་ས་སྟེ་བ

majority	mâng-che-wa	ཨང་ཆེ་བ
to make	so-wa	བཟོ་བ
make-up	gün-sâb	གྲུན་གསལ
man	pho	ཕོ
manager	u-zihn	དབུ་འཛིན
manual worker	nge-tsö lay-ka chay-khen	ངང་རྩོལ་ལས་ཀ་བྱེད་མཁན
many	mâng-po	ཨང་པོ
map	sâp-ta	ས་བཀྲ

Can you show me on the map?
(sâp-ta di-nâng) tön nâng-da   (ས་བཀྲ་འདི་ནང་) སྟོན་གནང་དང |

marijuana	nye-ta may-ra wa-na	ཉལ་མ་མེ་ར་ཝ་ན
marital status	châng-sa gyâb yö-may	ཆང་ས་བརྒྱབ་ཡོད་མེད
	nay-bâb	གནས་བབ
market	trom	ཁྲོམ
marriage	châng-sa	ཆང་ས
to marry	châng-sa gyâk-pa	ཆང་ས་རྒྱག་པ
marvellous	hang-sâng yâk-po	ཧང་སང་ཡག་པོ
massage	lü phur-nye tong-wa	ལུས་ཕུར་མཉེ་གཏོང་བ
mat	sa-den	ས་གདན
to match	chig-pa	གཅིག་པ
matches	tsâg-ta • mu-si	ཚག་ཏ • མུ་ཟེ

It doesn't matter.
kay chay-ki ma-ray   གལ་བྱེད་ཀྱི་མ་རེད |

What's the matter?
kâ-ray chay song   ག་རེ་བྱས་སོང |

mattress	bö-den	འབོལ་གདན
maybe	chig chay-na	གཅིག་བྱས་ན
mayor	dong-kay mi-pön	གྲོང་ཁྱེར་མི་དཔོན
mechanic	trü-lay-pa	འཁྲུལ་ལས་པ
medal	tâg-ma	རྟགས་མ
medicine	men	སྨན
meditation	gom	སྒོམ
to meet	thoog-tay chay-pa	ཐུག་འཕྲད་བྱེད་པ
member	tsog-mi	ཚོགས་མི
menstruation	dha-tsen	ཟླ་མཚན
menu	kha-la-tho	ཁ་ལག་ཐོ
message	kha-len	ཁ་ལན
metal	châg	ལྕགས
meteor	nâm-dho	གནམ་རྡོ
metre	mi-tar	མི་ཏར

midnight	tsen-goong	མཚན་གུང་
migraine	go-se na-tsa	མགོ་ཡེར་ནཚ
military service	dâ-mâg shâb-shu	དམག་དམག་ཞབས་ཞུ
milk	oh-ma	འོ་མ
millimetre	mi-li-mi-tar	མི་ལི་མི་ཏར
million	sa-ya-chig	ས་ཡ་གཅིག
mind	sem	སེམས
mineral water	te-chu	གཏེར་ཆུ
minute (time)	ka-ma-chig	སྐར་མ་གཅིག
in (five) minutes	ka-ma (ngay) nâng	སྐར་མ་(ལྔའི་)ནང

Just a minute.
teh-si gu-ah ཐེངས་ཅིག་བསྒུག་ཨ

---

mirror	shay-go	ཤེལ་སྒོ
miscarriage	pu-gu nge-nay shor-wa	ཕྲུ་གུ་ངེས་ནས་ཤོར་བ
to miss (feel absence)	den-pa	དྲན་པ
mistake	non-trül	ནོར་འཁྲུལ
to mix	se-wa • toog-pa	སྲེ་བ་•་དགུགས་པ
mobile phone	lâg-pa kye-ya kha-pa	ལག་པར་འཁྱེར་ཡ་ཁ་པར
modem	mo-dem	མོ་ཌེམ
moisturising cream	shâb-sö	ཞབས་སོས
monastery	gom-pa	དགོན་པ
money	ngü	དངུལ
monk	ta-pa	གྲྭ་པ
month	da-wa	ཟླ་བ
this month	da-wa-di	ཟླ་བ་འདི
monument	den-ten	རྟེན་རྟེན
moon	da-wa	ཟླ་བ
more	mâng-wa	མང་བ
morning	nga-toh	སྔ་དྲོ
mosque	kha-che lha-khâng	ཁ་ཆེ་ལྷ་ཁང
mosquito	duk-drâng	དུག་སྦྲང
mosquito coil	doog-dâng-pö	དུག་སྦྲང་པོས
mosquito net	nye-gur	ཉེ་གུར
mother	ah-ma	ཨ་མ
motorboat	trü-khor-dru	འཕྲུལ་འཁོར་གྲུ
motorcycle	bâhg-bâhg	སྤག་སྤག
mountain	ri	རི
mountain bike	ri shön-ya kâng-ga-ri	རི་འཞོན་ཡག་རྐང་སྐྱ་རིལ
mountain path	ri-lâm	རི་ལམ
mountain range	ri-gyü	རི་རྒྱུད
mountaineering	ri gâng zâg-ya	རི་སྒང་འཛེགས་ཡག
mouse	tsi-tsi	ཙི་ཙི
mouth	kha	ཁ
movie	log-nyen	གློག་བརྙན
mud	dâm-pâg	འདམ་འག

mum	ah-ma	ཨ་མ
muscle	sha-gyü	ཤ་རྒྱུད
museum	dem-tön-khâng	འགྲེམས་སྟོན་ཁང
music	rö-ja	རོལ་ཆ
musician	rö-ja tong-khen	རོལ་ཆ་གཏོང་མཁན
Muslim	kha-che	ཁ་ཆེ
mute	koog-pa	ཀུག་པ

N

name	ming	མིང
nappy (diaper)	chu-den	ཆུ་གདན
nappy rash	chu-den thor-sib	ཆུ་གདན་ཐོར་སིབ
national park	mi-mâng ling-ga	མི་དམངས་གླིང་ག
nationality	gye-khâb	རྒྱལ་ཁབ
nature	râng-joong	རང་བྱུང
nausea	kyoog-me lâng-wa	སྐྱུག་མེ་ལངས་པ
near	tih-la	ཐིག་ལ
necessary	gö ngay-chen	དགོས་ངེས་ཅན
necklace	ke-gyen	སྐེ་རྒྱན
to need	gö-pa	དགོས་པ
needle (sewing)	khâb	ཁབ
needle (syringe)	men-khâb	སྨན་ཁབ
neither	nyi-ka min-pa	གཉིས་ཀ་མིན་པ
never	tsa-wa-nay	རྩ་བ་ནས
new	sar-ba	གསར་པ
New Year's Day	lo-sar	ལོ་གསར
news	sân-gyur	གསར་འགྱུར
newsagency	tsâg-sho nyo-sa	ཚགས་ཤོག་ཉོ་ས
newspaper	tsâg-ba	ཚགས་པ
next	je-ma	རྗེས་མ
next month	da-wa je-ma	ཟླ་བ་རྗེས་མ
next week	dün-ta je-ma	བདུན་ཕྲག་རྗེས་མ
next year	lo je-ma	ལོ་རྗེས་མ
next to	je-la	རྗེས་ལ
nice	yâk-po	ཡག་པོ
nickname	ming-dok	མིང་འདོགས
night	gong-da · tsen	དགོང་དག · ཚན
no	min · may ·	མིན · མེད ·
	ma-ray · min-du	མ་རེད · མིན་འདུག
noise/noisy	kay-choh · kay-choh tsha-po	སྐད་ཆོར · སྐད་ཆོར་ཚ་པོ
none	chig-kyâng-may ·	གཅིག་ཀྱང་མེད ·
	chig-kyâng-min	གཅིག་ཀྱང་མིན
noon	nyin-goong	ཉིན་གུང
north	châng	བྱང
nose	na-khoog	སྣ་ཁུག
notebook	di-teb	འབྲི་དེབ
nothing	gâng-yâng-may ·	གང་ཡང་མེད ·
	gâng-yâng-min	གང་ཡང་མིན

not yet	tân-da-yâng may	དགྡ་ཡང་མེད
now	tân-da	དགྡ
nuclear energy	dü-tren nü-pa	རྡུལ་ཕྲན་ནུས་པ
nuclear testing	dü-tren tsön-cha	རྡུལ་ཕྲན་མཚོན་ཆ་ཚོད་
	tsö-ta chay-pa	ལྟ་བྱེད་པ
nun	ah-ni	ཨ་ནི
nurse	nay-yog	ནད་གཡོག

O

obvious	ngön-say tö-po	མངོན་གསལ་དོད་པོ
ocean	gyâm-tsho	རྒྱ་མཚོ
offence	phog-toog	ཕོག་ཐུག
office	lay-koong	ལས་ཁུངས
office work	lay-koong lay-ka	ལས་ཁུངས་ལས་ཀ
office worker	lay-koong lay-chay-pa	ལས་ཁུངས་ལས་བྱེད་པ
often	yâng yâng • yâng-se	ཡང་ཡང་ • ཡང་སེ
oil (cooking)	kha-noom	ཁ་སྣུམ
OK	di-gi-ray	འགྲིག་གི་རེད
old	nying-pa	རྙིང་པ
Olympic Games	oh-lim-pik tse-mo	ཨོ་ལིམ་པིག་རྩེད་མོ
on	gâng-la	རྐང་ལ
once; one time	teng-ray • teng-chig	ཐེང་རེ • ཐེང་གཅིག
one-way (ticket)	ya-lâm chig-po	ཡར་ལམ་གཅིག་པོ་འགྲོ
	do-ya ti-ka-si	འགྲོ་ཡི་ཏི་ཀ་སི
only	chig-po • ma-tog	གཅིག་པོ་ • མ་གཏོགས
open	kha-chay	ཁ་ཕྱེ
to open	kha chay-wa	ཁ་ཕྱེ་བ
opening	gon-zoog	དགོན་འཛུགས
opera	rö-gar tâb-tön	རོལ་གར་བཏབ་སྟོན
opera house	rö-gar-khâng	རོལ་གར་ཁང
operation	lay-gü	ལས་འགུལ
operator	trü-cha tong-khen	འཕྲུལ་ཆ་གཏོང་མཁན
opinion	sâm-tshül	བསམ་ཚུལ
opposite	gan-dha • dog-chog	འགལ་པ་ • ཕྱོགས་ཕྱོགས
or	yâng-na	ཡང་ན
oral	ngâg-tog	ངག་ཐོག
orange (colour)	li-ti	ལི་ཏི
order (stage)	bâng-rim	བང་རིམ
to order	kâ tong-wa	བཀའ་གཏོང་བ
ordinary	kyü-ma	དཀྱུས་མ
to organise	go-dig chay-pa	གོ་སྒྲིག་བྱེད་པ
original	ngo-ma	ངོ་མ
other	shen-da	གཞན་དག
outgoing	chee do-khen	ཕྱིར་འགྲོ་མཁན
outside	chi-log	ཕྱི་ལོགས
over	tog-la	ཐོག་ལ
overdose	men thün-tsay-lay ge-wa	སྨན་ཕུན་ཚད་ལས་བརྒལ་བ
overseas	chi-gye	ཕྱི་རྒྱལ

to owe	trö-jay chay-pa	སྐྱིན་འཛིན་བྱེད་པ
owner	dåg-po	བདག་པོ
oxygen	sog-zin-loong	སྲོག་འཛིན་རླུང

P

pacifier (dummy)	jib-ru	འཇིབ་རུ
package	chåg-pa • di-thoom	ཆགས་པ • སྒྲིལ་ཕུང
packet	chåg-pa chig • gåm-chig	ཆགས་པ་གཅིག • སྒམ་གཅིག
packet of cigarettes	tha-ma chåg-pa	ཐམ་ཁ་ཆགས་པ
padlock	gon-chåg	སྒོ་ལྕགས
page	shog-dång	ཤོག་གྲངས
pain	nay-soog	ན་ཟུག
painful	nâ-soog chem-po	ན་ཟུག་ཆེན་པོ
painkillers	nay-soog cho-ya	ན་ཟུག་གསོ་བའི་སྨན
to paint	tsön-tsi tong-wa	ཚོན་རྩི་གཏོང་བ
painter	tsön tong-khen	ཚོན་གཏོང་མཁན
painting (art)	rl-mo di-wa	རི་མོ་འབྲི་བ
pair (a couple)	cha-chig	ཆ་གཅིག
palace	gye-khång	རྒྱལ་ཁང
pan	tse-lång	ཙེ་ལང
pap smear	chay-shay-tog tåg-chay	ཁ་ཤས་ཤོག་བཀབ་དཔྱད
	chay-ya zay	སྦྱད་ཡག་ཟས
paper	shu-gu	ཤོག་གུ
paraplegic	may-dib	སྨད་གྲིབ
parcel	cha-låg • to-po	ཅ་ལག • ཏོ་པོ
parents	pha-ma	ཕ་མ
park	ling-ga	གླིང་ག
to park	mo-ta jog-pa	མོ་ཊ་འཇོག་པ
parliament	gya-yong trö-tshog	རྒྱ་ཡོངས་གྲོས་ཚོགས
part	cha-shay	ཆ་ཤས
party (fiesta)	thoog-toh	ཐུགས་སྤྲོ
party (politics)	si-dön tshog-pa	སྲིད་དོན་ཚོགས་པ
pass	pa-say • låg-kye	པ་སེ • ལག་ཁྱེར
passenger	drü-pa	འགྲུལ་པ
passport	pa-se-pot • chi-kyö låg-teb	པ་སེ་པོད • ཕྱི་སྐྱོད་ལག་དེབ
passport number	pa-se-pot ahng-dång	པ་སེ་པོད་ཨང་གྲངས
past	day-pa • ngön-ma	འདས་པ • སྔོན་མ
path	lâm-ga	ལམ་ག
patient (adj)	sö-sen-chen	བཟོད་སྲན་ཅན
to pay	rin trö-pa	རིན་སྤྲོད་པ
payment	rim-pa • la-phog	རིན་པ • གླ་ཕོགས
peace	shi-wa	ཞི་བ
peak	tse-mo	རྩེ་མོ
pedestrian	kång-tång dro-khen	རྐང་ཐང་འགྲོ་མཁན
pen (ballpoint)	nyu-gu	སྙུག་གུ
pencil	sha-nyoog	ཤ་སྙུག
penis	lig-pa • je	ལིག་པ • མཇེ
penknife	teb-di	ཏེབ་གྲི

pensioner	gen-yö	རྒན་ཡོལ།
people	mi-mång	མི་མང་།
pepper	ey-ma	གཡེར་མ།
period pain	dha-tsen bâ-kâb nay-soog	ཟླ་མཚན་འབབ་སྐབས་ནད་ཟུག
permanent	ten-châg	གཏན་ཆགས།
permission	chog-chen	ཆོག་མཆན།
permit	chog-chen trö-pa	ཆོག་མཆན་སྤྲོད་པ།
person	mi	མི།
personality	shi-ka	གཤིས་ཀ
to perspire	ngü-någ thön-pa	རྔུལ་ནག་ཐོན་པ།
petition	nyen-shu	སྙན་ཞུ།
pharmacy	men tsong-khång	སྨན་ཚོང་ཁང་།
phone	kha-pah	ཁ་པར།
phone book	kha-pah-teb	ཁ་པར་དེབ།
phone box	kha-pah tong-say khång-choong	ཁ་པར་གཏོང་ས་ཁང་ཆུང་།
phonecard	kha-pah tong-ya lâg-kye	ཁ་པར་གཏོང་ཡག་ལག་ཁྱེར།
photo	par	པར།

Can I take a photo (of you)?
(kay-rång) par-chig gyâb-na di-giy ray-bay

(ཁྱེད་རང་)པར་ཅིག་རྒྱབ་ན འགྲིག་གི་རེད་པས།

photographer	par-pa • par	པར་པ། • པར།
photography	par-lay • pâh gya-khen	པར་ལས། • པར་རྒྱག་མཁན།
pick/pickaxe	doog-pa • tog-tsay ko-wa	རྐོགས་པ། • རྟོག་རྩེ་ཀོ་བ།
to pick up	len-pa	ལེན་པ།
piece	toom-bu • cha-shay	དུམ་བུ། • ཆ་ཤས།
pig	phåg-pa	ཕག་པ།
pill	ri-bu	རིལ་བུ།
the Pill	kye-gok-men	སྐྱེ་འགོག་སྨན།
pillow	nyen-go	སྔས་མགོ
pillowcase	nyen-shoob	སྔས་ཤུབས།
pine	tång-shing	ཏང་ཤིང་།
pink	sing-kya	སིང་སྐྱ།
pipe	boob-dong	སྦུབས་གདོང་།
place	sa-cha	ས་ཆ།
place of birth	kye-yül	སྐྱེ་ཡུལ།
plane	nâm-du	གནམ་གྲུ།
planet	gyu-kar	རྒྱུ་སྐར།
plant	tsi-shing	རྩི་ཤིང་།
to plant	zoog-pa • deb-pa	འཛུགས་པ། • འདེབས་པ།
plastic	pö-kar	སྤོས་དཀར།
plate	tha-pa	ཐབ་པ།
plateau	sa-thö tang-shong	ས་མཐོའི་ཐང་གཤོངས།
platform	ding-cha	སྟེང་ཆ།
play (theatre)	tâb-tön	ལྟབ་སྟོན།

to play (a game)	(gyen) tse-wa	(རྒྱན་)རྩེ་བ
to play (music)	(rö-ja) tong-wa	(རོལ་ཆ་)གཏོང་བ
player (sports)	tse-mo-wa (tse-mo)	རྩེད་མོ་བ་(རྩེད་མོ)
playing cards	tah-se	དགའ་སེ
plug (bath)	trü-shong kha tig-ya	ཁྲུས་གོང་ཁ་དིག་ཡག
pocket	bâ-khoog	སྤ་ཁུག
poetry	nyen-ngåg	སྙན་ངག
to point	kha-chog tön-pa	ཁ་ཕྱོགས་སྟོན་པ
police	kor-soong-wa	སྐོར་སྲུང་བ
politics	si-dön • châb-si	སྲིད་དོན • ཆབ་སྲིད
politicians	si-dön-pa	སྲིད་དོན་པ
pollen	sen-drü-dü	སེ་འབྲུའི་རྡུལ
polls	wön-du	འོས་བསྡུ
pollution	du-lång-ki dib-pa	དུ་ལངས་ཀྱི་གྲིབ་པ
pool (swimming)	kye-zing	རྐྱལ་རྫིང
poor	kyo-po	སྐྱོ་པོ
popular	yong-ta	ཡོངས་གྲགས
possible	sih-pa	སྲིད་པ

It's possible.
si-ki ray

སྲིད་ཀྱི་རེད

It's not possible.
thoob-ki ma-ray

ཐུབ་ཀྱི་མ་རེད

---

post office	dåg-khång	དྲག་ཁང
postage	dåg-la	དྲག་ལ
postcard	dåg-shog	དྲག་ཤོག
postcode	dåg-chang ahng-dång	དྲག་ཅང་ཨང་གྲངས
poster	di-tåg jar-yig	རི་མོ་འགྲེམས་སྦྱར་ཡིག
pot (ceramic)	(zay) khog-ma	(རྫའི)ཁོག་མ
pottery	za-chay	རྫ་ཆས
poverty	wü-phong	དབུལ་འཕོངས
power	nü-shoog	ནུས་ཤུགས
prayer	mön-lâm • kha-dhön	སྨོན་ལམ • ཁ་འདོན
prayer book	kha-dhön-teb	ཁ་འདོན་དེབ
to prefer	dåm-ga chay-pa	འདམ་ག་བྱེད་པ
pregnant	pu-gu kye-ya yö-pa	ཕུ་གུ་སྐྱེ་ཡག་ཡོད་པ
premenstrual tension	dha-tsen må-bâb-gong ngång-tsåb	ཟླ་མཚན་མ་བབས་གོང་ངང་ཚབ
to prepare	da-dig chay-pa	གྲ་སྒྲིག་བྱེད་པ
present (gift)	ngen-pa • låg-ta	རྔན་པ • ལག་རྟགས
present (time)	tån-da	ད་ལྟ
presentation	ngo-trö	ངོ་སྤྲོད
presenter (TV etc)	ngo-trö chay-khen	ངོ་སྤྲོད་བྱེད་མཁན
president	si-zin	སྲིད་འཛིན
pretty	nying-jay-po	སྙིང་རྗེ་པོ
to prevent	ngön-gok chay-pa	སྔོན་འགོག་བྱེད་པ

price	gong • rim-pa	གོང་ • རིམ་པ
pride	nga-gye	ང་རྒྱལ
priest	la-ma	བླ་མ
prime minister	si-lön	སྲིད་བློན
print (artwork)	par-shü	པར་བཤུས
prison	tsön-khâng	བཙོན་ཁང
prisoner	tsön-pa	བཙོན་པ
private	gay	སྒེར
privatisation	gay-la gyu-wa	སྒེར་ལ་བསྒྱུར་བ
to produce	thön-kye chay-pa	ཐོན་སྐྱེད་བྱེད་པ
profession	tso-tâb lay-rig	འཚོ་ཐབས་ལས་རིགས
profit	keb-sâng	ཁེ་བཟང
profitability	keb-sâng yö-pa	ཁེ་བཟང་ཡོད་པ
program	lay-rig	ལས་རིགས
promise	kay-len	ཁས་ལེན
proposal	drö-shi	གྲོས་བཤི
to protect	kyob-pa-chay • soong-wa-chay	སྐྱོབ་པར་བྱེད • སྲུང་བར་བྱེད
protest	ngo-gö	ངོ་རྒོལ
to protest	ngo-gö chay-pa	ངོ་རྒོལ་བྱེད་པ
public toilet	mi-mâng sâng-chö	མི་དམངས་གསང་སྤྱོད
to pull	ten-par-chay	འཐེན་པར་བྱེད
pump	phun-dâ	ཕུ་མདའ
puncture	yi-koong • khor-lo dö-wa	ཡི་ཀོང • འཁོར་ལོ་རྡོལ་བ
to punish	nye-pa tong-wa	ཉེས་པ་གཏོང་བ
puppy	kyib-toog	ཁྱིའུ་ཕྲུག
pure	lhay-may • dâng-ma	ལྷད་མེད • དྭངས་མ
purple	mu-man	སྨུག་མན
to push	bü-gya tong-wa	འབུད་རྒྱག་གཏོང་བ
to put	jog-pa	འཇོག་པ

Q

qualifications (person's)	shay-tse	ཤེས་ཚད
quality	pü-ka	སྤུས་ཀ
quarantine	nay-yâm ngon-gok-che su-kâg chay-pa	ནད་ཡམས་སྔོན་འགོག་ཆེད ཟུར་བཀག་བྱེད་པ
quarrel	toog-pa gyâk-pa	འཐབ་པ་རྒྱག་པ
quarter	shi-cha-chig	བཞི་ཆ་གཅིག
queen	gyal-mo	རྒྱལ་མོ
question (topic)	leng-shi	གླེང་གཞི
question (enquiry)	di-wa	དྲི་བ
to question	di-da di-wa	དྲི་བ་འདྲི་བ
queue	len dig-pa • ray-mö chay-pa	ལན་སྒྲིག་པ • རེས་མོས་བྱེད་པ
quick	gyok-po	མགྱོགས་པོ
quiet (adj)	kha-khu sim-bu	ཁ་ཁུ་སིམ་པོ
to quit	pong-wa	སྤོང་བ

R

rabbit	ri-bong	རི་བོང་
race (people)	rig-gyü	རིགས་རྒྱུད་
race (sport)	gyook-tse den-du	རྒྱུགས་རྩེད་འགྲན་སྡུར་
racing bike	gyook-den kâng-ga-ri	རྒྱུགས་འགྲན་རྐང་གའ་རི་
racism	mi-rig ten-kay	མི་རིགས་ལ་བརྙས་བཅོས་
radio	hru-yin-ji • loong-tin	རུ་འཛིན་ • རླུང་འཕྲིན་
railway station	ri-lee bâb-tsoog	རི་ལའི་འབབ་ཚུགས་
rain	chah-pa	ཆར་པ་

It's raining.
chah-pa bâb-ki du   ཆར་པ་བབ་ཀྱི་འདུག

---

to rape	tsen-yem chay-pa	བཙན་གཡེམ་བྱེད་པ་
rare	kön-po	དཀོན་པོ་
rash	thor-sib	ཐོར་སིབ་
rat	tsi-tsi	ཙི་ཙི་
rate of pay	gong-tsay	གོང་ཚད་
raw	jen-pa	རྗེན་པ་
razor	ta-di	སྟ་གྲི་
razor blades	ta-di-kha	སྟ་གྲི་ཁ་
to read	log-pa	ཀློག་པ་
ready	da-dig	གྲ་སྒྲིག་
to realise	go-tön tog-pa	གོ་རྟོགས་རྟོག་པ་
reason	gyoom-tshen	རྒྱུ་མཚན་
receipt	choong-zin	བྱུང་འཛིན་
to receive	choong-wa • jor-wa	བྱུང་བ་ • འབྱོར་བ་
recent/recently	nye-char	ཉེ་ཆར་
to recognise	ngö zin-pa	ངོས་འཛིན་པ་
to recommend	ngo-trö gyâb-nye	ངོ་སྤྲོད་རྒྱབ་ཉེ་
recyclable	kyâr-tu bay-chö chay chog-pa	བསྐྱར་དུ་བེད་སྤྱོད་བྱེད་ཆོག་པ་
recycling	kyâr-tu bay-chö chay-pa	བསྐྱར་དུ་བེད་སྤྱོད་བྱེད་པ་
red	mah-po	དམར་པོ་
referee	tse-den dig-tim	རྩེད་འགྲན་སྒྲིག་ཁྲིམས་
	soong-khen	སྲུང་མཁན་
reference	ngo-jor	ངོ་སྦྱོར་
reflection (mirror)	sog-nyen	གཟུགས་བརྙན་
reflection (thinking)	sâm-lo ting-sâb tong-wa	བསམ་བློ་གཏིང་ཟབ་གཏོང་བ་
refrigerator	kyâk-gâm	འཁྱག་སྒམ་
refugee	kyâb-chö-wa	སྐྱབས་བཅོལ་བ་
refund	chi-log	ཕྱིར་ལོག་
to refund	chi-log chay-pa	ཕྱིར་ལོག་བྱེད་པ་
to refuse	kay-len mi-chay-pa	ཁས་ལེན་མི་བྱེད་པ་
regional	sa-khü-gi	ས་ཁུལ་གྱི་
registered mail	teb-kyel-dâg	དེབ་སྐྱེལ་དྭགས་
to regret	gyö-pa kye-wa	འགྱོད་པ་སྐྱེ་བ་

relationship	de-wa	འབྲེལ་བ
to relax	lhö-lhö chay-pa	ལྷོད་ལྷོད་བྱེད་པ
religion	chö-loog	ཆོས་ལུགས
religious	chö-loog-ki	ཆོས་ལུགས་ཀྱི
to remember	den-pa	དྲན་པ
remote	loong-koog • ta-kob	ལུང་ཁུག • མཐའ་འཁོབ
rent	kháng-la • yâr-la	ཁང་གླ • གཡར་གླ
to rent	yâr-wa	གཡར་བ
to repair	so-chö gyâk-pa	བཟོ་བཅོས་རྒྱག་པ
to repeat	kyar-dhö chay-pa	བསྐྱར་བཟློས་བྱེད་པ
republic	chi-thün gya-kâb	སྤྱི་མཐུན་རྒྱལ་ཁབ
reservation	ngön-ngâg	སྔོན་མངགས
to reserve	ngön-ngâg chay-pa	སྔོན་མངགས་བྱེད་པ
resignation	tsa-gong shu-wa	རྩ་གོངས་ཞུ་བ
respect	gü-shâb	གུས་ཞབས
rest (relaxation)	nge-so	ངལ་གསོ
rest (what's left)	lhâg-ma	ལྷག་མ
to rest	ngay so-wa	ངལ་གསོ་བ
restaurant	sa-kháng	ཟ་ཁང
resume (CV)	shay-tsay	ཤེས་ཚད
retired	gen-yö	རྒན་ཡོལ
to return	chih log-pa	ཕྱིར་ལོག་པ
return (ticket)	ya-lâm ma-lâm	ཡར་ལམ་མར་ལམ་འགྲོ
	do-ya ti-ka-si	ཡའི་ཊི་ཀ་སི
review	kyâr-shib	བསྐྱར་ཞིབ
rhythm	da-dâng chay-tsâm	སྒྲ་དབྱངས་བྱེད་མཚམས
rice	dray	འབྲས
rich (wealthy)	choog-po	ཕྱུག་པོ
rich (food)	kha-la shag-tsi-chen	ཁ་ལག་ཤ་ཚི་ཅན
to ride	shön-pa	བཞོན་པ
right (correct)	tâg-tâg • den-pa	ཐག་ཐག • འདྲེན་པ

You're right.
kay-râng tâg-tâg ray

ཁྱེད་རང་ཐག་ཐག་རེད

right (not left)	yeh	གཡས
right-wing	yeh-chog sho-kak	གཡས་ཕྱོགས་ཤོག་ཁག
ring (on finger)	tsih-kok	ཚིགས་ཀོག
ring (of phone)	kha-pah-kay	ཁ་པར་སྐད

I'll give you a ring.
ngay kha-pah tang-gi-yin

ངས་ཁ་པར་གཏང་གི་ཡིན

| rip-off | go-kor tong-wa | མགོ་སྐོར་གཏོང་བ |
| risk | nyen-ga | ཉེན་ག |

river	tsâng-po	གཙང་པོ
road (main)	lâm-chen	ལམ་ཆེན
road map	lâm-kay sâb-ta	ལམ་ཁའི་ས་བཀྲ
to rob	tog-chom chay-pa	འཕྲོག་བཅོམ་བྱེད་པ
rock	dâg	བྲག
rock climbing	dâg-la zek-pa	བྲག་ལ་འཛེག་པ
rolling	dil-wa	དྲིལ་བ
romance	pho-mo tse-doong	ཕོ་མོ་བརྩེ་གདུང
room	khâng-mi	ཁང་མི
room number	khâng-mi ahng-dâng	ཁང་མིའི་ཨང་གྲངས
rope	tâg-pa	ཐག་པ
round	go-gor	སྒོར་སྒོར
rowing	dru tong-wa	གྲུ་གཏོང་བ
rubbish	kay-nyig	གད་སྙིགས
rug	room-den	རུམ་གདན
ruins	shig-rü	ཞིག་རལ་པ
rules	dig-lâm	སྒྲིག་ལམ
to run	gyuk-sha lö-pa	རྒྱུག་ཤ་རྒྱོད་པ

S

sad	sem kyo-wa	སེམས་སྐྱོ་བ
safe (n)	rin-tâng chen-pö cha-la jog-sa	རིན་ཐང་ཆེན་པོའི་ཅ་ལག་འཇོག་ས
safe (adj)	nyen-ga may-pa	ཉེན་ཁ་མེད་པ
safe sex	nyen-soong tig-jor	ཉེན་སྲུང་འཇིག་སྦྱོར
saint	kye-bu dâm-pa	སྐྱེ་བུ་དམ་པ
salary	la-phog	ལཱ་ཕོགས
(on) sale	tshong(-chay)	ཚོང་(ཆེད)
salt	tsha	ཚྭ
same	chig-pa	གཅིག་པ
sand	chay-ma	བྱེ་མ
sanitary napkins	tsâng-day shu-gu	གཙང་དའི་ཤུའི་ཤོག་གུ
to save (money)	ngü sog-pa	དངུལ་གསོག་པ
to say	lâb-pa • shö-pa	ལབ་པ • ཤོད་པ
to scale (climb)	tsay jay-wa • zek-pa	ཚད་འཇལ་བ • འཛེགས་པ
scarves	kha-ti	ཁ་དཏིག
school	lob-ta	སློབ་གྲྭ
science	tsen-rig	མཚན་རིག
scientist	tsen-rig-pa	མཚན་རིག་པ
scissors	jâm-tse	ཇེམ་ཙེ
to score	ahng-dâng thob-pa	ཨང་གྲངས་འཐོབ་པ
scoreboard	ahng-dâng tsi-sa shog-pâng	ཨང་གྲངས་རྩིས་ས་ཤོག་པང
script	tsu-yig	སྐྱགས་ཡིག
sculpture	bu-kö	འབུར་སྐོས
sea	tsho	མཚོ
seasick	tsho-nâng do-nay shen-log gyâk-pa	མཚོ་ནང་འགྲོ་ནས་ཤེན་ལོག་རྒྱགས་པ

seat	koob-kya	སྐྱིལ་ཀྲུག
seat belt	koob-kya tâg-pa	སྐྱིལ་ཀྲུག་བཏགས་པ
second (n)	nyi-pa	གཉིས་པ
secretary	doong-yig	དྲུང་ཡིག
to see	mik tâ-wa	མིག་བལྟ་བ

S

self-employed	tso-wa rang-kyong	འཚོ་བ་རང་སྐྱོང
selfish	râng-shay tsâ-po	རང་ཤེད་ཚ་པོ
self-service	râng-gö rang-dem	རང་དགོས་རང་འདེམས
to sell	tsong-pa	བཙོང་པ
to send	tong-wa	གཏོང་བ
sensible	go-dön-chen	གོ་དོན་ཅན
sentence (words)	tsig-doob	ཚིག་གྲུབ
sentence (prison)	tim-tâg chö-pa	ཁྲིམས་ཐག་གཅོད་པ
to separate	ka-ka so-wa	ཁག་ཁག་སོ་བ
series	mu-tü gyü-del	མུ་མཐུད་རྒྱུད་འབྲེལ
serious	tshâb-che	ཚབས་ཆེ
service (assistance)	rog chay-ya	རོགས་བྱེད་ཡག
service (religious)	cho-ga tong-wa	ཆོ་ག་གཏོང་བ
several	ka-shay • ka-chen	ཁ་ཤས་ • འགའ་ཤས་ཆེན
to sew	tsem-po-gyâk-pa	འཚེམ་པོ་རྒྱག་པ
sex	pho-mo tâg	ཕོ་མོ་ཏག
sexy	châg-nyâm dö-po	ཆགས་ཉམས་དོད་པོ
shade/shadow	dib-nâg	གྲིབ་ནག
shampoo	ta-trü-ya shâm-bu	སྐྲ་འཁྲུད་ཡག་ཞམ་པུ
shape	sob-ta	བཟོ་བཏ
to share (with)	go-sha gyâk-pa	བགོ་བཤའ་རྒྱག་པ
to share a dorm	chi-khâng-nâng nyâm-tu dhö-pa	སྤྱི་ཁང་ནང་མཉམ་དུ་སྡོད་པ
to shave	shar-wa-chay	གཤར་བ་བྱེད
she	mo	མོ
sheep	loog	ལུག
sheet (bed)	cha-tah	ཉལ་གདན
sheet (paper)	shog-leb	ཤོག་ལེབ
shelves	bâng-ti	བང་ཁྲི
ship	dru-zing	གྲུ་གཟིངས

to ship	tong-wa	གཏོང་བ
shirt	tö-toong	སྟོད་གྱོགས
shoe shop	lhâm-ko tsong-khâng	ལྷམ་གོག་ཚོང་ཁང
shoes	lhâm-ko	ལྷམ་གོག
to shoot	phen-pa	འཕེན་པ
shop	tsong-khâng	ཚོང་ཁང
to go shopping	nyob-cha gya-ga-do	ཉོ་ཆ་རྒྱག་ག་འགྲོ
short (height)	mâ-po	དམའ་པོ
short (length)	toong-toong	ཐུང་ཐུང
short films	log-nyen toong-toong	གློག་བརྙན་ཐུང་ཐུང
short stories	doong toong-toong	སྒྲུང་ཐུང་ཐུང
shortage	ma-dâng-pa • nyoong-ta-pa	མ་འདང་པ • ཉུང་དྲགས་པ
shorts	ha-pan • gö-toong wog-dho	ཧ་པན • གོས་ཐུང་འོག་དྲོ
shoulders	poong-pa	ཕྲག་པ
to shout	kay-cho gyâk-pa	སྐད་ཆོ་རྒྱག་པ
show	tay-mo	ལྟད་མོ
to show	tön-pa	སྟོན་པ

Can you show me on the map?
(sâp-ta di-nâng) tön nâng-da   (ས་བཀྲ་འདི་ནང་)སྟོན་གནང་དང |

shower	soog-po tru-ya tor-cho	གཟུགས་པོ་ཁྲུས་ཡ་རྟོར་ཆ
shrine	lha-khâng	ལྷ་ཁང
to shut	kha gyâk-pa	ཁ་རྒྱག་པ
shy	ngo tsha-wa	ངོ་ཚ་བ
sick	nah-wa	ན་བ
sickness	na-tsa	ན་ཚ
side	chog	ཕྱོགས
sign	tâg	རྟགས
to sign	sa-yig gyâk-pa	ས་ཡིག་རྒྱག་པ
signature	sa-yig	ས་ཡིག
silk	dru-zi	གྱུར་ཙི
of silver	ngü-gi	དངུལ་གྱི
similar	chig-pa	གཅིག་པ
simple	lay la-po	ལས་སླ་པོ
sin	dig-pa	སྡིག་པ
since (May)	(chin-da nga-pa) nay	(ཟླ་བ་ལྔ་པ)ནས
to sing	shay tong-wa	གཞས་གཏོང་བ
singer	shay tong-khen	གཞས་གཏོང་མཁན
single (person)	mi-hreng	མི་ཧྲེང
single (unique)	chig-kyâng	གཅིག་རྐྱང
single room	khâng-mi-chig	ཁང་མི་གཅིག
sister	pün-kya bu-mo	སྤུན་སྐྱ་བུ་མོ
to sit	dhö-pa	སྡོད་པ
size	tsay	ཚད
to ski	gang-shü-tong	གངས་ཤུད་གཏོང
skiing	gang-shü tong-wa	གངས་ཤུད་གཏོང་བ

skin	påg-pa	པགས་པ་
sky	nåm	གནམ་
to sleep	nyi nyay-wa	གཉིད་ཉལ་བ་
sleeping bag	nye-koog	ཉལ་ཁུག
sleeping pills	nyi-men	གཉིད་སྨན་
sleepy	nyi doh-po	གཉིད་འོང་པོ་
slow/slowly	ka-lee ka-lee	ག་ལེ་ག་ལེ་
small	choong-choong	ཆུང་ཆུང་
smell	ti-ma	དྲི་མ་
to smell	ti-ma noom-pa	དྲི་མ་སྣོམ་པ་
to smile	gay-mo tse-tse chay-pa	གད་མོ་ཚེ་ཚེ་བྱེད་པ་
to smoke	tha-ma ten-pa	ཐ་མག་འཐེན་པ་
smoking	tha-ma ten-pa	ཐ་མག་འཐེན་པ་
soap	yi-tsi	ཡི་ཙི་
soccer	kång-pol	རྐང་པོལ་
social sciences	chi-tsog rig-nay	སྤྱི་ཚོགས་རིག་གནས་
social security	chi-tsog de-soong	སྤྱི་ཚོགས་བདེ་སྲུང་
social welfare	chi-tsog de-dön	སྤྱི་ཚོགས་བདེ་དོན་
socialist	chi-tsog ring-loog-pa	སྤྱི་ཚོགས་རིང་ལུགས་པ་
solid	tråg-po	བྲིགས་པོ་
some	ka-shay	ཁ་ཤས་
someone	mi-chig	མི་གཅིག
something	gang chig	གང་ཅིག
sometimes	tshåm-tshåm	མཚམས་མཚམས་
son	bu	བུ་
song	lu	གླུ་
soon	gyok-po	མགྱོགས་པོ་

| **I'm sorry.** | | |
| gong-da | | དགོངས་དག |

sound	da	སྒྲ་
south	lho	ལྷོ་
souvenir	dren-ten cha-låg	དྲན་རྟེན་ཆ་ལག
souvenir shop	dren-ten cha-låg tsong-khång	དྲན་རྟེན་ཆ་ལག་ཚོང་ཁང་
space	bar-nång	བར་སྣང་
to speak	kay-cha shö-pa	སྐད་ཆ་ཤོད་པ་
special	mik-say	དམིགས་བསལ་
specialist	mik-say kay-pa	དམིགས་བསལ་མཁས་པ་
speed	gyok-po	མགྱོགས་པོ་
speed limit	gyok-tsay	མགྱོགས་ཚད་
spicy (hot)	men-na	སྨན་ན་
sport	lü-tsay	ལུས་རྩལ་
sportsperson	lü-tsay kay-pa	ལུས་རྩལ་མཁས་པ་
sprain	tsig chü-pa	ཚིགས་འཁྱུད་པ་
spring (season)	chi-ka	དཔྱིད་ཀ

square (shape)	toob-shi	གྲུ་བཞི
square (in town)	(dong-kay)	(གྲོང་ཁྱེར་)
	zom-sa te-wa	མི་འདུགས་འཛོམས་ས་སྟེ་བ
stadium	lü-tsay tang	ལུས་རྩལ་ཐང་
stage	ding-cha	སྟེངས་ཆ
stairway	kay-zek-lâm	སྐས་འཛེགས་ལམ
stamp	dåg-tåg • ti-ka-si	སྦྲག་ཏགས • ཊི་ཀ་སི
standard (usual)	tsay-den	ཚད་ལྡན
standard of living	tso-way nay-tång	འཚོ་བའི་གནས་སྟངས
stars	kar-ma	སྐར་མ
to start	go zoog-pa	འགོ་འཛུགས་པ
station	båb-tsoog • ti-sing	བབས་ཚུགས • ཊི་སིང
stationery shop	yig-chay tsong-khâng	ཡིག་ཆས་ཚོང་ཁང
statue	ku-da	སྐུ་འདྲ
to stay (remain)	dhö-pa	སྡོད་པ
to steal	ku-wa	རྐུ་བ
steam	lâng-pa	རླངས་པ
steep	sah-po	གཟར་པོ
step	gom-pa	གོམ་པ
stomach	drö-kog	གྲོད་ཁོག
stomachache	drö-kog na-soog	གྲོད་ཁོག་ན་ཟུག
stone	dho	རྡོ
stop	tsâm jog-pa	མཚམས་འཇོག་པ
to stop	kåg-pa	བཀག་པ

Stop!
kha kåg .... ཁ་བཀག

---

stork	toong-toong kâ-mo	གུང་གུང་དཀར་མོ
storm	char-loong dåg-po	ཆར་རླུང་དྲག་པོ
story	doong	གྲུང
stove	tâb	ཐབ
straight	ka-toog	ཁ་ཐུག
strange	ken tsâ-po	ཁྱད་མཚར་པོ
stranger	gyü may-pay-mee	རྒྱུས་མེད་པའི་མི
stream	gyoog-chu	རྒྱུག་ཆུ
street	lâm-ga	ལམ་ག
strength	tob	སྟོབས
strike	lay-tsâm ngo-gö	ལས་མཚམས་ངོ་རྒོལ
on strike	lay-tsâm ngo-gö chay-pa	ལས་མཚམས་ངོ་རྒོལ་བྱེད་པ
string	kü-pa	སྐུད་པ
stroll	châm-châm	གོམ་པ་བགྲོམས
strong	shoog chen-po	ཤུགས་ཆེན་པོ
stubborn	go teg-po •	མགོ་མཁྲེགས་པོ •
	wu-tsoog tsa-po	ཨུ་ཚུགས་ཙ་པོ
student	lob-toog	སློབ་ཕྲུག
studio	par-khâng •	པར་ཁང •

	ri-mo di-khâng	རི་མོ་བྲི་ཁན་
stupid	koog-ta-chen	གླགས་དགས་ཅན་
style	sob-ta	སོབ་བཀོད་
suburb	dong-kay sa-kü	གྲོང་ཁྱེར་ས་ཁུལ་
suburbs of ...	... gi dong-kay sa-kü	...གྱི་གྲོང་ཁྱེར་ས་ཁུལ་
success	doob-day thön-pa	གྲུབ་འབྲས་ཐོན་པ་
to suffer	doog-nge nyong-wa	སྡུག་བསྔལ་མྱོང་བ་
sugar	chay-ma-ka-ra • chi-ni	ཕྱི་མ་ཀ་ར་ • ཅི་ནི་
suitcase	gâm	སྒམ་
summer	yar-ga	དབྱར་ག་
sun	nyi-ma	ཉི་མ་
sunblock	nyib-ta gok	ཉི་བཀག་འགོག
sunburn	nyib-ta teb-pa	ཉི་བཀག་འཐེབས་
sunglasses	mik-shay nâg-po •	མིག་ཤེལ་ནག་པོ་ •
	nyi-dib mig-shay	ཉི་སྒྲིབ་མིག་ཤེལ་
sunny	nyin-ma tsa-po	ཉི་མ་ཚ་པོ་
sunrise	nyi-shar	ཉི་ཤར་
sunset	nyi-noob	ཉི་ནུབ་

<hr>

Sure.
ngön-nay • yin-dâng-yin   དངོས་གནས། • ཡིན་དང་ཡིན།

<hr>

surface mail	sa-tog tong-ya-dâg	ས་ཐོག་གཏོང་ཡ་བརྡག
surname	kyim-ming	ཁྱིམ་མིང་
surprise	ha lay-pa • hâng sâng-wa	ཧ་ལས་པ་ • ཧང་སངས་བ་
to survive	sön-pa	གསོན་པ་
sweet	ngah-mo	མངར་མོ་
to swim	chu-kye gyâk-pa	ཆུ་རྐྱལ་རྒྱག་པ་
swimming pool	kye-zing	རྐྱལ་རྫིང་
swimsuit	kye-chay	རྐྱལ་ཆས་
sword	di	གྲི་
sympathetic	sha-tsay	ཤ་ཚེ་
synagogue	ju-yi lha-khâng	ཇུ་ཨི་ལྷ་ཁང་
syringe	men-khâb	སྨན་ཁབ་

T

table	chog-tse • gya-chog	ཅོག་ཙེ་ • རྒྱ་ཅོག
table tennis	ping-pong	པིང་པོང་
tail	nga-ma • shu-gu	རྔ་མ་ • གཤུག་གུ
to take (away)	kyer-wa • len-pa	བཀྱེར་བ་ • ལེན་པ་
to take photographs	par gyâk-pa	པར་རྒྱག་པ་
to talk	kay-cha shö-pa	སྐད་ཆ་བཤད་པ་
tall	ring-po	རིང་པོ་
tampons	ma-kha gok-chay sin-bay	མ་ཁ་འགོག་བྱེད་སྲིན་བལ་
tasty	to-wa chen-po	བྲོ་བ་ཆེན་པ་

tax	tay	ཁྲལ
taxi	tek-si	ཊེག་སི
taxi rank	tek-si dhö-sa	ཊེག་སི་སྡོད་ས
teacher	gay-gan	དགེ་རྒན
teaching	lob-ti	སློབ་ཁྲིད
team	ru-kâg	རུ་ཁག
tear (crying)	mik-chu	མིག་ཆུ
technique	tâb-tsü	ཐབས་ཚུལ
teeth	so	སོ
telephone	kha-pah	ཁ་པར
telephone centre	kha-pah lay-khoong	ཁ་པར་ལས་ཁུངས
to telephone	kha-pah tong-wa	ཁ་པར་གཏོང་བ
telescope	gyâng-shay	རྒྱང་ཤེལ
television	dian-shi •	ཌེན་ཥི •
	soog-tong nyen-tin	གཟུགས་མཐོང་མཉན་འཕྲིན
to tell	lâb-pa	ལབ་པ
temperature (fever)	tsha-wa	ཚ་བ
temperature (weather)	nâm-shi	གནམ་གཤིས
temple	lha-khâng	ལྷ་ཁང
tennis	te-ne-si	ཊེ་ནི་སི
tennis court	te-ne-si tse-tâng	ཊེ་ནི་སི་རྩེད་ཐང
tent	gur	གུར
tent pegs	phoor-pa	ཕུར་པ
tenth	chu-pa	བཅུ་པ
terrible	pay dhuk-cha	དཔེ་སྡུག་ཆགས
test	tsö-ta	ཚོད་ལྟ
to thank	tu-jay-chay shu-wa	ཐུགས་རྗེ་ཆེ་ཞུ་བ

Thank you.
tu-jay-chay   ཐུགས་རྗེ་ཆེ

theatre	tâb-tön-khâng	བཏབ་སྟོན་ཁང
thermos flask	cha-dâm	ཇ་དམ
they	khong-tso	ཁོང་ཚོ
thick	thoog-po	མཐུག་པོ
thief	ku-ma	རྐུ་མ
thin	tâb-po	ཊབས་པོ
to think	sâm-lo tong-wa	བསམ་བློ་གཏོང་བ
third	soom-pa	གསུམ་པ
thirsty	kha kom-po	ཁ་སྐོམ་པོ
this (one)	di (chig)	འདི (གཅིག)
thought	sâm-lo	བསམ་བློ
throat	mik-pa	མིད་པ
ticket	ti-ka-si • pa-say	ཊི་ཀ་སི • པ་སེ
ticket collector	ti-ka-si shib-shay chay-khen	ཊི་ཀ་སི་ཞིབ་ཤེར་བྱེད་མཁན
ticket office	ti-ka-si lay-khoong	ཊི་ཀ་སི་ལས་ཁུངས

tide	dü-lâb	རྫུས་རབས
tight	dâm-po	དམ་པོ
time	dü-tsö	དུས་ཚོ
on time	dü-tog	དུས་ཐོག
timetable	dü-tsö re-mig	དུས་ཚོ་རེ་འུ་མིག
tin (can)	châg-tin	ལྕགས་ཏིན
tin opener	châg-tin kha chay-ya	ལྕགས་ཏིན་ཁ་ཕྱེ་ཡག
tip (gratuity)	ngen-pa • sö-ray	རྔན་པ • གསོལ་རས
tired	tâng chay-pa	ཐང་ཆད་པ
tissues	tsâng-ta shu-gu	གཙང་སྦྲ་ཤོག་གུ
toast	may-ta bâk-lay	མེ་བཀོལ་བག་ལེབ
tobacco	doh-thâg	ཐོ་རྡེག
today	te-ring	དེ་རིང
together	nyâm-du	མཉམ་དུ
toilet	sâng-chö	གསང་སྤྱོད
toilet paper	sâng-chö shu-gu	གསང་སྤྱོད་ཤོག་གུ
tomorrow	sa-nyin	སང་ཉིན
tomorrow afternoon	sa-nyin chi-toh	སང་ཉིན་ཕྱི་དྲོ
tomorrow evening	sa-nyin gong-da	སང་ཉིན་དགོང་དག
tomorrow morning	sâng-nyi nga-to	སང་ཉི་སྔ་དྲོ
tonight	toh-gong	དོ་དགོང
too (as well)	yâng	ཡང
too expensive	gong chay-tâg-pa	གོང་ཆེ་དྲགས་པ
too much/many	mâng dâg-pa	མང་དྲགས་པ
tooth (front)	(dün) so	(མདུན་) སོ
tooth (back)	(gyâb) so	(རྒྱབ་) སོ
toothache	so na	སོ་ན
toothbrush	so-trü	སོ་འཁྲུད
toothpaste	so-men	སོ་སྨན
torch (flashlight)	log-shu	ལོག་ཞུ
to touch	reg-pa • châng-wa	རེག་པ • འཆང་བ
tour	ta-kor	བལྟ་སྐོར
tourist	yu-kor to-châm-pa	ཡུལ་སྐོར་ལྟོ་འཆམས་པ
tourist information office	yu-kor to-châm-pay lay-khoong	ཡུལ་སྐོར་ལྟོ་འཆམས་པའི་ལས་ཁུངས
towards	chay-tu	ཕྱེད་དུ
towel	ah-choh	ཨ་ཅོ
track (car-racing)	(den-tse mo-ta) gyuk-sa	(བདེན་རྩེ་མོ་ཊ་) རྒྱུགས་ས
track (footprints)	(kâng-je) shü-lâm	(རྐང་རྗེས་) ཞབས་ལམ
track (sports)	(den-tse) gyuk-lâm	(བདེན་རྩེ་) རྒྱུག་ལམ
track (path)	kâng-lâm	རྐང་ལམ
trade union	so-lay kyi-doog tsog-pa	བཟོ་ལས་ཀྱི་མཐུན་ཚོགས་པ
traffic	dim-drü	འགྲིམ་འགྲུལ
traffic lights	dim-drü log-da	འགྲིམ་འགྲུལ་འོད་རྟགས
trail (route)	lâm-shü • lâm-chog	ལམ་ཤུལ • ལམ་ཕྱོགས
train	ri-li	རི་ལི
train station	ri-li bâb-tsoog	རི་ལི་འབབ་ཚུགས
transit lounge	drü-pa nye-so gyâk-sa dön-khâng	འགྲུལ་པ་ངལ་གསོ་རྒྱག་ས་མགྲོན་ཁང

to translate	phâb-gyur chay-pa	ཐབ་འགྱུར་བྱེད་པ
to travel	drü-shü chay-pa	འགྲུལ་བཞུད་བྱེད་པ
travel agency	dim-drü lay-koong	འགྲིམ་འགྲུལ་ལས་ཁུངས
travel sickness	drü-shü-la ten-nay	འགྲུལ་བཞུད་ལ་བརྟེན་
	go-yom dâng	ནས་མགོ་ཡོམ
	kyoog-may lâng-wa	དང་སྐྱུག་མེར་ལང་བ
travellers cheques	drü-shü ngü-zin	འགྲུལ་བཞུད་དངུལ་འཛིན
tree	shing-dong	ཤིང་སྡོང
trek	ri-loong-doh-wa	རི་ལུང་འགྲོ་བ
trendy (person)	mi ta-so dö-po	མི་བཀྲ་བཟོ་དོད་པོ
trip	drü-shü	འགྲུལ་བཞུད
trousers	gö-toong • dho-ma	གོས་ཐུང་ • དོར་མ
truck	do-kye lâng-khor •	དོར་སྐྱལ་ལངས་འཁོར་ •
	lo-ri	ལོ་རི

It's true.
ngön-nay ray • den-pa ray

དངོས་གནས་རེད • འདེབ་པ་རེད

trust	yi-chay	ཡིད་ཆེས
to trust	yi-chay chay-pa •	ཡིད་ཆེས་བྱེད་པ •
	lo gay-wa	བློ་བགལ་བ
truth	den-pa	བདེན་པ
to try (to taste)	tsö-ta chay-pa	ཚོད་བལྟ་བྱེད་པ
to try (to attempt)	bay-tsö chay-pa	འབད་རྩོལ་བྱེད་པ
T-shirt	gong-may tö-toong	གོང་མེད་སྟོད་ཐུང་བྱེད
	phu-che	
tune	da-dâng	སྒྲ་གདངས

Turn left.
kha yön-la kyog

ཁ་གཡོན་ལ་བཀྱོག

Turn right.
kha ye-la kyog

ཁ་གཡས་ལ་བཀྱོག

TV	dian-shi •	ཊེན་ཤི་ •
	soog-tong loong-tin	གཟུགས་མཐོང་ཀླུང་འཕྲིན
twice	teng-nyi	ཐེངས་གཉིས
twin beds	nye-ti cha-chig	ཉལ་ཁྲི་ཆ་གཅིག
twins	tsib-toog	མཚེ་ཐུག
to type	châg-par gyâk-pa	ལྕགས་པར་རྒྱབ་པ
typical	trü-may	འཕྲུལ་མེད
tyre	gyik-gi khor-lo	འགྱིག་གི་འཁོར་ལོ

U

umbrella	nyi-du	ཉི་གདུགས།
to understand	ha go-wa chay-pa	ཧ་གོ་བར་བྱེད་པ།
unemployed	lay-ka may-pa	ལས་ཀ་མེད་པ།
unemployment benefits	lay-may-phog	ལས་མེད་ཕོགས།
unfurnished	nâng-chay may-pa	ནང་ཆས་མེད་པ།
universe	jig-ten-khâm	འཇིག་རྟེན་ཁམས།
university	tsoog-la lob-ta	གཙུག་ལག་སློབ་གྲྭ།
unsafe	nyen-ga yö-pa	ཉེན་ཁ་ཡོད་པ།
until (June)	(chin-da doog-pa) bah-tu	(ཕྱི་ཟླ་དྲུག་པ)བར་དུ།
unusual	cha-chen min-pa	ཕལ་ཆེར་མིན་པ།
up	yah • gâng-la	ཡར་ • གང་ལ།
uphill	ri gâng-la	རི་གང་ལ།
urgent	kay chen-po	གལ་ཆེན་པོ།
useful	bay-chö-chen	བེད་སྤྱོད་ཅན།

V

vacant	tong-pa	སྟོང་པ།
vacation (holiday)	goong-seng	གུང་གསེང་།
vaccination	nay ngön-gok men-khâb	ནད་སྔོན་འགོག་སྨན་ཁབ།
valley	loong-shong	ལུང་གཤོང་།
valuable	rin-tâng chen-po	རིན་ཐང་ཆེན་པོ།
value (price)	gong-tsay • rin-tâng	གོང་ཚད་ • རིན་ཐང་།
vegetable	ngo-tsay	སྔོ་ཚལ།
vegetarian	sha mi-sa-khen	ཤ་མི་ཟ་མཁན།

I'm vegetarian.
nga sha mi-sa-khen yin ང་ཤ་མི་ཟ་མཁན་ཡིན།

vegetation	tsi-shing	རྩི་ཤིང་།
vein	tâg-tsa	ཁྲག་རྩ།
venereal disease	tig-jor-lay choong-way gö-nay	འབྲིག་སྦྱོར་ལས་བྱུང་བའི་འབྲེག་ནད།
venue	zom-sa • tsog-sa	འཛོམས་ས་ • འཚོགས་ས།
very	shay-ta	ཞེ་དྲག
view	tong-tsül	མཐོང་ཚུལ།
village	dong-seb	གྲོང་གསེབ།
vine	gün-doom	རྒུན་འབྲུམ།
vineyard	gün-doom shing-ra	རྒུན་འབྲུམ་ཤིང་ར།
virus	nay-bu ta-mo-shig	ནད་འབུའི་རིམ་ཞིག
visa	vi-za • tong-chen	ཝིས་ • མཐོང་མཆན།
to visit	do-wa • thoog-tay	འགྲོ་བ་ • ཐུག་འཕྲད།
vitamins	tob-kye-men	སྟོབས་སྐྱེ་སྨན།

voice	kay	ཤད་
volume	da-shoog	སྒྲ་ཤུགས་
to vote	wö-shog loog-pa	འོས་ཤོག་བླུགས་པ་

W

Wait!
gu-dâng-da ... སྒུག་དང་།

waiter	se-dim shâb-shu-wa	ཟས་འབྲེལ་ཞབས་ཞུ་བ་
waiting room	drü-pa gook-dhö-khâng	འགྲུལ་པ་སྒུག་སྡོད་ཁང་
walk	châm-châm	འཆམ་འཆམ་
to walk	gom-pa gyâk-pa	གོམ་པ་རྒྱབ་པ་
wall (inside)	gyâng	རྒྱང་
wall (outside)	châg-ri	ལྕགས་རི་
to want	gö-pa • dhö-pa	དགོས་པ་ • འདོད་པ་
war	mâg	དམག་
wardrobe	du-log jog-sa al-mi-ra	དུག་ལོག་འཇོག་ས་ཨལ་མི་ར་
warm	drö-po	དྲོད་པོ་
to warn	nyen-da tong-wa	ཉེན་བརྡ་གཏོང་བ་
to wash (something)	trü gyâk-pa	ཁྲུས་རྒྱབ་པ་
to wash (oneself)	soog-po tru-wa	གཟུགས་པོ་འཁྲུ་བ་
watch	chu-tsö	ཆུ་ཚོད་
to watch	mik ta-wa	མིག་བལྟ་བ་
water	chu	ཆུ་
mineral water	tay-chu	གཏེར་ཆུ་
water bottle	chu shay-tâm	ཆུ་ཤེལ་དམ་
wave	ba-lâb	རྦ་རླབ་
way	lâm-ga	ལམ་ག་

Please tell me the way to ...
...-la do-ya-gi lâm-ga tön
nâng-da ...ལ་འགྲོ་ཡག་གི་ལམ་ག་སྟོན་
གནང་དང་།

Which way?
lâm-ga ka-gi ལམ་ག་ག་གི་

Way Out
chi-lo dön-sa ཕྱི་ལོག་དོན་ས་

we	ngân-tso	ང་ཚོ་
weak	soog-po kyo-po	གཟུགས་པོ་སྐྱོ་པོ་
wealthy	choog-po • gyu chen-po	ཕྱུག་པོ་ • རྒྱུ་ཆེན་པོ་
to wear	gyön-pa	གྱོན་པ་

weather	nâm-shi	གནམ་གཤིས་
wedding	châng-sa	ཆང་ས་
week	dün-tâ	བདུན་ཕྲག་
this week	dün-tâ di	བདུན་ཕྲག་འདི་
weekend	sa pen-pa dâng nyin-ma	གཟའ་སྤེན་པ་དང་ཉིན་མ་
to weigh	ji-tse dheg-pa	ལྗིད་ཚད་འདེགས་པ་
weight	ji-tse	ལྗིད་ཚད་
welcome	ta-shi de-lek •	བཀྲ་ཤིས་བདེ་ལེགས་ •
	ka-su-shu	དགའ་སུ་ཞུ་
welfare	de-dhuk	བདེ་སྡུག་
well	de-po	བདེ་པོ་
west	noob	ནུབ་
wet	lön-pa	རློན་པ་
what	kâ-ray	ག་རེ་

What is he saying?
khö kâ-ray lâb-ki-du
ཁོས་ག་རེ་ལབ་ཀྱི་འདུག

What time is it?
chu-tsö kâ-tsay ray
ཆུ་ཚོད་ག་ཚོད་རེད།

wheel	kho-lo	འཁོར་ལོ་
wheelchair	kho-lö koob-gya	འཁོར་ལོའི་ཀུབ་རྒྱ་
when	ka-dü	ག་དུས་

When does it leave?
ka-dü tön-gi ray
ག་དུས་འཐོན་གྱི་རེད།

| where | ka-bah | ག་བར་ |

Where is the bank?
ngü-khâng ka-bah
དངུལ་ཁང་ག་བར།

| white | kar-po | དཀར་པོ་ |
| who | su | སུ་ |

Who is it?
su yim-pa
སུ་ཡིན་པ།

Who are they?
khong-tso su ray
ཁོང་ཚོ་སུ་རེད།

W

english–tibetan

235

| whole | tshâng-ma | ཚང་མ |
| why | kâ-ray chay-nay | ག་རེ་བྱས་ནས |

Why is the museum closed?
kâ-ray chay-nay dem-tön-khâng
goh gyâb yö-ray

ག་རེ་བྱས་ནས་འགྲེམ་སྟོན་
ཁང་སྒོ་བརྒྱབ་ཡོད་རེད།

wide	gya-chem-po	རྒྱ་ཆེན་པོ
wife	kye-man	སྐྱེ་དམན
wild animal	ri-dâg	རི་དྭགས
to win	gya-ka tob-pa	རྒྱལ་ཁ་ཐོབ་པ
wind	loong	རླུང
window	gay-koong	སྒེའུ་ཁུང
to go	trom-la ta-ga-si	འཁྲོམ་ལ་འགྲོ་ག་ས་འགྲུལ
window-shopping	kyâm-kyâm do-wa	འགྲིམ་འགྲིམ
wine	gün-doom châng-râk	ཀུན་འཛོམ་ཆང་རགས
winery	châng-râk so-sa	ཆང་རགས་བཟོ་ས
wings	shog-pa	གཤོག་པ
winner	gya-ka tob-khen	རྒྱལ་ཁ་ཐོབ་མཁན
winter	gün-ga	དགུན་ཁ
wire	châg-kü	ལྕགས་སྐུད
wise	lo-drö-chen • kay-pa	བློ་གྲོས་ཅན • མཁས་པ
to wish	re-wa chay-pa	རེ་བ་བྱེད་པ
with	nyâm-tu	མཉམ་དུ
within	nâng-ngö-su	ནང་འོད་སུ
within an hour	chu-tsö-chig nâng	ཆུ་ཚོད་གཅིག་ནང
without	may-pa • min-pa	མེད་པ • མིན་པ
woman	kye-man	སྐྱེ་དམན
wonderful	ha lay-pay yâk-po	ཧ་ལས་པའི་ཡག་པོ
wood	shing	ཤིང
wool	bay	བལ
word	ming-tsig	མིང་ཚིག
work	lay-ka	ལས་ཀ
to work	lay-ka chay-pa	ལས་ཀ་བྱེད་པ
work permit	lay-ka chay-ya chog-chen	ལས་ཀ་བྱེད་ཡག་ཆོག་མཆན
workshop	so-lay-khâng	བཟོ་ལས་ཁང
world	zâm-ling	འཛམ་གླིང
worms	bu-sin	འབུ་སྲིན
worried	sem-tel chay-pa	སེམས་འཁྲལ་བྱེད་པ
worship	châg-chö mön-lâm	ཕྱག་མཆོད་སྨོན་ལམ
worth	pen-tog • rin-tâng	ཕན་ཐོགས • རིན་ཐང
wound	ma-may	རྨ་རྨས
to write	ti-wa	འབྲི་བ
writer	tsom-pa-po	རྩོམ་པ་པོ
wrong (fault)	non-trül	ནོར་འཁྲུལ

I'm wrong. (my fault)	
ngay non-trü ray	ངའི་ནོར་འཁྲུལ་རེད།
I'm wrong. (not right)	
ngay nor sha	ངའི་ནོར་ཤག

Y

year	lo	ལོ་
this year	lo-di	ལོ་འདི་
yellow	say-po	སེར་པོ་
yesterday	kay-sa	ཁ་སང་
yesterday afternnoon	kay-sa chi-toh	ཁ་སང་ཕྱི་དྲོ་
yesterday evening	kay-sa gong-da	ཁ་སང་དགོང་དག
yesterday morning	kay-sa shoh-gay	ཁ་སང་ཞོགས་གས་
yet	ta-toong • tân-da yâng	ད་དུང་ • ད་ལྟ་ཡང་
you (pol)	kay-râng-tso	ཁྱེད་རང་ཚོ་
young	shön-shön	གཞོན་གཞོན་
youth (collective)	shön-kye	གཞོན་སྐྱེས་
youth hostel	shön-nü don-khâng	གཞོན་ནུའི་མགྲོན་ཁང་

Z

zodiac	kar-kyim chu-nyi	སྐར་ཁྱིམ་བཅུ་གཉིས་
zoo	chen-sig-khâng	སྲུན་གཟིགས་ཁང་

SIGNS

Closed	goh-gyâb	མོ་རྒྱབ་
Cold	dâng-mo	གྲང་མོ་
Danger	nyen-ga	ཉེན་ཀ་
Entrance	zül-sa	འཛུལ་ས་
Exit	dön-sa	དོན་ས་
Hot	tsâh-po	ཚ་པོ་
No Entry	zül mi-cho	འཛུལ་མི་ཆོག་
No Photographs	pâh gyâb mi-chog	པར་རྒྱག་མི་ཆོག་
No Smoking	tâ-ma tehn mi-chog	ཐ་མག་འཐེན་མི་ཆོག་
Open	goh chay	མོ་ཕྱེ་
Prohibited	kâg-dom-yö	བཀག་སྡོམ་ཡོད་
Stop	kâh kâg	ཁ་བཀག་
Toilets	sâng-chö	གསང་སྤྱོད་